BEAUTY, DIS- RUPTED

BEAUTY,
DIS-

Carré Otis

RUPTED

with Hugo Schwyzer

itbooks

AN IMPRINT OF HARPERCOLLINS PUBLISHERS

This book is not intended to harm anyone in my past. In sharing my life experience with readers, my aim is to foster self-awareness and a measure of self-protection in young women of the present and future. In a few places, I've changed or left out entirely the names of individuals who have played a role in my life in order to protect their privacy. I have also, in some places, altered details, locales, and other specifics to be sure these people are not recognizable, but in no instance have I altered or changed the stories that I am sharing with you.

HarperCollins books may be purchased for educational, business, or sales promotional use. For information please write: Special Markets Department, Harper-Collins Publishers, 10 East 53rd Street, New York, NY 10022.

FIRST EDITION

Designed by Renato Stanisic

Library of Congress Cataloging-in-Publication Data has been applied for.

ISBN 978-0-06-202445-9

11 12 13 14 15   OV/RRD   10 9 8 7 6 5 4 3 2 1

*This book is dedicated to my teachers,
past, present, and future.
May we all be so blessed to cross paths with
the Wise Ones . . . those who remind us of
the inherent wisdom we all possess . . .*

Contents

1

False Starts

2

Early Modeling Years

3

The Mickey Years

———

4

On My Own

———

5

A New Beginning

————

1

False Starts

BARELY OF AGE

I could feel my sixteen-year-old breasts bouncing against the cool, soft silk camisole I was wearing, the whiskey I'd just downed burning in my throat, and my knees nearly buckling with every step I took down the rickety tabletops lined up to form a makeshift runway. Phil Collins's "Sussudio," the sound track for my walk, was pulsing to the beat of my heart and even shook the platform beneath my feet, making my gait even more unstable. My face was flushed with the realization that I was too young for men to be leering at my body, too young to be in this godforsaken bar. This runway was no place for anybody, even for a runaway scraping to get by.

Twenty bucks, I reminded myself. *Twenty bucks, and tonight for the first time in weeks I can eat something that hasn't been salvaged from a Dumpster.* That thought kept me focused as I pivoted awkwardly in my kitten heels and made my way back down the line of tables. With every step I took, I dug deeper to find my dignity. I pulled myself taller, hoping my face reflected a calm I didn't feel inside. Through the smoke, the blaring music, and the jarring catcalls, one thought pushed stubbornly past all the others: *How in hell did I end up here?*

Every life is filled with turning points, decisive instants that determine the direction we will ultimately take. Many such moments had already led me to this bar and my first modeling gig. And as I started to think back to where the journey first began, my mind flashed to a time a dozen or so years prior and a dozen or so miles away, back to San Francisco, the summer of 1973, and what was the original turning point.

MARIN

I was sprawled out on the grass in the little yard behind my family's Clay Street flat, staring up at the gray sky. The lonely sound of foghorns echoed throughout the city. Almost everywhere else in America, August is hot, but in my hometown it was invariably dreary, cold, and overcast. I daydreamed as I lay there, fantasizing about a place my parents had talked about all summer, the sunny place we were moving to. It was somewhere, I was sure, that my family would be happier. Somewhere called Marin County. And though I hadn't ventured there yet, I'd already invested a lot of hope in that place.

We were going to see our new house that day for the very first time.

For my parents Marin symbolized success. A short drive north of San Francisco, it's where many affluent Californians live. Almost all the other attorneys where my father worked commuted from homes outside the city, as the suburbs were warm and bright, the schools were top tier, and the streets were safe. As I neared kindergarten age, my parents wanted to give my sister and me a chance to grow up away from the crime, the mist, and the cramped apartments that were the norm in San Francisco. Moving to Marin meant giving their children the best—more than they had been given. And it meant giving themselves and their marriage a second chance, too.

My parents were both from the East and had moved to San

Francisco only so my father could go to law school there. I was born in 1968, just eighteen months after my sister Chrisse and just one year after Dad passed the bar exam. Money had been tight during those early years, which caused all kinds of stresses, but by 1973 my father's career was finally starting to take off. In Marin we could have a house of our own, big enough for my sister and me to each have a room and secure enough for my parents to lay down roots. That sounded like heaven to me.

When Mom was ready to go, I slipped from my momentary reverie, clambered to my feet, and ran to the car. We were off to check out Greenbrae, a town right in the heart of Marin. We drove Mom's yellow Volvo across the Golden Gate Bridge and up through the rainbow-painted tunnel on the other side. Every time we passed through that tunnel, Chrisse and I would count to three and inhale dramatically, competing to see who could hold her breath all the way to the other side. But on that August day it was as if we'd taken the whole ride with bated breath.

The whisper of promise in the air actually sent a tingle right through me. I thought about the new friends I'd make and all the open spaces in which I'd have to play. I thought about feeling warmth inside and out. And in the Volvo, as we climbed up a winding hill and turned onto Corte Lodato, I knew that my mother, father, and sister were deep in their own fantasies, too. Their silence told me that.

Chrisse and I both squealed with delight as the car rolled to a stop. There was a small knoll dotted with low-hanging oak trees in the center of the street; to get to the house, you had to drive slowly around it, making a wide circle so as not to clip the curb. I leaped from the backseat and raced to our door. I reached up and lifted the brass knocker that was shaped like a smiling dolphin.

I rapped on the door with that dolphin several times, until my mother said, "Carré, that's enough!" I exhaled impatiently, fidgeting and listening for footsteps approaching from inside the house. When the door swung open, the owner greeted us. Introducing herself as Martha, she flashed a broad smile. She had pink frosted lips that twisted in a strange way every time she spoke. Chrisse and I were fascinated by her to the point of distraction, like Charlie Brown listening to his teacher, unable to understand a word she was saying.

We were finally given permission to explore, while my parents stayed behind to talk with Martha. Chrisse and I raced through the house and bolted out onto the back deck, where we were surprised to see an enormous yard, so much bigger than any yard we'd ever seen in San Francisco.

From the deck I could glimpse the pool my parents had promised. Separated from the house by a grove of oak and eucalyptus, it was in the shape of a kidney bean. As I ran toward it, leaving Chrisse behind, I saw that an old cover lay over the top, partly submerged in what looked to be murky brown water. The closer I got to it, the scarier it seemed. I felt a weird sense of dread as I inched nearer still. I circled the pool warily, my footsteps loud on the concrete that surrounded it. Taking a deep breath, I lifted the cover—and just as quickly I gasped, dropped it, and fled. The corpses of bugs, mice, and birds floated and bobbed in the filthy water below. The stench of death was overpowering. All the optimism I'd felt in the car ride there left me instantly. I didn't like this place at all, with its cold, dark interiors and its foreboding pool. But the deal was already done. We were moving. This was to be our new home.

By the middle of September, we were settled in. I'd gotten the room my mom had promised to me—the one with an orange shag rug. It had a bunk bed, a bookshelf my dad had built, and a desk situated near a set of windows that overlooked a small garden alongside the driveway. From there I could easily see who was coming and going. I had one of those old reading pillows with armrests built into it, a soft yellow blanket and a tattered but much beloved, stuffed rabbit. I pressed rainbow stickers onto the ceiling next to images of shooting stars and flying unicorns. I had made the space my own. When I fell asleep at night, my new digital clock radio glowed, its steady green light offering reassurance from the darkness. I would have this clock for many years, its light a dependable guardian against whatever frightened me and its clicking a reminder that, like the hour, all fears ultimately pass.

One of the great draws to Marin County was the famed Marin Country Day School in nearby Corte Madera. MCDS, as it was called, enrolled students from kindergarten to the eighth grade and was one of the few private schools in the area. It was a mark of status for a family's child to attend MCDS. But that wasn't the only reason so many people, including my parents, struggled to pay the steep tuition. In addition to a great academic program MCDS offered students all the attributes of a close-knit community. What it didn't offer, however, were the resources needed to deal with troubled kids. And my troubles at school, as it turned out, began very early.

With the start of our first term there, Dad headed back across the bridge every morning to a new job at a prestigious law firm. And when Mom wasn't shuffling us off to MCDS and preparing for the birth of my little brother, Jordan, she worked part-time at Dominican College in San Rafael. Meanwhile Chrisse and I were adjusting in our own manner—and growing steadily apart in the process. Each morning when we were dropped off at school, we'd head our separate ways, a sadness befalling me as she'd quickly run off to greet her new friends.

Chrisse was almost instantly popular, whereas I was the complete opposite. And the comparisons that put a wedge between us didn't stop there. She'd been a beautiful baby, but as she got older, she developed a bad overbite that had to be corrected with the infamous headgear of 1970s orthodontia. My teeth were better behaved, and so in the same way that her popularity made her my rival, my smile made me hers. We were close enough in age to have bonded very tightly when we were small and close enough to become intensely competitive as we got older.

Bad overbite aside, Chrisse always had an easy time making new friends. I was beyond shy, painfully introverted, and willing to do whatever I could to remain unnoticed. While girls like my sister slid easily into and out of cliques, I would break into a cold sweat just thinking about the prospect of speaking to anyone I didn't know. From the very start, my days at MCDS were filled with schemes to get out of class. I'd fabricate reasons to go to the nurse's office—or, if necessary, do something that assured detention. While Chrisse was affable and excelled academically, I was angst-ridden and withdrawn to the point where my grades soon began to plummet. We seemed to move in tandem, just in opposite directions. Each of Chrisse's successes was matched by one of my setbacks.

In retrospect I understand that we didn't fall into this strange rhythm because we were close in age and were trying to define our individuality; we did so because we had each internalized our dysfunctional family dynamics in different ways. It was pretty obvious to all of us during those first few weeks in the new house that our move didn't hold as much promise for my parents as we had secretly hoped it would. Their tensions still remained. As Dad drank and Mom found her own ways to check out, Chrisse turned stress and anxiety into performance. The worse things got at home, the better, more productive, and more accomplished she became. What drove her to succeed was the same thing that left me feeling overwhelmed with despair and sadness. She got A's and made friends easily, while I slipped further and further into my own world, shutting out everyone and everything else.

However, there was one very real reason why adopting Chrisse's strategy for coping couldn't work for me: I had dyslexia.

The signs had emerged early. From the time I started school, it was clear to everyone that I wasn't learning at the same pace as other kids. I just didn't process information the way they did; I could learn quickly through song and rhythm, but the typical academic setting didn't provide the opportunity for alternative methods like that. Things that other children seemed to understand readily went over my head. My teachers became increasingly irritated with me, assuming that I wasn't trying hard enough—or, worse, that I was deliberately attempting to aggravate them. As it became more obvious that I was different, my shame and humiliation grew.

I can still recall that awful day when I was asked to stand in front of my first-grade class and recite the alphabet. It is so seared into my memory. I was terrified. I had no choice but to try. I made it through the beginning but then I began to make up the rest. The order of the letters simply eluded me. The classroom erupted in laughter. The childish jeers followed: "Carré doesn't know the alphabet!" "Carré, you're so dumb!"

I burst into tears. After that, I did everything possible to avoid being put into a humiliating situation like that again. I grew fiercely sensitive and even shyer than I'd already been. The last thing I wanted was the kind of attention that might lead to my being mocked. If I could disappear by hiding in a group, so much the better. This is certainly not a quality one expects in a future model.

It was my father who first discovered that there was a problem. He, too, had struggled with dyslexia as a boy, and he still has trouble with spelling as an adult. (That's the story behind the unusual spellings of both my name and my sister's.) One day he sat me down and gently asked a few questions. In a calm and encouraging voice, he walked me through the general concepts that he knew other kids my age were grasping. My answers confirmed that something was seriously amiss. So he took me to see the MCDS headmaster, Malcolm Manson. Mr. Manson arranged for a battery of tests, which ultimately revealed dyslexia. And on the advice of the learning specialists, I was told that I would need to repeat the third grade. It was a devastating blow.

That diagnosis marked me as a problem child not only for the school but for my family as well. Though my parents assured me over and over again that I wasn't stupid or slow, I sensed that my dyslexia was now a stigma on all of us. We were no longer the perfect family. We never had been, of course, but the revelation of my disability somehow seemed to bring our imperfections out into the open. My problem had a name, and that name was on everyone's lips. The most frustrating thing of all is that no one else's problem had a name yet. But my parents' problems were just as real as mine.

Thankfully, we recognize today that almost everyone's family is dysfunctional in one way or another. And except for extreme cases of abuse, it's usually not worth arguing about whose family is unhealthier. As is true for most people, my family's particular dysfunctions shaped my life and the choices I would make for many years to come. I don't hold my mom and dad fully responsible. They, too, had their own memories of childhood pain, complex memories they carried with them into their marriage and into their parenting. Of course, I knew nothing of that then.

My father, as I later found out, was the son of a man who'd narrowly escaped the Holocaust, though this truth about his Jewish heritage was hidden from my dad for years. My grandfather saw his Jewish identity as a liability and did everything he could to disguise that aspect of his being and of my father's, too. Known by the very American-sounding name "Lee Otis" until the day he died, my grandfather never addressed the subject once, not even with his son. Sadly, instead of teaching my dad about his roots, my grandfather unwittingly taught him how to hide from the things that frightened him most. But what my grandmother did hurt even more.

My grandmother came from the Appalachian foothills of western North Carolina. Her name was Augusta Bay Young.

Bay, as she was called, was a devout Christian Scientist, having converted to that faith when she was very young. Followers of this religion are most reluctant to see doctors or to be treated in the ways of modern medicine when they're ill, preferring the power of prayer instead. Perhaps as a result of her refusal to seek medical help, two of my dad's eight siblings died in infancy and one, Colleen, died at age seventeen.

Colleen had been born with cystic fibrosis, which in the 1940s meant near-certain death at a very young age. Miraculously, she lived until late adolescence, but due to Bay's Christian Science beliefs she was barred from taking any medication and subsequently endured years of unnecessary agony. My father and his siblings were torn, desperate to alleviate Colleen's suffering while fearing that to do so would be to go against their mother's wishes—and against God.

I have come to believe that a huge and unnecessary burden of guilt associated with his sister's suffering and death, coupled with the legacy of hiding one's true self, was at the core of the alcoholism that ruled my father's life until he finally became sober in 1988.

While my mother's family was small by contrast—she grew up with just one brother—oddly enough she lost this beloved sibling at a relatively young age, too. My uncle Ray fought in Vietnam and came home suffering from a serious case of post-traumatic stress disorder. In time he died of Guillain-Barré syndrome, which my mother always believed was brought on by exposure to Agent Orange. But my mother's hardship didn't begin and end there. My maternal grandmother, who went by the name Moonga, was mentally unstable throughout her life. She engaged in serial infidelities, was deeply depressed, periodically suicidal, had terrible boundaries and was estranged from the family for a long period of time, all of which left my mother perpetually yearning for something more.

As I see it, both of my grandmothers did tremendous damage to their children.

It is no wonder that when my parents met in college they fell in love very quickly. My father was just twenty-two years old and my mother only twenty. Both were truly longing for stability and happiness, and both wanted to raise a family very differently from the ones they'd grown up in. But what, more likely than not, attracted them to one another was a hint of familiarity each saw in the other. (My mom has often said that my father and her mother were two of the most depressed people she's ever known.) So there they were: a young couple, both of whom had been reared in an atmosphere of silence, secrets, and inexplicable rules that had to be obeyed no matter what, trying to navigate an adult relationship. My father's drinking and my mother's withdrawal from him were predictable strategies for coping.

They simply didn't have the insight or the tools to change the dysfunctional blueprint upon which their marriage was built. But as dramatic as their stories are, they weren't so unusual in Greenbrae, California, during the 1970s. Or anywhere else, for that matter.

So wearing the label "dyslexic" at age eight, when no one else was owning their labels—not even the adults—did nothing for my already fragile self-esteem.

We know so much more about learning disabilities today than we did then. Now kids with dyslexia have access to specialists and sophisticated treatments that were unimaginable just a few decades ago. We don't confuse dyslexia with laziness or stupidity anymore, and techniques exist to help even severely afflicted kids keep pace with their classmates. But those techniques weren't available to me or other kids in my generation. And that meant I would spend years dealing with the damaging consequences of having been called "slow" from an early age.

Being perceived that way robbed me of the little confidence I had. So at the start of my second year in third grade, I made a decision about myself: Since I was already different from other kids, I was going to define myself on my own terms. If I was going to be labeled at all, I wanted to be known as a rebel or a troublemaker. Even being called a loser, because I would not conform, beat being called slow.

Despite my status as an outcast, I ultimately developed my own way of making friends. By the time I was in sixth grade, boy-girl parties were all the rage—though only a few parents were "cool" enough to host them. My mom and dad were definitely not in that narrow set, but after some subtle and persistent pressure on my part they agreed to let me have what I promised would be a "small" mixer. For as long as I could remember, I'd been a very good manipulator, with an uncanny ability to exploit the insecurities of my predictable parents. I was especially good at working on my dad. When he wasn't drinking, his guilt made him an easy mark. Extracting his permission to have a small group over on a Friday evening was contingent on getting him in one of these moments, and so I did. As I walked into the living room, his brows furrowed, his mouth set, and a sad, faraway look settled on his face. He loved me dearly, but he was so clearly uncomfortable in my presence. And though I would much rather have had his reliability, I accepted what I could get. I played on his apparent remorse for my own purposes, and I got what I wanted at the moment: my party.

After being excluded from so many things at MCDS, I took as much pleasure in making a list of the kids I *wouldn't* invite as I did choosing the ones I would. I kept it to a group of five: three boys and two other girls.

Jared, Tyler, and Mitch were inseparable; they were a natural choice. Cathy and Kara were "in" girls, very popular, more likely to be friends with people like my sister than with me. But the promise of alcohol and a few hours' break from their parents was too good to pass up. Plenty of us had already started drinking by the beginning of junior high; for kids like me, a party without alcohol was no party at all.

Jared was my first kiss, my first crush, the first boy who made my heart beat faster. He was short and pudgy, but cute and witty, too. He could charm kids, parents, and teachers alike with his fierce but strangely kind sense of humor. Unlike so many other boys his age, he never felt the need to be cruel to make a point or win a cheap laugh. Everyone adored Jared. I couldn't wait to have him at my party, in my house, and to feel that he was mine.

As soon as I got home from school that day, I immediately went to work. With care and consideration, I pulled out the records I wanted to play, lining them all up in order: *Van Halen I* and *II;* the Police's *Zenyattà Mondatta,* and the indispensable early-eighties party album, AC/DC's *Back in Black.* And, of course, I made the drinks. Or, to be precise, the drink. Before my dad got home from work, I discreetly confiscated a fair amount of his booze from the stash he hid in the basement. I'd taken a little bit from each bottle, eventually mixing together vodka, gin, whiskey, and tequila in one giant mason jar that I stored in the back of my closet. Obviously, we weren't drinking for taste. What mattered was the wicked buzz that this concoction was sure to deliver.

That basement liquor cache was always a source of tension—and, in a strange way, hilarity—for our family. My mother was determined to stop my father from drinking but wasn't quite brave enough to throw the booze out. So she set up all kinds of silly traps, designed to make a loud noise or a huge mess if he (or I) broke into the supply. The traps were crude and obvious, and it made me laugh to think that she believed either of us would actually be deterred by them. They were much too easy to replace, making it seem as if we'd never been in the basement at all. Meanwhile the level of liquid in the bottles declined at a steady, unceasing rate. And as with so many other things, we never talked about either the bottles or the ineffective snares designed to keep us from them. I was my father's daughter, and by the time I was twelve, I knew every one of his tricks. And I had his habit, too.

With the music and the beverages taken care of, I began pulling together my outfit: my Converse high-tops with their glittery purple laces, my crisp striped Lacoste shirt, and my brand-new Gloria Vanderbilts. It took me a few minutes of wrestling on my bed, flat on my back, to get the zipper up on those skintight jeans. Underneath it all I wore an overstuffed bra, having carefully smoothed out any lumps. One quick look in the mirror and I was ready. My guests were due at seven.

Waiting sucked. At six-thirty, antsy with anticipation, I tiptoed to the closet, quietly pulled out the mason jar, and unscrewed the golden lid. Holding my nose with one hand, I forced myself to take a big gulp of the pale amber potion. I exhaled dramatically, breathing fire. I tucked the jar back beneath the pile of dirty socks and T-shirts, shut the door, and checked the mirror one last time. My mouth was numb from the alcohol as I tried to smear my favorite root-beer-flavored Bonne Bell gloss over my tingling lips. I smiled at the image of myself staring back at me, gave her a confident wink and a nod, and squirted three quick shots of Binaca into my mouth. Game on.

A moment before seven, a squeal of brakes announced the arrival of the boys. I ran to the front door and peered through the peephole. Jared's dad drove a Porsche 911. When the coupe roared to a stop in front of our house, Jared bounced out, followed by Mitch and Tyler. My heart leaped a bit when I saw them, though whether it was Jared who caused this reaction or the huge shot I'd just taken was anybody's guess. I opened the door wide, giving what I hoped was a self-assured grin. "Hi," I managed.

Kara and Cathy arrived just as the boys were entering the house. They were wearing matching pink Polos, and their hair was pulled back in identical ponytails, secured with giant pink tassels. It was an unfortunate choice; as popular as they were, they looked a little too much like a pair of dorky twins that night. I was relieved. It's always reassuring to see flaws in "perfect people." Girls are taught early on to be relentlessly competitive with one another, and I was no better than anyone else when it came to the comparison game. But as they drew closer, my judgment quickly turned back to envy. I couldn't believe it. They were wearing matching diamond earrings! Despite my pleas, my mother still hadn't let me pierce my ears.

But with only three hours to party, I decided to let my insecurities go. Everyone had to be out by 10:00 P.M. The only other rules my father insisted upon were that the lights needed to stay on and my bedroom door needed to remain unlocked. I'd thought it all through and was well prepared. We could still get a lot done within those limitations.

I wanted to get this party started, so I directed everyone into my room and told Jared to put on Van Halen. I ran back to the kitchen and collected my carefully prepared hors d'oeuvres. Salami, cheese, and crackers on one plate and Hostess Ho Hos (my favorite) on another. I balanced them together with two six-packs of Tab hanging from my fingers, and as I made my way back down the hallway, I heard the whir of the turntable, a slight hiss, and then David Lee Roth's voice open "Ice Cream Man." Jared was a boy who dug the blues.

"Okay, I got the goods," I announced, placing the plates on my

desk and discreetly adjusting the jeans that kept riding up my butt.
"Now . . . who would like a cocktail?" It was a line I'd prepared, knowing that it would give me instant clout. I knew what this little group
wanted, and not only was I going to give it to them, I was going to give
it to them with style.

The line worked. Everyone grinned. I told Jared to stand guard at
the door as I turned up the music and poured the contents of the mason
jar into plastic cups.

"Straight up or mixed?" I asked each guest in turn, diluting the
booze with cola for those who chose the second option. I felt high, my
heart pounding; I was on a roll. The party was on. The Binaca spray
was close by, as was the food. If a parent came in and we had to cover
for ourselves, we knew just what to do. With the drinks in hand, I sur-
veyed the group and experienced a rush of accomplishment. It felt so
good to belong.

Mitch turned off the overhead light, leaving only my desk lamp on
to comply with my dad's rule. We drank the first drink together. "One,
two, three, bull's-eye!" The first person to drain his or her glass got to
start the game we all knew we were there to play: Truth or Dare. Mitch
won, and dared Jared to French-kiss me. And off we all went.

The hours passed in a blur. We paired off quickly: Jared and I took
the top bunk, Mitch and Cathy got cozy down below, and Tyler and
Kara stayed on the floor. We moved from our places only to get fresh
shots and to change the music. Hardly anyone spoke. After a while
my face was raw from making out and my jaw hurt from keeping my
mouth open for so long. It didn't seem to matter. I loved lying next to
Jared, feeling him against me. It was as if I'd thought about this forever and part of me couldn't believe that it was finally happening. Our
clothes stayed on, of course. While we were wild kids on one level, we
were all pretty innocent on another. I was barely thirteen.

A loud knock at the door startled me. "Carré? Carré! Open this
door. Now." My father's voice rose above the sound of "Back in Black"
on its third or fourth rotation.

I was disoriented. The room was dark, my skin was clammy, my hair was plastered to my neck and forehead. I felt vaguely nauseous. "Let's go, Carré," Jared whispered, helping me down from the top bunk. "Be cool," he said softly, deftly unwrapping and then popping a Ho Ho into my mouth. "Keep eating." And with a wink and an achingly sweet smile, Jared pushed me toward the increasingly impatient sound of my dad's voice. The boy was smooth. The light from the hallway flooded into the room as soon as I opened the door. I had this weird feeling of being under arrest. "Hey, Daddy," I managed. My father just looked at me, his brows furrowed again. I swallowed quickly and flashed him my best smile, letting him know I was so happy he'd let me throw this party. Though we'd never said it aloud, there seemed to be an unspoken understanding that this was his penance for things he failed to be or do while drinking. My smile was meant to remind him of that. But my grin was drunken, too, and my teeth were caked with chocolate Ho Hos. My father simply shook his head and reached his hand inside the room, flicking the light switch back on.

"I said lights on, Carré. Is that understood?" He wasn't trying to be mean, but it came out harsher than he probably intended. My father always seemed so uncertain of what role to play or what tone to take. Boys were in my room, it was dark, and it was obvious enough that we'd been drinking. So he was firm, but this time it felt like he was overcompensating for the increasingly frequent times when he hadn't been attentive to what was going on with me.

He turned on his heel and headed down the hall, staggering slightly. "Anyway," he muttered, "it's time for you all to go home. Party's over, kids." Grasping the handrail carefully, he made his way back down the stairs to the basement.

Though my father and I were the serious drinkers in the family, we weren't the only partiers. As she got into high school, Chrisse started to host some mixers of her own. One warm summer evening in 1982, she threw a party that changed my life. My parents were away on one of their weekend vacations, taking some time to work on their marriage as best they could and to have a break from us, too. We had the house to ourselves. And, of course, to anyone else my sister chose to invite.

It was a Saturday night. A warm wind gently rustled the old oak tree that sheltered our suburban home. I was out back on the redwood deck, listening to the sounds of laughter and shrieks coming from the downstairs room that had become my sister's sanctuary. Elvis Costello ballads poured from Chrisse's new stereo system, and the steady crack and fizz of beer cans being opened could be heard from where I was. I sat in the dusk, debating whether I could get away with joining the older crowd of high school students who had infiltrated my playroom. I let a few more minutes pass, and then on a dare to myself I ventured in.

I wasn't there to socialize. I was there to snag some beer from the coolers on the basement floor. Although I wasn't that far from their age group, this wasn't really my crowd. They knew it, and so did I.

I had on my favorite Ditto jeans and a purple alligator shirt. Purple was my color. On some days I dressed head to toe in it, mixing up the uniform with only a rainbow ribbon tied around my head to hold back my long brown hair. It was my fashion statement. I felt put together and special in it. It completed me, like carrying a lucky charm or a rabbit's foot.

Unnoticed, I waltzed over to the ice chest and pulled out a Michelob. *I'll just enjoy this in my room,* I told myself. At the time, I was too shy to move to the music the way the other girls did. Some danced with partners, some alone. They grooved and swayed with a freedom and ease I had yet to experience with my body. A part of me just wanted to sit and stare for a while, to be a fly on the wall and gather clues about how to be comfortable in my own skin. But the risk was too great. I couldn't chance my sister busting me for just hanging out at her party and publicly humiliating me. In all fairness, this was not my turf. Even living under the same roof, there were spots that were definitely off-limits. The basement—at least when Chrisse and her friends were there—was one of those places.

So I went back to my room and sat alone in the dim green light cast by my digital alarm clock. I raised the beer to my mouth and chugged. I was drinking not for the taste but for the delicious feeling that trickled down my neck and shoulders, relaxing every knot of tension along the way. As the beer flowed, I shuddered. It was like that divine moment when I'd stand over the heater in the early morning and the chill would give way to a sublime warmth. I took another swig, trying to lengthen my swallows. I'd been taught that I could get more down if I just loosened up my throat.

Two gulps in and my eyes fell onto my most prized possession, a ceramic unicorn that sat on a piece of purple velvet fabric on my shelf. I reached out to touch the cool arch of its back, the graceful point of its horn, and launched into a fantasy that took me far, far away to a place of willow trees and brooks, grassy knolls, and a tall blond knight in shining armor. I yawned dreamily. It was time to either sleep or make another risky trip downstairs for more beer. I crept back down the steps in the hope that I would remain unnoticed.

I wouldn't be lucky twice.

Chrisse zeroed in on me, digging her nails into my arm as she pulled me aside. "Just what do you think you're doing?' she hissed. "Get lost, Carré. Now!"

I was dismissed, as quickly as that. I could have been dying for all she knew, or have been delivering some important information to her, but she couldn't have cared less. I bit back the anger. I needed to stay cool.

"I'm going, I'm going. I just left some homework down here," I said expertly. I knew how to lie, even to a suspicious older sister. And I knew how to do it effectively. Especially if it meant I could get my hands on some more alcohol.

"Whatever . . . just do it already and get lost!" With that she turned and hurried back to her hard-partying guests. That was my cue. I raced to the cooler and pulled out not one, not two, but three beers. Fast as lightning I slid them under my shirt and bolted back up the stairs, two at a time.

Safely in my own space again, I decided to put one of my records on to drown out the thumping noise below. My room felt like a cocoon now, completely detached from the rest of the house and its inhabitants. At the same time, I secretly longed to be part of the crowd downstairs, laughing and flirting and moving to the rhythm of the music as effortlessly as the others. I wished my name weren't Carré, but something more common, like Jane or Linda. I wished that I had long blond hair and soft, pale skin. Sometimes I'd imagine what my life would be like if I'd been born somewhere else, to another family, with another sister and brother. I imagined a different set of parents, with a mom who stayed home and helped me with my homework and lovingly brushed my hair before bedtime and with a dad who didn't drink. But I knew the odds of that happening were nil. The closest I would ever come to that existence was in my head.

Since I knew in my heart that I would never fit in with the crowd downstairs either, I dropped *Sticky Fingers* onto the turntable and cranked up the volume. That did the trick. I couldn't hear a thing. Another beer and I had completely disappeared into a strange, fuzzy world of my own, an ever-more-distant place. But one still defined by the simple desires of a not-so-simple thirteen-year-old girl.

An hour or so must have gone by. I slouched in my chair, drunkenly staring at the pile of stickers I had successfully divided into categories. There were the "scratch 'n' sniffs," the "glitters," and then my favorites, the "puffy" stickers. They were made of soft, padded plastic, and my collection of them was impressive. I had Hello Kitty, peace signs, rainbows, and moonbeams. I had unicorns, slogans, kissing lips, and I also had a cola bottle. But divvying them up and arranging them had gotten old quickly. I was tired and bored. I needed to move. The buzz from the beer had worn off, and I decided I needed more. Time for one last run.

As I shoved myself away from the desk, my chair toppled over behind me, and I giggled stupidly as I attempted to right it. "Ooops," I said, speaking to no one in particular. I knew I needed to get myself together before I tried my luck again at the coolers. But chances were that everyone else downstairs was getting as goofy as I was, and that meant that my success rate had potentially improved. I fumbled in my pocket for a piece of gum, I brushed my bangs out of my eyes, and I slowly opened my bedroom door.

Something felt different in the house. Things had quieted down, and there was a hush in the air. The music that came from below was now slower, moodier. The overpowering smell of cigarettes and pot hung in the air and clung to the walls, and I wondered to myself how the hell Chrisse would manage to explain that to our parents when they came home the next day. Standing in my doorway, I was suddenly aware how full my bladder was from all the beer I'd drunk. Deciding to use my parents' bathroom, I closed my door carefully behind me and stepped out into the hall.

Their room was just a few steps away. I used my "superglide" to move along the floor silently. Once I reached their blue shag carpet, I tiptoed to the bathroom door. Why was I being so quiet? So on guard? Sneaking about made even the simplest tasks much more exciting. I felt as if I were fine-tuning some skill I might need later as an adult.

When I finally made it to my parents' bathroom, I switched on the light and raced to the toilet, forgetting to close the door behind me. By this point I had to pee so badly that as soon as my butt hit porcelain, I let loose in a flood of ecstasy. *Phew,* I thought. *That was close.*

And then I saw him.

He was at the bathroom door, one hand on the knob, one foot still in my parents' bedroom, staring at me with a strange, sheepish grin on his face. He was Chad, a senior at a neighboring school. He was popular, and he flaunted it. Lots of girls had the hots for him, my sister among them.

Seeing Chad standing there, I immediately stopped peeing. I wanted to die of embarrassment. I was frozen. My face must have blanched, because Chad quickly stepped all the way into the bathroom, shutting the door behind him. His fingers found the lock in an instant, and I heard him jiggle the knob to test it.

"What . . . what the fuck are you doing?" I stammered. It was a huge effort to get these words out. They didn't sound as tough as I wanted them to sound, but it was a strain to speak at all. I reached down to pull up my panties, trying to cover myself as quickly as possible.

I wasn't fast enough. Chad lunged toward me, grabbing my hand before I could yank up my underwear. "Don't," he said. "They're cute. . . . You're cute."

What the hell does that mean? I wondered.

"No, I mean, just let me . . . get them . . . up!" I squawked. Part of me was furious with myself for not handling this better while another part of me was shocked that Chad, the boy so many girls wanted (including my sister), was after me. What more should I want? Terror and confusion mixed with the sense that this was some important opportunity I shouldn't blow, and yet I didn't know how not to blow it. My heart was pounding a million miles an hour, my stomach doing triple flips. I was frozen, my hands still on my panties, his hand on mine.

Without ever letting go of me, Chad pulled me up off the toilet and backed me into the corner. I could smell the alcohol on him. For the first time, I realized how drunk he was. "You have little titties, don't you?" he said, laughing softly to himself. I cringed. "I bet you don't even have any hair down there. Come on, baby, let Chad take a little look." With that, he pulled up my shirt, forcing my hand away, defeating my best attempt to block his view. Chad studied me.

"Oooh, baby, a bald eagle!" He whooped and slapped his thigh, as if this were the funniest discovery he'd ever made. I felt light-headed and queasy. I wondered if I were about to be sick. Despite my efforts, tears of shame started rolling down my cheeks. I could taste the salt.

"Well . . . let's see how you like this. A taste of the goods to come." Then he pushed his hand between my thighs and gave me the finger.

I froze. Next, he raised his hand to his mouth, taking one long, slow, dramatic suck of what had just been inside me. "Nice and easy, little girl," he said as his hand disappeared again and I felt it poking, groping between my legs.

"Spread those legs open a little more, soldier." He kicked my left leg open wider; I nearly fell to one side. *Soldier?* Off balance and unprotected, I had nothing with which to stop him as he made his move again, pushing more of his fingers inside me. I felt a sharp pain ripping through my center.

A screeching gasp of breath escaped my mouth, my head banging back against the wall as I furiously tried to move my feet and body away from his. But Chad's big shoes were on my feet, and the crushing weight pinned me in place. At the same time, his hand nearly lifted me off the ground from the sheer force he used as he shoved it deeper into me. He panted and groaned as he pushed himself against me.

"You like it, baby girl. You like it, little slut," he repeated over and over.

The tears were now rolling, big and salty as they hit my lips. But I made no more noise. I refused to speak. It actually never even occurred to me that I could, and not once did I say no or stop.

Chad rubbed his jeans against me, pushing and jerking and grunting, until, finally, he gave a long, groaning exhale. I felt a shudder go through him, and he dropped away from me. Just like that, his hand was out and I could feel a place where my insides were torn.

Without looking me once in the eye Chad lifted his hand and once again took a long sniff. "Now, that stinks like a baby's butt, little girl. Didn't your mama teach you how to wash?" Before his laughter died, he turned and walked back out of the bathroom.

And I collapsed onto the open toilet, my favorite purple panties still down around my ankles. I was numb. I was silent. I could feel my mouth drawn in a tight little line, and I didn't want to let it go for fear I would make a sound . . . and that once I did, the sounds that erupted would not stop.

I tried to relax my bladder to finish my pee. I could feel a searing pain burning inside me. And that's when I began to cry. Throwing my arms around my knees and falling forward, I rested my chest against my legs. My whole body shuddered with the pain, the despair, the terror.

Wiping myself carefully, I lifted my panties back up. I felt how much this hurt, too, having them there against my skin. I pulled up my cords and, leaving the zipper undone, moved silently back down the hall to my room. Locking the door behind me, I found the ladder of my bunk bed in the dark and climbed up, into the safe arms of my stuffed animals, the soft, feathery down of my pillows and their familiar sweet scent. I didn't wipe the tears from my eyes or the snot from my nose, even though it made big booger bubbles with each breath I choked out.

It is here I finally let go, and between my moans and coughs and shame, I fitfully fell asleep.

What happened to me with Chad would shape my sexual relationships for years to come. Like so many other victims of sexual abuse, I blamed and second-guessed myself. I had lost my voice when I needed it most and been unable to protect myself from what happened. That pattern of voicelessness would return again and again, as would the victimization at the hands of men. It would take me nearly twenty-five years to heal from the cycle that began that night in my parents' bathroom.

But this "voicelessness" with men didn't mean I turned into a silent girl in every other area of my life. In the aftermath of my assault, my anger and pain over that and other issues began to manifest outwardly in bursts of unpredictable behavior. My acting out took place mostly at school. I soon became very familiar with the yellow walls and the woven earth-toned tapestries that decorated the small office of the school counselor, Ms. Tinder.

On my last day at MCDS, my mother had dropped me off as usual. I'd begged her not to step out of the car and expose her too-short miniskirt, knee-high socks, and Birkenstocks to my world, and on that day at least she gave in to my pleas. Having narrowly escaped embarrassment in front of my friends, I grabbed my backpack, said a quick good-bye, and instead of going to homeroom I snuck around to the back of the auditorium and waited for some of the older girls to arrive.

Jennifer and Tracy were eighth-graders and outcasts, too. They were the first and last friends I would make at MCDS. I saw in them the kind of potential that I sensed in myself. They were rebels eager to buck the system, troublemakers, and oddballs. They found the same ways as I did to carve a niche for themselves within that privileged environment. We all knew that quietly flying under the radar would get us by. We shared a lack of interest in school and an awareness of what little we had in common with our popular, promising, praiseworthy classmates. Jennifer, Tracy, and I also shared a smoking habit. And after waiting for the first bell to ring, we slipped into the upper school's bathroom, pulled out a few cigarettes, and lit up.

We were asking for trouble. Tracy swore that the smoke would be gone before anyone else came in, but I think we all knew we were taking a huge risk. Predictably, we were busted. Caught puffing away by the headmaster himself. Within minutes I was back in the familiar confines of the counselor's office. In trouble again.

Ms. Tinder turned to face me. Her pretty brown hair was swept away from her face, and a light coat of mauve lipstick had just been applied to her lips. She was impeccably dressed as always.

"What have we gotten ourselves into, Carré?" she inquired with a steady but calm look in her eyes. It wasn't the first time she'd asked that question. As on previous occasions, I could only gaze at the floor, my cheeks slowly reddening. The truth was, I didn't know why I kept getting into trouble. I had no answer for her, only a strange and terrible mix of regret and fear. I was desperately sad, and I truly wanted to communicate that to her. But today, like so many other times, the words wouldn't come. *What's the point?* I asked myself. *This woman isn't going to understand.* My walls stood tall.

But I had to say or do *something*. I could feel Ms. Tinder's expectant patience wearing thin. I took a deep breath. *This one's for you*, I thought, silently addressing myself to no one and everyone all at once. A nasty smile spread across my face as I lifted my right hand and boldly went where no student in the history of MCDS had dared to go before. My middle finger shot up, and with it I raised a defiant gaze to meet Ms. Tinder's shocked expression. She froze for a moment, then tilted her head to one side, studying me. With a sigh of both exasperation and decisiveness, she picked up the phone, never once breaking eye contact, and pressed the button for her secretary.

"Please call Carré's parents immediately. She is expelled and must be promptly escorted off campus." And with that, the receiver was gently placed back on its cradle and I was dismissed to sit in the hall.

My mother said nothing to me. I had nothing to say to her either. We just rode in silence side by side back to Greenbrae. As soon as we got home, I raced once more to the safety of my room and listened for the sound of my father's old Plymouth rolling up the driveway. I heard my mother talking on the phone to someone, hysteria in her voice. I caught every few words. "Expelled . . . out of control . . . I can no longer . . ." I was numb to it all.

Chrisse opened my door and stuck her head in. "You stupid thing, Carré! You really fucked it all up, didn't you?" Then she slammed the door without waiting for a reply. I rolled to face the wall and pulled the blankets over my head. *I wish I were dead*, I thought. The anxiety about what would happen next was making me drowsy, as if by going to sleep I could slip away from the consequences of what I'd done.

When my father arrived, I listened for what his footsteps might reveal. Had he been drinking? Had he heard the news yet? And as soon as the front door slammed, I decided upon both. He knew. And he had been drinking. I heard him shout, "Get her out of her room! In the kitchen—now!"

I didn't even wait for the messenger to deliver his words. I flung myself over my bunk, using the rail for leverage, and landed with a thump on the rug. I left the door to my room open behind me and tried to stand up straight and tall as I walked down the stairs and entered the kitchen.

They were both standing there, Mom leaning against the counter and Dad with a beer in hand, one arm raised to loosen the tie around his neck. That tie had been a gift from me a few years back. By now it had faded in color from a rich fern green to a hue that no longer flattered him, especially on that night.

"Jesus Christ! What the hell have you done?" he demanded, a wild look in his eye as if I had humiliated him in front of the world. He didn't want an explanation, and drunk as he was, he was beyond reasoning with. I felt betrayed. I wanted to break him, tear at him, make him stop judging me and become the ally who'd been missing since the day we moved into this horrible house. The day he started withdrawing deeper and deeper into that wretched basement liquor cabinet of his. If anyone in the world could understand why I had done what I'd done, it should have been him. But my father was lost to me at that moment and at so many others before then. Lost in his own pain and rage—a rage that unintentionally fueled mine, too. "What the fuck, Daddy?" I shrieked. "What the fuck is your problem?"

And with that, he slapped me. Hard. My father had never laid a hand on me before, but I had goaded him beyond his limit. As angry as we both were, the blow was shatteringly unexpected. I fell back, landing in a heap at the base of the stove. I remember my sister racing to my side, gently reaching out her hand to help me up, and softly pushing me down the hall and into the abyss of my room.

As I lay in bed, a hand to my swollen, tear-streaked face, a memory came to me. It was from a few years earlier, not long after I'd been diagnosed with dyslexia. I was nine, perhaps ten.

It was December, almost time for winter break. The days were getting darker earlier and earlier. As the sun began to set in the cold blue sky, slipping behind the western ridge of Mount Tamalpais, I'd raced from school, up the long hill and into the warmth of home. As I passed the Landons' house, I saw my father's car in our driveway and felt a sudden rush of excitement. I knew well by then that if it was early enough in the day, I'd have some time with the "old Dad," the one who existed before the booze, the one who was—and still sometimes could be—present in the moment. The Daddy I needed and longed for so desperately.

I was led to him by the sounds of crumpling newspaper in the living room, as he rolled pieces of the *Marin Independent Journal* to stoke a fire. His back was to me as I walked in, and I watched him quietly for a moment as he reached first for a poker and then for a small broom to sweep away stray ash. I walked up behind him, stretching my arms their full length so I could place them around his burly shoulders. He turned halfway toward me and smiled, placing a free hand to meet mine, patting it lovingly. He was still sober. My body tingled with relief.

Although still in his work clothes, he was rumpled from his day and his long commute home. His hair, the subject of our incessant teasing, rose up in what he called his "Jewfro," an unruly and wildly dark, thick halo. His familiar Dad smell mixed wonderfully with the scent of wood smoke. It was comforting beyond words.

I stepped back, and as I plopped onto our old couch, Draco, our dog, shimmied up to me, wagged his big butt, and nuzzled in for a scratch. Crackling pops and hisses escaped from the fire. Satisfied that it would burn for hours, my father stood and turned toward the records lining the wooden shelves beside him, reading their labels aloud as he scanned the selection. "What will it be?" he asked. "The Beatles? Simon & Garfunkel? Carly Simon?" This was a rare but familiar moment, and I beamed at him, knowing immediately what he wanted me to say.

"Beatles, Papa. Let's have the Beatles!" I was up on my feet now, skipping toward him, ready and eager for what I knew was coming. Daddy slipped the shiny black disc from between the covers, then carefully held the edges with his thumbs and forefingers as he ceremoniously blew on one side, then expertly flipped it to blow on the other. Of course there was no dust, since no one was permitted to touch his records but him, and he treated all of them like gold.

He positioned the record on the turntable, gently dropped the needle into place on the third track. I waited, eyes shut, counting down for the crackle that always preceded the music by an instant.

Picture yourself in a boat on a river

My father motioned for me, holding his arms up and out as an invitation for me to come closer to him, to place my feet atop his and begin our waltz around the living room, which for the moment was our very own magical dance floor.

Somebody calls you, you answer quite slowly.

My eyes locked onto his, trying to impress upon him the deep love and need I had for these very moments. How I tried to hold their gaze. How they were like the flavors of my favorite dessert. It was far better even than Mom's chocolate mousse. I would have given anything to be suspended forever in that moment. For time to stand still. As he lifted his feet and mine, we waltzed back and forth, in sync with each other and the music. He held me firmly in the safe arms of a father, and I let my eyes close and my head fall back in absolute trust. *Remember this,* I thought. *Burn this memory forever in your heart.*

When I looked up again, I saw tears in my father's eyes. And I knew he felt it, too. We each had an innate understanding of how much this dance meant. This one moment seemed to have more than made up for all the disappointments, all the betrayals, and all the broken promises. I held on to this experience tightly, in the hope that I could call on the memory of it later. I wanted to be able to recall the true nature of this precious man who just by taking a few steps with me had lifted me up and showed his love for me so dearly.

Even after he sent me sprawling to the floor, I would remember this moment. And I would remember it again later, when another man I loved so much did the same.

I slept that night with my hand to my cheek and my wounded heart pressed to my ratty old stuffed rabbit. *Someday I will get out*, I promised myself. *Please, God, let it be soon.*

Although MCDS had been around for twenty-five years, it turns out that I was the first student ever to be expelled from it. Rumors about what I'd done spread rapidly. My mother swears that the real reason for my expulsion was the school's inability to cope with my severe dyslexia, but that's not what the story was on the street. Everyone in Marin seemed to have heard about it. I saw the looks and heard the whispers. Privately, I thought there was only one way I could survive—and that was to give up. I decided that I was damaged goods, untouchable and unsalvageable. I saw it as a plain and simple truth, like a fact you find in a math book. I no longer fretted over it. Once in a while, a sharp pang of sadness would seize me, but for the most part I was filled with a steely resignation, just as I'd been whenever a teacher would place a test in front of me. No answer of mine ever fit in the endless columns of check boxes. I already knew that I would fail, so with some disconnected sense of duty I made it look as if I'd tried, randomly filling in those dots and creating patterns that zigzagged in all directions. Still, a faint hope lingered that by some stroke of luck I might just get a few right. But I rarely passed.

My parents laid down the law with me. After the MCDS debacle, I would be going to Kent Middle School, the county's largest public junior high. My life was to be focused solely on education, not on socializing. Everyone I knew from MCDS was off-limits, and my phone privileges were suspended indefinitely as well. Not that I had many friends from there that I wanted to keep. Secretly I was happy to be moving on, glad to make a clean break from everyone and everything.

It was then, too, that my parents sent me to see my first therapist, Dr. Nathalie O'Bourne. Twice a week for an hour, her office was the one refuge I had from the world and my growing depression. But despite even Dr. O's help, I was withdrawing quickly, distancing myself from my family, friends, and life itself. I felt like a snail that had just had salt poured all over it. I wanted the pain to stop, and if receding into my shell did the trick, then so be it.

I may not have been the only girl to feel neglected or to struggle with dyslexia or the aftermath of sexual assault, but I was the only one I *knew* of. At Kent I did enough to get by. At home, like so many middle children, I found it easy to disappear. Alcohol was one comfort. Increasingly, boys were another. Until I moved beyond boys.

I had just turned fourteen when I met Elliott. He was working a birthday party at which I was a guest. His family owned a novelty gift store called Balloon Dreams, and he drove the company van. I still remember the image of balloons painted on the side and the cheery slogan promising a personalized delivery. Lots of girls had the hots for him: He was wiry, with dark, curly hair, a dead ringer for INXS's Michael Hutchence, a resemblance he made every effort to exploit. He was also thirty years old.

When Elliott left the party to return to his van, I followed and stopped him with a question: "Got a cigarette?"

He turned, cocked his head to one side. Squinted at me and asked, "How old are you?"

"Sixteen," I lied. But as the blood rushed to my cheeks, exposing my lie, I decided to come clean. "Fourteen, really." I shrugged, letting my shoulders fall dramatically. And waited.

Elliott just looked at me. His gaze made my heart lurch and my skin grow warmer. No other girl my age I knew of would have followed Elliott like that. But I was bolder. By now I knew the allure I had. I might not have been confident in other areas of my life, but my desirability was rising on a very short list of the things I could trust. "Getting Elliott" was now my project. I knew that our age difference made

us off-limits to each other. In my parents' eyes, my having a relationship with a male of any age was unacceptable. While that made the
challenge more appealing, it was still terrifying.

As we stared at each other, I slowly fingered the unicorn medal-
lion that hung around my neck on a thin silver chain, twirling it, then
lifting it to my lips. I knew that the ball remained in my court. So I
pressed: "What about that cigarette?"

I could see he was intrigued. More than intrigued, he was fascinated.
But also appalled and unnerved. I had him believing that I knew what
I wanted—and that what I wanted was dangerous. Taboo. Forbidden.
Pulling a pack of Marlboro Reds from his back pocket, he expertly
shook one to the surface and held it out for me. Without fumbling, I
took the cigarette, placing it between my teeth, all the while continuing to hold his gaze. I thought of Debra Winger in *Urban Cowboy* and
waited for my man to light me up.

"I don't get something," Elliott said, having lit my cigarette. "Here
you are at this party full of kids. But you're obviously not like them,
are you?"

I smiled, silently urging him on.

"So you see me, and when you should be enjoying birthday cake
and Pin the Tail on the Donkey, you follow me out here. Couldn't just
be for a cigarette, huh?"

I had him. I grinned, leaning back on the hood of the van, turning
my gaze skyward, letting the rays of sun splash across me, conscious
of how I hoped I looked. I knew I still had to play another move. The
only way I could see Elliott would be if I got his number; it would be
a disaster if he called my house and one of my parents answered. I
raised my head, meeting his eyes, and in a steady voice asked him for
it. He tossed his cigarette away and scribbled it on the inside cover of a
matchbook, pressing it into my ready little palm. As coy as could be, I
waved at him, then walked back into the house, knowing that his eyes
were on my ass the entire time.

Under my parents' strict curfew, there was only one time I could see Elliott: in the middle of the night. We developed a routine. I would sneak out of the house after everyone was asleep and meet him, returning home before dawn without fail. I needed Elliott and the freedom and excitement he represented, more than I needed sleep. And night after night, week after week, I got away with it.

I had carefully planned rituals to ensure my safe escape from the house. I always waited until after midnight, when the :00 on my digital clock radio flipped to :01 and P.M. changed to A.M. I'd climb out of my bunk, still wearing the street clothes I'd worn to bed. Most nights the outfit was the same: tight jeans and a sweatshirt with Mickey Mouse on the front. The jeans were my stab at looking sexy, the sweatshirt my threadbare attachment to childhood. Even at fourteen I could sense the conflict between these two aspects of myself—the confident sexuality I was trying to display and the innocent girlishness that was still very much a part of who I was.

I would arrange my pillows into the shape of a slumbering body and pull the covers up over them. I'd tiptoe to the window, straining to hear if anything was amiss. I'd open it just wide enough to squeeze my slender body through, and then I'd drop a few feet to the ground, leaving the window slightly ajar for my return. At this point I'd always pause and listen once more to be sure that the thud of my landing hadn't roused my parents or my sister. It never did.

It was not so much where I was going, or even who I was going to see, that gave me such a rush. What I loved most about these escapes was the game, the art, the science, and yes, the experience of just setting myself free. To make it all that much more exciting, I'd pretend I was a princess narrowly slipping through the clutches of evil captors, risking death if I were to be caught. The thrill was tremendous. Once I was in the clear, I'd be off and running.

Elliott and I always met at the same place: a 76 station on Sir Francis Drake Boulevard, less than a mile down the hill from my house. I didn't dare let him drive any closer for fear that a neighbor might see us. The gas station was the nearest safe place. And at the end of our nights together, it was at the 76 that Elliott would leave me to climb back up the hill and into my house alone.

One unforgettable night I reached Elliott's car just before twelve-thirty. When I stood at the door of the old Toyota Supra (he wasn't forced to drive the family delivery van all the time!), I found him fast asleep with the driver's seat fully reclined. The engine was running, the stereo was pumping. The car shook from the pulsating bass that rumbled through his prized speakers. And the backseat was filled with helium balloons, as it so often was. The balloons seemed to cradle Elliott's head and torso as he lay there, oblivious to my insistent rap on the window. I figured out what had happened pretty quickly. Elliott usually passed the hours waiting for me by getting drunk and high; by the time I made it to him most nights, he was already loaded. But this time he was passed out cold. A half-smoked joint in a roach clip sat in the ashtray.

I pounded on the window with a closed fist. No response. I pushed up and down on the hood of the Supra, trying to rock the car more than the bass already was. Still nothing. I was at a loss. I knew from experience that the cops would drive by every so often; I needed the shelter of being inside the car, and soon. And it wasn't only the cops I sought shelter from—the late hour brought with it all kinds of fears.

Headlights blinded me momentarily as a huge gasoline delivery truck slowly pulled into the station. It wasn't unusual for them to come by at this time of night, but I felt afraid, exposed, still very much left out in the cold even though my boyfriend was only inches from me. I watched the truck's cab as the engine shut down, seeing only the red ember of a cigarette inside. I turned back to Elliott's window, hitting it as hard as I could, bruising my knuckles in the process. Still nothing.

The driver of the truck climbed out of the cab and began walking slowly toward me. He was tall and lean, wearing jeans and cowboy boots and a T-shirt that read COCA-INE written in Coca-Cola script. He was older than Elliott, and I sensed by his approach that he wasn't going to leave me alone.

"Whatcha doing there, young lady?" He slurred his words as if he'd been drinking.

"Just waiting for my boyfriend," I replied. As soon as I said that, I realized how stupid it sounded.

Cowboy looked past me, into the driver's seat. "Yeah. Seems your boy's out like a light. Stone-cold stoned." His expression changed from feigned concern to an unmistakable leer. He moved closer. I backed away, praying for Elliott to wake up.

Just then my prayers were answered. I heard the door to the Supra open and a sudden burst of music pour forth from within the car. I only half turned to face my boyfriend, not wanting to take my eyes off the trucker.

"What's up, girl?" Elliott asked, making eye contact with me, trying to assess the situation as quickly as he could. "What's going on here?"

I moved to get behind him, and instinctively Elliott stepped forward as if to shield me from harm's way. There was something impressive about his fearlessness, something that made me want to curl up in his lap and wrap my arms around his strong neck. He was everything my father wasn't: assertive, defiant, brave, protective. But I could see Elliott's temper rising by the second. I already knew his reputation for violence, and though I'd not yet been one of his targets, I'd seen him throw some wicked punches that had knocked even sizable men out cold.

Cowboy trucker stood his ground. "Your girl was trying to get into that car of yours. Just making sure she was all right. Strange to be out at this hour, such a young lady and all. And strange she couldn't wake you either."

"I don't see how that's any of your fucking business," Elliott snarled, the words coming out slowly and rising with emphasis as he at first walked toward the trucker and then broke into a run, almost charging him.

In a split second, I saw a flurry of movement as the trucker reached behind his back and whipped something shiny from his waistband, something that stopped Elliott dead in his tracks. Cowboy pointed a .357 Magnum right at Elliott's forehead, cocking the gun.

"Step the fuck back, boy. You don't want to come any closer."

I could see the wheels turn in Elliott's head. I prayed frantically, silently, *Just step back, Elliott, step back*. But I could see that he was lost to his rage and his toxic pride. Drawing himself up tall, he stared straight at the trucker and spit.

"Go for it, motherfucker."

It was my first time seeing a man I loved facing death. It wouldn't be the last either. Quicker than I knew I could move, and without any hesitation, I ran in between Elliott and the gun, turning to face him.

"Elliott, step back. Just do it." At that moment I could hear my voice, strong and sure, a voice I hadn't exercised with Chad or my family or anyone else, for that matter. Inches from a gun pointed at the back of my head, I had found it. And with it I felt how wildly out of control my whole situation had become. I was fourteen years old. It was nearly one in the morning on a school night, and I was standing between my boyfriend and a deadly weapon. It was crazy. And more than that, it was downright terrifying. So near death, I was alive.

I spoke again. "Elliott, step back. Get in the car. Let's just go." I turned to the cowboy, face-to-face with the gun, my eyes now pleading with his. I had always known how to rescue, fix, or manipulate people and circumstances. But this expertise was definitely being put to the test.

I heard Elliott exhale behind me, trying to right himself, weighing the options. "Fuck it," he said, and with that I could feel my insides sag in relief. I kept my eyes trained on the cowboy until I heard the driver's-side door of the Toyota open and close. I gave the trucker the most thankful smile I could manage and backed quickly toward the Supra, sliding into my seat and slamming the door once inside. Elliott revved the engine and peeled out of the lot.

As we hit the boulevard, he rolled down his window and screamed, "Motherfucker!" I moaned in fear, turning to look behind me. The trucker stood framed in the orange glow of the mammoth 76 globe. As we tore off down Sir Francis Drake, Cowboy raised his gun and fired a single bullet straight into the sky. That should have been my warning shot. It was not.

My last night out with Elliott came a few months later, the night before my eighth-grade graduation. I followed the same routine that had worked for me so often before. After the episode with the trucker, I had decided that I needed to get to Elliott earlier in the evening so he had less of a chance to drink and smoke himself into a stupor. Instead of meeting him at midnight, I began sneaking out nearly an hour before that. My new magic time became 11:07 P.M. These numbers proved reliably lucky every time.

Some of my fellow eighth-graders at Kent were holding a pregraduation party at Muir Beach that night. I knew better than to ask my parents for permission to go. Elliott had promised to take me, and I suspected that it would be raging until well past midnight. I found him at the 76 station as always; he wanted to keep meeting there, even if it meant risking another confrontation with the trucker. Thankfully, we never saw that cowboy again.

As soon as I climbed into the Supra, Elliott handed me a beer. We chugged the better part of a six-pack as we drove over the windy roads to the beach. When we got there, I was relieved to see a bonfire; the party wasn't over yet. I was already very tipsy, and as soon as we stopped, I climbed onto the roof of the car, yelling and signaling to my friends. I began to do a little provocative dance, swiveling my hips, the beer easily in my grasp as I raised my arms over my head. Suddenly I was in a very real spotlight. Flashing red lights followed a second later. The unmistakable sound of a police car loudspeaker crackled.

"Get off the car, ma'am. Now."

I thought about making a run for it but realized the futility in that idea almost instantly. I was caught. I could barely climb off the Toyota's roof at that point. Elliott staggered out of the car, and before I knew what was happening, he charged the cops, two of whom drew their guns and ordered him to the ground. Fortunately, he obeyed and was quickly handcuffed.

There was more than one police car, and in no time at all another cop was at my side. He asked me for identification. I had none.

"How old are you?"

"Old enough," I said smartly. He wasn't impressed.

Elliott and I were taken back to the station in separate cars. My parents were called. A young officer with a bushy mustache spoke to my sleep-addled mother, who apparently insisted that I was still in my bed.

"Ma'am, I apologize, but we do in fact have your daughter here with us. You need to come pick her up. Right now." The officer looked at me as he spoke. I squirmed under the bright fluorescent lights. Somewhere Elliott was being interrogated. I silently hoped he wasn't getting himself into more trouble. I could guess what the cops thought of a thirty-year-old man caught in the middle of the night partying with a fourteen-year-old girl.

The mustachioed one hung up the phone with my mom. "Your mother says you have graduation tomorrow," he said, shaking his head. "Uh, I guess make that later today, huh?"

I shrugged. "Yeah." I stared at the clock above the cop's desk— 4:25 A.M.

My father arrived angrier than I'd ever seen him before. He'd been to jails many times as a lawyer visiting his clients. But he'd never had to release his daughter from one, until now. He walked past without even looking at me.

The officer behind the desk handed him some papers. "If you'll sign here, Mr. Otis, you'll be free to take your daughter. But we need you to decide if you want to press charges against the man she was with."

My father looked taken aback. "Charges for what, Officer?"

The cop hesitated, clearing his throat awkwardly. "Well, sir, for . . . um, statutory rape."

Great. I'd only said Elliott was my boyfriend. God knows what Elliott had told them. He was foolhardy enough to tell them the truth.

My father went white. With his fists clenched at his sides, he slowly turned toward me, cocked his head, and looked me right in the eyes. I didn't want to meet his gaze, but I couldn't help it. We stared at each other for a moment.

"No. That won't be necessary."

Relief. Then confusion. *Why the hell not, Daddy?* I wondered. *Don't want the family reputation spoiled any more than it already is?* I stood quietly looking at him. Searching for an answer.

My father turned back to the cop. "Just tell that motherfucker if he comes anywhere near my daughter again, he'll have a shit storm to deal with."

My father signed the papers and left. He didn't wait for me. He walked briskly to the car, got in, and started the motor.

Tears rolled down my cheeks as I slowly followed him. The air remained thick with silence the whole drive back.

The sun was rising as we arrived home. My father shut off the engine and spoke to me for the first time.

"Get yourself washed up for graduation. I never want to speak of this again. You will graduate, and then you will be grounded. The entire summer."

I sat staring straight ahead, forcing myself not to sob.

Then he opened his door, put one foot out, and turned back to me. "And by the way, kid, you got off easy." He walked into the house, slamming the door behind him.

I was crushed. As inadequate as his response had been, he'd done the best he could do with the tools he'd been given. And who's to say which was greater: his disappointment in me or my pain at having disappointed him once again.

A few bleary hours later, I sat with my classmates in the school gym as we graduated from Adeline E. Kent Middle School. On our drive to and from the ceremony, my parents said nothing about what had happened. Simply one more denial in a long string of them.

Just as perplexing was the sight of Elliott standing defiantly in the doorway staring at me, a faint smile on his lips as I walked across the stage to receive my diploma. I never saw or spoke to him again after that day.

The summer of 1983 was a hard one. My parents and I barely spoke. I had already been grounded, so there weren't many more privileges they could deprive me of. Clearly they were running out of ways to control me. Hoping that another private school might do the trick, they enrolled me in Marin Academy in nearby San Rafael.

Academically, it didn't matter much if I was there or at any other private school. But there was one difference that did matter to me. I started as a freshman at Marin Academy with a boyfriend. And not a boyfriend like Elliott either. This boyfriend was someone I could see in the daylight hours. Scott Hamilton Chase was everything Elliott wasn't. He was bright and athletic, and he came from a well-known family in the community. He was heading into his junior year at Branson, Marin Academy's elite rival in nearby Ross. Scott was also handsome, charming, and age-appropriate. Miraculously, even my parents approved of him.

I met Scott at one of my sister's parties just before the start of my freshman year. We bonded over our mutual love of ska music. My favorite album that summer was the English Beat's *Special Beat Service;* Scott was into another English group, too, called Madness. He rode a Vespa, the signature ride of all the cool kids. We quickly became a couple. For the first time, I was allowed to date openly. My parents were so relieved that I was seeing someone still in high school and someone from a well-to-do family that they agreed to relax some of the restrictions they'd imposed on me at the start of the summer.

I loved Scott, and I loved the attention we got as a couple. But he was also a mystery to me. He kept a lot hidden behind his popular, happy-go-lucky persona. One thing I did find out quickly: Scott used a lot of drugs, even more than Elliott. I wasn't always sure if it was because of or despite being high on cocaine that he managed to make it through his rigorous classes and varsity sports so successfully. He was a golden boy who got away with everything. Or so we all thought.

I'd been in high school less than two weeks when Scott showed up at Marin Academy unexpectedly one afternoon. I was on the track for PE when I heard him calling my name. As I walked over to him, I saw that he was sweating profusely. A thick, white, foamy paste caked the sides of his mouth. His eyes were wild and unfocused. He grabbed me by the hand and led me away, his grip damp and hot.

Scott tried to speak, but nothing came out. His mouth moved but could only form shapes around a disobedient tongue. There was a silent, desperate exchange between us, with me knowing he was in trouble yet also knowing I was completely in over my head. I had no idea what to do. He was high, higher than I'd ever seen him. Much too high.

My hand reached up to touch his forehead. I gently wiped the trickling sweat from it, pressing the moisture into my now-dampened sweatshirt. He leaned back against a redwood tree, staring off into space, his body shaking.

"Are you okay, Scott?" It was all I could get out, the answer obvious before the question was asked.

He grabbed me with a trembling hand, his eyes briefly focused. In a flat and cold yet clear voice, he got out one sentence: "I lost my soccer match."

And with that, Scott ran, breaking into a sprint, heading for home. I took his place against the redwood tree, watching as he disappeared. I could have run after him. I could have told someone. I could have seen the obvious warning signs. But he hadn't been my boyfriend for long. I didn't know him as well as I had wanted. And it was just a soccer game, I reasoned.

After school I hung out with a few friends before heading to the bus stop. It was nearly seven; the sun was starting to set as I took my seat on the plastic bench and waited. I hadn't been sitting for more than a minute when instead of a yellow school bus I saw my mother's old yellow Volvo approach. Both my parents were inside. My first reaction was pleasure at the thought that they'd come to pick me up. My second was confusion. My mother and father were very rarely in the same car these days unless they had to be. I stood up and walked toward them. I saw my mother's expression, her mouth pulled tight, her hand inexplicably gripping my father's, her knuckles white. I took a step back, inhaling sharply, knowing that news I didn't want to hear was coming.

My father leaned over toward me, his voice a single crackling whisper. "Scott's dead."

I remember my body beginning to shake as my insides unraveled. The rest was a blur: my mother's mouth moving, my dad lifting me in his arms, placing me gently into the car, helping me out again when we arrived home, and carrying me to my room, where only my bunk bed, a heating pad, and my stuffed rabbit consoled me.

When Scott left me that day, he ran straight home. After eating a chocolate chip cookie with his mother and sister, he went up to his room and wrote a note on his monogrammed Ralph Lauren stationery. He then took a handgun from his father's dresser and shot himself in the head. He had died instantly.

The note he left contained messages for his parents and his sister, but it was addressed to me. He had signed his name and added in parentheses, *"See you later, maybe."* The police showed it to me, hoping I could shed some light on what Scott had been thinking and doing in his final hours. But I had no explanation to give them. We'd been together barely a month, this beautiful, funny, golden sixteen-year-old boy and I. What I did know was that he had come to me seeking my help that afternoon, but whatever it was that he'd needed from me I clearly hadn't been able to give him. I also knew that on one occasion before this I'd been capable of standing squarely between Elliott and a gun, yet I couldn't do the same for Scott. In my mind and heart, I felt partly responsible for saving one life and equally responsible for *not* saving another.

I would never let that happen again.

Soon it seemed as if everyone in the county knew that Scott's note had been addressed to me. Some people were sympathetic, others judgmental, and of course there were those who just gossiped behind my back. Two weeks into my high-school career, I was desperate to get out of a very unwelcome spotlight. Because of the circumstances of Scott's death, a lot of kids at Branson and Marin Academy pledged never to do cocaine again. I, on the other hand, couldn't take that pledge. Scott was gone. The new friends I'd made through him were gone, too. But the impressive stash of coke that Scott had given to me was not. And in the days and weeks after his suicide, I slowly but steadily made my way through his supply.

One blustery late-September afternoon, desperate to get off campus, I invited an older fellow student to share a few lines with me. We drove her car to a tree-lined street above the school and parked under an old oak stand. Using her open glove compartment as a make-shift table, I cut two long lines of coke, pulled out a straw, and snorted. As I lifted my head, I came face-to-face with a cop, who was staring straight through the passenger's-side window. I was busted again.

It was in everyone's best interest to keep the misdeeds of the town's rich kids out of the courts and the newspapers. So rather than arresting us, the cops drove us back down to campus and turned us over to the headmaster.

Marin Academy was a "progressive" school. Rather than dismissing me in private, I recall the administration gathering the student body together the next day to settle my punishment. I was made to stand at a podium in the auditorium before my classmates as they voted to expel me. The results weren't even close. My career at Marin Academy ended nearly unanimously, less than a month after it began.

By the start of the ninth grade, my formal education was over. At this point I was numb. Scott's suicide, my guilt, and my public scapegoating for his death had done more than enough damage. Being kicked out of my second private school in three years seemed to have hardly made an impact on me. (Of course, now I know how far from the truth that statement really is!) I was so overwhelmed by the drama and the disasters that I didn't even react when my parents told me they were sending me away.

True to their liberal beliefs, they had no intention of shipping me off to a traditional reform school. But they were at their wits' end, and in all fairness they were truly worried about me. So they sent me to a place where parents like them had sent kids like me before: to John Woolman, an unconventional Quaker boarding school in the Sierras. Woolman had a history of dealing with troubled teens, but in a countercultural fashion. Rather than taking away their freedoms, Woolman gave young people far more freedom than they'd ever had before, hoping that it would lead to a willingness to take responsibility for themselves. For some kids it worked. In a way it did for me, too. In fact, it gave me enough clarity and courage to drop out of school altogether.

While I know now that my parents didn't see their actions as abandonment, I sure as hell felt as if it was when they left me off at Woolman after the long drive up from Marin. Yes, they had tears in their eyes as they headed back to their car; but my eyes were completely overflowing. I wanted to run to them, to tell them I was sorry, to beg them to do anything but leave me behind. Instead I simply watched as their car rounded the corner and pulled away.

The school had the feel of a hippie commune. Girls and boys lived in A-frame cabins. The showers were single-sex but communal. The students cooked the meals, cleaned the cabins, maintained the grounds, and grew vegetables and fruit in Woolman's gardens and orchard. The faculty and administration practiced a deeper democracy than even Marin Academy. Every major decision was made with student input, and every student was invited and encouraged to be heard. We were given rights, and yes, responsibilities. We learned that our voices mattered.

A lot of the students at Woolman were like me: misfits from well-off Bay Area families. Not surprisingly, there were as many drugs at Woolman at the time as there had been at Marin Academy or Branson. But the drug of choice among the kids I knew wasn't something as suburban as cocaine. Here in the mountains, the drugs were designed to do more than get you high. They were intended for exploration and discovery. One of those drugs was LSD.

I first did acid shortly before Thanksgiving break in 1983. I'd been at Woolman just over a month, and I'd already been teased quite a bit about my LSD "virginity." A large group of us crowded into the little cabin I shared with my beautiful earth mama of a roommate, Andrea. We lit candles and put them on every inch of flat surface. The Grateful Dead played on the stereo. Our friend Troy pulled a sheet of paper out of a little plastic bag. There was a giant image of Mickey Mouse on the sheet, made up of tiny perforated square images of Minnie Mouse. Cooper handed me one little square.

"Seriously, Coop, is this enough?" I asked naïvely. It looked so tiny.

"Hell yeah. More than enough. Girl, you'll be flying high and right within the hour. Stick out your tongue."

I did. And soon the tapestries on the walls turned to waves and the music from the stereo began to ripple with light. All night long we tripped and bonded with one another. When daylight finally came, I felt as if a huge burden had been lifted from my shoulders. For the first time in a very long time, I was happy. It wasn't just the LSD that was liberating. It was everything about the place: the nature, the democracy, the students, the relentless encouragement, the absence of judgment. My dyslexia didn't matter, my past didn't matter, all my perceived shortcomings didn't matter. What mattered was my ability to grow and to feel more connected to others.

I spent less than one full year at Woolman, marinating in its hippie broth. They were wild times, when lifelong friendships were formed and when I experienced more laughter than I ever had before. But it couldn't last. By the time spring rolled around, the magic was wearing off. The LSD trips weren't the same; the periods after coming down were growing more prolonged and depressing. And seeing one of my stoned classmates climb on top of the biology teacher's car, drop his pants, and take a shit on the hood certainly sealed my disenchantment.

I began to spend as much time as I could in nearby Grass Valley, the closest town to the school. Tired of tripping, I moved on to the risky routine of hiking through the forest, crossing the streams on the other side, and jumping a fence to get to Highway 49, where I could usually thumb a ride for the twenty-minute drive into town. In the spring of 1984, Grass Valley had a thriving music scene and some great coffee shops. I became a regular. One night near the end of the school year, a small group of us from Woolman caught a visiting band from San Francisco, the Guardians. They played infectious and infinitely danceable world-beat music. During their set my eye kept wandering to a guy with a star-shaped tattoo who stood near the stage swaying to the music, his gaze increasingly directed back at me. As soon as the set break arrived, I introduced myself. He was Kenny, and he was with the band. He seemed to ooze trouble. I was instantly infatuated.

When the spring semester ended and I'd moved back to Marin, I broke some unsettling news to my parents. They were on the verge of divorcing, and when they asked me what I planned to do next, I told them I'd made my decision: I was dropping out of Woolman, dropping out of school altogether, and I was moving to Berkeley to live with Kenny.

I was sixteen. I had a ninth-grade education, but I had another adult boyfriend and a hunger to leave Marin once and for all. "That's the plan," I repeated stubbornly to my exasperated parents. What other plan did I need?

THE FIRST RUNWAY

Living on my own at sixteen turned out to be nothing like what I thought it would be. I discovered that it wasn't only a plan that I lacked, I had no money to pay for food or rent either. I had dropped out of high school and moved in with a guy who was a good ten years older than me.

Kenny shared a rental in Berkeley with three roommates: Vicky, a cute blond lesbian with a lisp; Janelle, her tough, punk girlfriend; and Les Claypool, the bassist and lead singer of the cult punk band Primus. It was a wild group. Kenny was a roadie for various East Bay musicians, including the Guardians, and while he was working, I tried desperately to get my feet back under me. I didn't know whether or not anyone frowned on Kenny for bringing a minor into the house to live, but I did know that my lack of money was a real issue for the others. Everyone there slaved to make ends meet, and I was the only one who was unemployed. Most of the jobs I applied for required someone of legal age, and I was shy of that by a good year and a half.

Under that one roof, everyone was an artist of some kind or another. It was very intimidating. On the nights when we'd go out to the clubs and hang backstage with Kenny, I would always borrow a pair of his Danskin leggings and wear them with a long men's shirt and my soft-soled jazz shoes. The best and only look I had was the borrowed look. I couldn't afford anything else.

With so few prospects for earning money available to me, I found any number of ways to score a meal. Behind the Berkeley co-op was a Dumpster, and in it were all the items that had "expired." But that didn't necessarily mean that the food was bad. I would gather up the day-old bread and muffins in a sack and bring them home for my housemates. I'd also pare away the rotten bits from the fruits and vegetables to salvage what was still perfectly edible. For many months this helped me to supplement my diet and stock our refrigerator. I don't think anyone in the house had any idea where these things really came from!

I tried my hand at the one store willing to hire me. It was a small Berkeley clothing boutique named Suki. But I failed there, too, because I didn't have the basic math skills needed. My lack of confidence soon got in the way. I was petrified of adding numbers, counting bills, and giving change. The owner didn't care about my age, but she cared that all the cash that should be in the register at the end of the day was! I was always on the verge of tears. Soon enough I was let go.

One night backstage at a Metallica concert, a woman approached me. She had an enormous eighties-style blond perm and was wearing big hoop earrings. Dragging heavily on a smoke, she looked me up and down and nodded.

"Are you with the band?" she asked.

"Um . . . sort of," I replied.

She extended her hand and offered me a smile. "I'm Chantal. Pleased to meet you."

She waited for a name.

"Yeah, I'm Carré," I said, grabbing her hand.

"Anyone ever told you you should model?" she asked.

I choked on the soda I was drinking, then laughed. "Yeah, right. That's funny." I started to turn away. But Chantal grabbed my arm.

"No, I'm serious. Carré? You said your name was Carré, right?" She knew she had but a moment to get her point across. I wasn't buying it, and besides, I needed to make a quick exit—I could see Kenny motioning to me from across the stage.

"Look, I gotta go," I said.

Glancing at my boyfriend, Chantal pressed a card into my hand. "Here's my number. Kenny knows me. I'm having a fashion show at my club next Wednesday. Come and walk the runway," she said.

"Yeah, sure." I laughed her off again.

"For pay," she added firmly, staring me straight in the eye.

I stopped in my tracks. "How much pay?" I asked in a cocky tone, my hope and curiosity just beneath the surface.

"Twenty bucks for the evening."

Hmmm. That was more than I'd made in a while. "Just for the night?" I asked.

"Yep." She nodded. "The address is on the card. See you next Wednesday at five P.M. Okay?"

"Um, yeah. Okay. " I turned to get back to Kenny, who was waiting for me with a scowl on his face.

"What the fuck did Chantal want with you?" he hissed through his missing front tooth.

"Nothing. Just being friendly," I lied. I wasn't sure why I didn't tell him. For whatever reason, I didn't want him to know what I was up to. I needed something for me.

The week passed quickly, and by Wednesday I found myself frantically searching for the card Chantal had given me at the concert. I hadn't been making any money and knew that my welcome at the house was wearing thin. Twenty bucks would go a long way.

I hopped on Kenny's bicycle and pedaled across town through a light drizzle. By the time I found the place, I was soaked to the bone. I looked up at the sign. This was no club. It was a total dive bar. But I had already committed, so I locked Kenny's bike to the nearest pole and entered. Though night was just falling outside, the sun had clearly set long ago inside this bar. I coughed as I walked into the darkness and smoke.

"Hey there!" I heard Chantal call. She was arranging folding tables to create a makeshift runway. *Oh, boy,* I thought. *A real class act.*

As I walked toward her, I noticed an area that was curtained off. She pointed and said, "That's the changing room. Your outfit's in there."

"Oh, okay," I said, trying to sound nonchalant. I entered and saw a dozen or so high heels, all with marabou feathers at the toe, stacked in the corner alongside a few silk teddies, a bra, matching panties, and some sort of corset contraption. *Yikes.*

"These are the outfits?" I stammered, poking my head out from behind the curtain. "Like the outfits we wear and walk down the . . . um, runway in?"

"Yeah, Carré, this is all for the Ashby Street Lingerie store. I didn't tell you that? Oops!" She laughed. She already had a drink in her hand. I stared at it longingly. She looked down and then back at me. "You want one?" she asked.

"Yeah," I exclaimed, relieved that she'd gotten the hint, unsubtle as it was. There was only one fucking way I was going to be able do this, and that was loaded.

I stepped into the curtained room again and began to strip down. As Madonna's "Dress You Up" boomed over the sound system, I pulled the teddy on and stepped into the heels. I sighed. I barely filled out the form-fitting cami, but then again, there really wasn't much material there to cover up what I did have.

As the crowd gathered, I peeked out from behind the curtain again.

Thankfully, Chantal kept the booze flowing. I laughed and shuddered as the small bar filled up quickly with mostly men. I stood next to two other girls, noticing that I was by far the youngest. The music quieted, and Chantal stepped up onto the table, clapped her hands, and announced the evening's lineup. There were raucous cheers from the patrons, and the next thing I knew, one of Phil Collins's classic anthems began to rock the house. A shove to my back propelled me out onto the wobbly runway, where I stood there near naked for the world to see.

And though I didn't know it that night, as I struggled to remain sure-footed and to retain some semblance of self-worth, I'd just stumbled onto a platform that would alter my life forever.

SAN FRANCISCO

Not long after my first moment on the runway, Kenny and I moved to San Francisco—ironically, the city I was so eager to leave as a young girl. We both wanted our own place, away from roommates. Since most of Kenny's gigs were in the city anyway, it made sense. But rents were higher there than in Berkeley. All we could afford was a tiny apartment on Rose Street, not quite under the 101 freeway but close. Our neighbors were prostitutes and drag queens. All too often I would see one of them taking a dump between the parked cars in front of our building. I can't even begin to count the number of times I was asked for toilet paper. But at least the place was ours.

I was lonely and still too young to work most places. My days were long and dull. My nights were usually spent roaming the streets and frequenting dance clubs where I was admitted despite my age, thanks to Kenny. One night he and I were at the Station, a hot new club that had recently opened. While I was dancing, I could see Kenny talking with a man at the bar. They both nodded in my direction, and I glimpsed something exchange hands. I couldn't see what it was and didn't really care. I assumed Kenny was scoring some blow.

Lou Reed's "Walk on the Wild Side" was playing, and since it was my favorite song at the time, I stepped into the center of the floor and got into a solitary groove. I didn't need a partner in order to shake my ass; I just loved to dance. Suddenly I felt a hand on my lower back. Turning in surprise, I stood face-to-face with the guy from the bar.

"Hey there," he said, smiling at me.

"Hi," I said, my tone both questioning and dismissive. *What's up with him?* I wondered as I turned away again. A second later his hand was on my ass.

I spun around. "Dude! What's *up?*" I was angry now. I slapped his hand off me. I looked around for Kenny. He stood in the darkness, on the outskirts, watching me.

"Your pimp said you were cool. You *are,* right?" He looked defensive and confused more than hostile.

"What the fuck? Not right, asshole." I couldn't believe him. There was no way Kenny could have done that to me. Could he? I stormed over to my boyfriend, demanding to know what was going on. "Did you take that guy's money?"

Kenny shrugged, avoiding my gaze. "Carré, we need the cash. He just wants to feel you up. It's no big deal. Do it for me. For us." He raised his eyes to meet mine, his tone pleading.

Speechless, I cocked my head to one side, trying to understand how this man, who I thought loved me, could have done such a thing. And then I raised my hand and slapped him across the face as hard as I could. I began to stalk off. A second later Kenny grabbed me by the hair, and with one vicious yank I was on my back. The potential john came running up, trying to protect me. "Man, take it easy!" he yelled at Kenny. Kenny shoved the guy backward, pulled me up by my roots, and began dragging me out of the club.

I could see people watching, their eyes wide with alarm. But no one else ran to help.

Out on the street, under the glare of a streetlamp, Kenny pushed me up against a telephone pole. Pointing a finger in my face, spit flying from his mouth, he raged on and on, accusing and threatening me. I stood motionless and silent. It was the only way I knew to remain safe. But I also knew I was in real danger if I stayed with Kenny. I needed a way out.

I spent the night on our threadbare couch, listening to the sound of the foghorns merge gloomily with the sound of Kenny's snoring. His duffel bag was packed and ready by the door. He was heading out of town again with the band. I sensed that this was my moment to make a break. I just didn't know what that break would be. As the rain poured down outside, streaking the windows and casting shadows on my naked legs, I realized I had two options: prostitution or modeling. I knew I couldn't do the former. And while that twenty-dollar walk down the runway in Berkeley was hardly what I envisioned for myself, it was at least bearable. Fucking someone for money was not. Thus began my modeling career.

AGENTS OF CHANGE

As soon as Kenny had left the next morning, I pulled out the phone book and started searching, looking under "Models" or "Modeling Agents." One listing jumped out at me: Gary Loftus Model Management. That one sounded more professional than sleazy. And the office was close, just up the way in the Castro. I put on the best outfit I had, smeared on some lipstick and blush, and headed out to catch the bus up Market Street.

Some girls dream of modeling from the time they're small. I wasn't one of them. I clearly chose that option out of need, out of a desperate desire to make it on my own. That fleeting moment on the makeshift runway in Berkeley hadn't made me long for fame as a cover girl. What it had done, though, was open a door of possibility in my mind. A door I was now ready to walk through with determination.

As I entered the quaint little office, I saw a short, balding man sitting behind an enormous wooden antique desk. He wore an earring in his right ear and a gold ring on his pinkie finger. Gary Loftus gave a vigorous wave to invite me in, his eyes assessing every inch of me as he continued his phone conversation. His would be the first pair of eyes to subject me to an agent's professional scrutiny. I didn't feel at all uncomfortable. I had been stared at before with lust (usually from men) and with hostility (usually from other women). But there was something comfortingly businesslike about this man's gaze. Besides, I was certain he was gay.

"Gary will be off in a moment," a cheerful voice said from behind me. I hadn't noticed anyone else but that small magnetic man. I turned around in surprise and saw a strikingly beautiful, statuesque woman sitting at another desk. She stood up and extended a delicate hand. "Hi. I'm Dawn," she said.

"Oh. Hi. Sorry, I hadn't even noticed you there."

"You are . . . ?"

"Duh. Carré . . . Carré Otis. Pleased to meet you," I sputtered. I was sure I was making a lousy first impression. I reached out and took her hand. She held it longer than normal, long enough to send a shiver through me. *Wow,* I thought. *That was strange.* Dawn nodded and looked as if she were licking her lips. However awkward my introduction had been, she seemed to like what she was seeing.

"Do you have an appointment?" Dawn asked.

"No. Should I have made one? Should I go? Come back another time?" I was babbling, and I knew she could hear the slight desperation in my voice. We had this strong vibe together. I couldn't explain it. Before Dawn could answer, I heard Gary hang up the phone. Spinning around to face him, I grabbed the initiative and introduced myself.

"Well, doll, have a seat." He motioned to the chair in front of his desk, and I quickly sat down. I wanted to make an impression, but I didn't want to take up too much of his time.

"So, kid, tell me your story. You are . . . let me guess. Sixteen? Seventeen? Does your mother know you're here?" He gave me a not-unkind smile, but it was clear he'd heard every story in the book. I knew I would have to make this one good.

"Eighteen, actually," I lied. "And it's Carré. Carré Otis." I was a lot smoother with Gary than I'd been with Dawn. I was still unnerved by the electricity I'd felt with her.

Gary nodded slowly, looking me straight in the eye, trying to decide whether to believe me. "Do you have some photos for me to look at today?"

I gulped. It hadn't even occurred to me to bring anything except my face.

"No. I don't. I have nothing." I swallowed hard to contain the emotions that were surfacing. I felt like bursting into tears. Considering what I'd been through during the previous twelve hours, this felt like my only shot. I was desperate. And I needed someone to believe in me without trying to fuck me over one way or another.

Gary just watched me for a while. I could feel Dawn's eyes on us, too. Gary was smart enough to know that I wasn't your average eighteen-year-old. (As he would tell me later, he was smart enough to know that I wasn't eighteen at all.) He also knew I had a tough story. But he didn't need the details. What he needed was to decide if I had "it."

"What do you think, Dawn? Should I give this kid a break?" His eyes never left mine while we waited for Dawn to respond. Time stopped. I held my breath.

"She's a beauty, Gary. Let's give her a go and see what she's got. I'll set up some shots with Carolyn for tomorrow morning."

Gary smiled, just a little. "Whaddaya think, kid? Can you get yourself to this address tomorrow? Eight A.M.?" He handed me a piece of paper, and I looked down, my hands trembling.

"Yes. Of course," I said, my eyes welling with tears. I quickly raised a hand and wiped them dry. Gary saw them anyway.

"No promises, kid, so don't get your hopes up. Let's just wait and see what we get back. Oh, and clean face, no makeup—and clean hair, Carré. Got it?"

I nodded yes. Gary led me to the door, his hand kind and supportive on my shoulder. I stepped outside, turned around, and thanked him.

"Sweetheart, I don't know where you're from, or what you're up to," Gary said quietly, "but I'm gonna do my best to help you out. For the love of God, don't you dare screw me."

I nodded and tried to speak, but he just shook his head and waved good-bye, closing the door. "Have a fab day, my dear! And an even better one tomorrow!"

And with that, I was back on the bus, excitedly making my way to my tiny dive of an apartment. In less than twenty-four hours, I'd finished my first photo shoot.

I called Gary's office every day for a week, asking if the photos Carolyn had taken were in yet. Dawn flirted with me on the phone, patiently reminding me I needed to wait. Finally, on a Friday morning, she called before I could call her. The pictures were in. Gary wanted to see me right away.

I burst into the office, filled with a mix of excitement and anxiety. I wanted to say something, but I just stood there trembling. When Gary saw me, he stood up from behind his desk and walked toward me, his expression unreadable. The anticipation was killing me.

"They look good, kid," he said, breaking into a broad smile. "Really, really good."

I squeaked and jumped up and down in my spot. But what did "really good" really mean?

Dawn sidled next to me, her shoulder nearly touching mine, beaming from ear to ear. "We need to know something, Carré. Are you ready?"

"Ready for what?" I demanded.

"For New York City?" Gary asked with a grin.

As soon as Gary had seen my test shots, he'd sent them to Elite in Manhattan. John Casablancas, the president of the agency, liked what he saw. He wanted to fly me out at once.

"Oh, my God!" I shrieked. If Gary and Dawn had had any doubts that I'd been lying about my age, they vanished. I was almost childlike with giddiness. This was my shot to get out, far away from Kenny, and away from the troubles with my family. This was a real plan. And then it hit me. This was impossible.

"Wait . . . Gary, I can't afford that. I have no money. I mean, *no* money. I have nothing." Tears of excitement changed to tears of embarrassment and frustration.

Gary stepped forward, putting his arms around me, giving me the safest hug I'd had from a man in years. Maybe ever.

"Shh, sweetie, it's okay. You don't need money now. Elite will pay for everything. They see something in you worth the expense."

I cried harder, sobbing on Gary's shoulder, even though I had at least three inches on him. It felt so good to have someone believe in me at last. Perhaps there'd been others who had seen my potential before, but, for whatever reason, *I* hadn't sensed it or trusted it. I trusted this sweet and gentle man, though. He had given me my chance. The phrase "overwhelmed with gratitude" is trite, but it truly describes how I felt at that moment. I could barely speak.

Gary gently extricated himself from my embrace and stepped back, his smile as wide as ever. Reaching into his wallet, he peeled off three crisp twenty-dollar bills. "A little something to get you through," he said. I saw tears in his own eyes as he pressed the money into my hand and gave me a peck on the cheek.

"Dawn will give you all the details. Flights, bus stations, the models' apartment. Congrats, kid. You did good. Now you better go knock 'em dead."

I went home that day and packed my little bag. I would be gone long before Kenny got home from his tour. Getting away from him wasn't my only reason for going to New York, but it was high on the list. I didn't leave a note, didn't tell my parents where I was going. I didn't feel like I had to now that I was really on my own.

Sadly, I never saw Gary again. This lovely man who gave me my first break died of AIDS just months after I left for New York. He was the first of many dear friends who would lose their lives to that dreadful disease. To this day I have never once forgotten his kindness or his faith in me.

I would not find either of those qualities in a man again for a very long time.

2

Early Modeling Years

THE BIG APPLE

New York was a whirlwind of surprises. With just the money that Gary had given me in my pocket, and a few more pennies I had saved up, I was living on the low end of a pauper's budget. Unprepared for winter weather, I was cold to the bone. Colder than I'd ever been before.

Finding my way to the models' apartment was a terrifying journey. New streets, yellow cabs, fast drivers, all a swirl of unknowns. Elite's model apartments were way up on the twenty-second floor of a high-rise on Manhattan's famed Park Avenue. San Francisco didn't have many buildings like this. I wasn't used to the towering heights, nor was I used to the city lights, which never seemed to dim long enough for anyone to sleep. That old feeling of homesickness permeated every cell in my body. I ached for familiarity. But instead, when I rang the buzzer on apartment D, I was met by a woman with a stiff smile who efficiently proceeded to tell me the rules and regulations of the housing arrangement I'd just entered into.

Trudi Tapscott was in charge of the New Faces division at Elite, and all the new girls stayed with her. The place was depressing: There was a stark living room with a glass table and a lone ficus tree standing sadly in a bare corner. A kitchen completely devoid of any basics, even salt and pepper, lent itself easily to the new diet all the girls seemed to be on. Trudi's apartment adjoined the models' quarters, and although she couldn't have been older than thirty, her impressive stature easily had us all assuming that "big sister" was watching. Although it remained unspoken, I'm pretty sure we all thought that a favorite of Trudi's would have a lot more casting opportunities in a day than would a girl who rubbed her the wrong way. So we learned to live with her and love her. And those who didn't, pretended to.

I was "odd girl out" again. My style wasn't "sorority." My differences had already found their way into how I related to others. This housing arrangement wasn't going to lead to forming any close or lasting friendships. It was clear to me that my personal history wasn't exactly like that of most of the other girls. I was a runaway. I had no money, nothing cool in my bag of tricks, nothing fancy in my wardrobe. And, most painfully, unlike the others I wasn't calling home on Sundays to report my week's victories to my loving and excited family. I was just hoping to get by.

The day I arrived, I dragged my exhausted self and my small bag into the bunk room. I was barely given a nod by the others, all of whom were newcomers themselves.

"Hi," I tried shyly. "I'm Carré."

Nods all around. Stephanie was a brunette on the top bunk, Tiffany a blonde on the lower bunk. And Fiona walked in with a towel wrapped around her tall, slender body. "Oh!" she declared excitedly. "I'm not the new one anymore! That's a fucking relief!"

Great, I thought. *This ought to be fun.* Pulling out my toiletry bag, I headed to the bathroom to get washed up. Tomorrow morning I would have to be at the Elite headquarters to meet the man in charge.

Afterward, climbing onto the small bottom bunk, I could hear the girls whispering and laughing. They had already met the Boss, John Casablancas, and were well into their first weeks of endless castings and test shoots. If you managed to nail a job, you were as good as gold, but so far none of the new girls had. Listening to their conversations, I gathered that there was a four-week rule. If you hadn't scored something (or someone) by then, chances were you would be "sent back." That banishment loomed over all our heads as the minutes, days, and weeks ticked by. It was an interesting hell for a teenager to have to endure. Already we were on the clock, with a definite expiration date.

As the sun rose over the Big Apple, movement in the small apartment had purpose. The occupants made themselves busy preparing for the rounds of the day. Hair dryers buzzed, mascara was applied, lip gloss dabbed, and hefty streaks of rouge were smudged on. Apparently, barefaced castings were not really done in New York, or perhaps everyone just had her own interpretation of what "bare" meant.

I threw together the only outfit I had that might be hip enough to wear to a meeting with the president of Elite: an oversize silk navy button-down man's shirt and my only pair of black leggings that weren't yet threadbare. Pulling on my socks and boots, I gazed out at the city streets below, noting that a light rain had begun to fall. I didn't have an umbrella, and I certainly didn't have a fancy overcoat. Looking on as my fellow models buttoned up their formal "best," I felt small and inadequate. Fiona must have noticed my wistful expression and threw me a long black trench coat.

"Here," she said. "You don't have one, do you?" Her look was inquisitive, and maybe a bit concerned. Shaking my head in disbelief and gratitude, I stood up to try it on. It was a perfect fit. And a perfect addition to my one and only outfit.

"Seriously? I can borrow it?" I asked.

"No prob," Fiona answered with a smile. That coat was an absolute gift, and it got me through my first freezing weeks in Manhattan.

I made my way to the agency and prepared myself for the worst. I was certain that John Casablancas would see me and realize that he'd made a terrible decision in flying me out. I sat quietly in the waiting room playing with the buttons on Fiona's coat, watching the doors open and shut, seeing faces and hearing accents from all over the world as people passed through like waves in an undulating ocean. The walls were covered with posters of Kim Alexis, Joan Severance, and Janice Dickinson. Paulina Porizkova lay sandy-bottomed for a *Sports Illustrated* cover. It was all tremendously impressive as well as tremendously intimidating.

Suddenly the large doors onto the waiting room opened and Trudi's familiar face poked in.

"Carré, John will see you now."

I gulped. Stood. And followed Trudi through the doors and into absolute mayhem. Bookers were on phones, all speaking in different languages. Head shots and composites lined the walls. Notes and client names were pinned to an enormous bulletin board. It was loud. Unbelievably loud. These were the days before computers and e-mail. The noise was unforgettable.

Trudi opened another large wooden door leading to a spacious office, and as I stepped in, she closed it firmly behind me. I held my breath. Here it was. The moment of truth. Sitting behind a beautiful mahogany desk was a dark-haired man. He swiveled his chair around to face me. He had such a magnetic smile. He beamed broad and bright; John Casablancas was a handsome and gregarious man.

"Hello, my dear," he said as he stood up. He walked across the carpet toward me. Just when I thought I would shake his hand, his cheek met mine in what I would soon come to know as the "Euro air kiss." Both sides were quickly pecked, and then he just as quickly backed off, retreating to his lush seat behind the desk.

"Sit. Sit down." John smiled, nodding to the chairs that surrounded him. I sat, trying to cross my legs elegantly and look sophisticated. Shit, I was so far out of this league it was painful. I was certain my cover was about to be blown.

"Let me tell you how this works, Carré," he said. "You will stay here, with us, and we will begin by sending you out for some test shoots. All I have here are these." He slapped the test photos I had taken in San Francisco onto the table. "Of course we can tell you are a pretty girl. But the question remains . . . do you have it?"

I nodded dumbly. "It." Did I? I wasn't certain at all.

As if reading my thoughts, he gave a small laugh. "Even if you think you don't have it, my dear, act like you do. And let me be the judge."

"Also, I hear you have no money. Is this true?"

I nodded and stared.

"We will provide you a small allowance every week. This will be on your tab of what you will owe us as your agents. And this money . . . well, Trudi will give you all the details you need. We expect you to show up on time. Be professional." He turned his attention to a small photo on his desk. I recognized the face. It was a young up-and-coming model, Stephanie Seymour.

"Let me tell you a story. This girl, Stephanie, came to me only six months ago. With her mother. She was an unknown. And soon she will be world-famous. In just a year. Ahhh . . . Stephanie." He looked longingly at the picture. "She sends me the sweetest cards, with glitter and stickers spilling out. She's in Marbella right now, shooting for French *Elle*. My little star."

I was confused. But soon it would be clear. Stephanie was John's girlfriend—despite their nearly twenty-seven-year age difference.

He placed his hand on the intercom and paged Trudi.

"So let's give you a few weeks and see what we have. Perhaps you will be my next little star," he said, in what sounded to me an almost conspiratorial tone.

Just then Trudi walked in.

"Come along with me, Carré," she said. "Let me show you around. You will be 'mine.'" There was something caring and protective about both her manner and these words.

I stood and thanked John. I was genuinely grateful, just unsure.

As we walked back through the office and the hustle and bustle, Trudi pointed out all the big agents. "There is Monique Pillard. She handles all the stars." As we passed a glass-encased office, I could see a small, pudgy, wire-haired woman pacing. She looked like someone's grandmother. But Monique was a big shot. Not to be fooled with.

After my tour I was a given a map of the city and a list of the subways I'd need to take to get to my first test shoot. It was with Rocco Laspata, a photographer who would later go on to found the Laspata DeCaro agency. Rocco had been sent my one picture from Gary's test and had liked it enough to agree to shoot me. Working with him was my initiation into life as a model in the big city.

There were many, many test shoots in the weeks to come, but few pictures actually made the cut. It was the hair, or the makeup, or the lighting—or, even worse, just me. I wasn't quite right. I was too this or too that. I was too plump, my face too fat, my smile too crooked, or my nose too difficult to light. My pout at that time was too big, my tits too small. Despite all the hope in my heart, there was an inevitable sinking feeling at day's end, knowing as I did that the clock was ticking and my time was running out.

One evening Trudi asked if I wanted to come over for a glass of wine. *Wow. This must mean she likes me,* I thought. I happily agreed, and as I knocked on the door that led from the models' apartment to hers, I felt my first sense of triumph in the big city.

I sat with Trudi on her white couch, listening to music, sipping wine. And as we both loosened up, she began to share with me details of her love life. Her boyfriend had just sent her a gift, she told me. "Wanna see?" she asked sloppily. I laughed, eager to please, and said, "Of course."

But mortification took over as she pulled off her pressed pants and underwear and stood there bottomless. (Modesty, as I'd be reminded many more times in my career, really is overrated in the modeling industry.) Embarrassment then turned to confusion when Trudi opened a box and pulled out a pair of panties. Or were they? What the hell? They were "half panties." My brows must have furrowed in uncertainty. I tried to act cool and nodded, encouraging her to try them on. That, of course, was my first introduction to the thong. Neither of us were very clear on how to wear one, so the next few minutes were spent in trial and error.

"Well, wait," she said, struggling. "I think this string goes here and that one goes there." She wiggled the panties around, but no matter how she situated them, they still looked totally wrong.

We laughed and at that point I stood, figuring this was a good time to leave. "Oh, they're cute," I assured her. "Really cute. He must be a doll."

"Wait, Carré, before you go. . . . Let's hang out again. Maybe we could have drinks with Eric. My boyfriend?"

"Yeah. That would be great." I lied. I sensed that Trudi was lonely and looking for a friend but I also sensed trouble. *Lord knows, I don't need any more of that now,* I thought.

"Cool. Tomorrow at seven. Okay?"

"Sure." I smiled. I was tired. Ready for my day to end.

The next day came, and eventually I found myself back at Trudi's with a glass of Fumé Blanc in my hand. Her boyfriend was there, too. We hung out and ate Chinese food ordered from the corner restaurant. But every time Trudi left, Eric would stare at me, inching closer and closer on the couch. It was all too awkward. I liked Trudi a lot, but spending time with her and her boyfriend was weird. He made me feel uneasy.

I ended up hanging out with them again . . . and again. Every night the same thing happened. But I couldn't resist. The models' apartment was dull and lonely. Of course, it didn't take long for my involvement in the "world next door" to get the other girls furiously whispering every time I made a late-night return.

A couple of weeks into my stay, I was called into the Elite headquarters. Waiting in Trudi's office, I was surprised to see John himself walk in. He had a series of my test shots in his hand.

"Carré, we have a problem."

Oh, no. This wasn't going to be good.

"Your look isn't it, my dear. It's not catching on. We haven't one really solid shot of you in all of these," he said, waving the pile of pictures. I swallowed hard.

"You look too . . ." He paused.

"I know," I said. I finished the line: "Fat, pouty, angry, plump, dark, exotic. I've heard it all." It sounded like a list of dwarfs from an alternative Snow White movie. And I was grumpy, too, tired of being endlessly picked apart.

"Now, now," John scolded. *He* was supposed to say these things. Not me. "I will give it one more week. On my dime. If we can't get something good, something really good, then I'm afraid you will have to move on."

"Shit," I muttered under my breath.

"Pardon?" He shot me a stern look.

"Nothing. Of course, Mr. Casablancas. Thank you. I will give it my all." Not that I hadn't been. I had. It was just that—once again—I was "wrong." All wrong.

John left, and I sat alone in Trudi's office, tears streaming down my face. I didn't have a fallback. I didn't have another plan. This had been the whole plan. I was fucked.

"Hey, Carré." Trudi waltzed in. "What's up?" She saw my stricken face. "Oh, honey, it's okay. It's going to be okay." She drew me into a hug, and I cried for a moment, then looked her in the eyes.

"Sweetie, listen to me," she said. "He won't just let you go. You'll be sent to Paris. Milan. You *will* make it." I felt momentarily comforted. "You! You are special, Carré, you have that look," she assured me. Then she asked me to do her a favor.

"What is it?" I said between sniffles and blotting my tears.

"Can you meet Eric at my apartment? He doesn't have the keys, and I have a late meeting."

Without thinking, I said yes. Why? I'm not sure. I wanted to help. I felt vulnerable, and I was grateful for her support. But something in me was flashing a warning sign.

When Eric showed up around seven, I did as I was told and let him in. Comfortable in Trudi's apartment by this time, I turned on the music and opened a bottle of wine, offering him a glass.

"Here you go, Eric," I said, smiling cheerfully and handing it to him. "Thanks, Carré." As he took it, his hand touched mine and our eyes met. His gaze lingered a moment too long. I pulled away and looked at the floor. *That was awkward,* I thought.

"Come," he said, as he patted the couch next to him. "Sit by me for a moment."

I was unsure of what to do, yet I didn't want to be rude. And so I sat. Casually and utterly predictably, Eric put his arm over the back of the couch, his hand touching my shoulder. I stiffened. A moment later he swiveled around so that we were nose to nose. I held my breath, praying he would go away. And then he did it. He kissed me. I pulled back on impulse, totally mortified. I was considering slapping him when Trudi walked in and stood, mouth agape, staring at the two of us sitting much too close together on her couch.

"What the fuck is going on?" she yelled. I could see the fury course through her, the rage welling up as her cheeks flushed. "You didn't just do that again, Eric?" She was demanding an answer and begging him to be something other than what he was. I could feel her pain, her sense of betrayal.

"Trudi!" I cried, rising from the couch. "It's not what it looks like!" *What a pathetic line,* I thought as soon as it came out of my mouth. Like she'd ever believe that one.

She stomped over to me and pushed me. "What the fuck are *you* doing? You treat me like this? You treat me like shit? I invite you into my home and you do this?" Spit was flying. Her voice was escalating. I knew that the girls next door had their ears to the wall.

"Wait! I didn't do anything. He—" I cried, pointing a finger. "*He* tried to kiss *me*. I only did what you said. I opened your door for him!" I was desperate. But I knew I wouldn't be believed. I was telling the truth and it didn't matter. My lifeline was being severed.

Trudi looked like she wanted to slap me first and then smack Eric, too. Instead she grabbed me by the arm and practically dragged me to the door that separated the apartments. She opened it and pushed me through.

"Get out of here, Carré! Get the fuck out. And don't you ever fucking set foot in here again." She looked at me with disbelief and hurt. And then it turned to disgust.

I felt like shit. I had disappointed her and myself. And with that, she slammed the door, leaving me face-to-face with a roomful of models, each silently staring at me. We all stood motionless, amid the yells and the thumps and the shattering of glass as Eric and Trudi argued in the next room.

In my bed I pulled the covers around me and listened to the drone of city traffic, then a pounding rain. I blew it. I could see Trudi's expression over and over in my head. I couldn't imagine exactly what my fate would be after this, though I had my fears. As it happened, I wouldn't have to wait long to find out.

The next morning the phone rang in the models' apartment.

"Carré, it's for you."

It was Trudi's assistant.

"Pack your bags. You're heading out."

"Wait . . . what?" I stammered. "Where to?"

"Paris, France." I knew after my meeting with Mr. Casablancas that this call would be coming, but I had hoped it wouldn't be so soon . . . and that the incident with Eric didn't hasten it. What would have been welcome news yesterday sounded more like a death sentence today. I knew the truth and it hung over me like a black cloud.

I had blown it. Again.

PARIS, TAHITI, MILAN

The next night I took the red-eye on Air France. It seemed to last forever—hour after hour, flying through darkness. By the time we landed at Charles de Gaulle just before dawn, I was exhausted and disoriented. Some people imagine that traveling must be a particularly glamorous perk for a model. Many assume that models all fly first class. There would come a time when I would travel in the front of the plane, and even on private jets. But in 1985 I traveled the way most models did and still do: in coach. Luxuries in the industry were reserved for a lucky few, and John Casablancas wasn't going to spend more than he had to on sending a difficult young model off to Paris.

What little sleep I got had been in some cramped and compromised position. Even for my young body, that flight was a haul. I got off the plane, every bit of me aching, and trudged through a maze of escalators and moving walkways. I longed for a soft bed. A flat bed. But as I arrived at the baggage claim, I saw through the windows that the sun was already rising. The airport was a long distance from the city. I would catch my first glimpse of it in broad daylight. In spite of my exhaustion, I began to wake up. It was too noisy not to. De Gaulle was a cacophony of sounds. The strange language and the overpowering smells of smoke, perfume, and espresso all hung heavy in the air.

My one bag came around on the carousel, and I swung it over my shoulder and headed through customs. As I walked toward the glass doors that divided new arrivals from the outside world, I saw the waiting and expectant faces on the other side. I didn't know what face to look for. I had only a name. I prayed that I would find him; I realized that I had no idea how to use a French pay phone, and I didn't even have a number to call.

I stepped out into a sea of people and looked around. I didn't see my name on a sign or anyone waving at me. I walked slowly toward the street exit, holding on tightly to my bag. As I pivoted to avoid getting run over, I saw a short man with a round and flushed face come my way. He had on an old-fashioned cap, a corduroy blazer, a button-down shirt, and a colorful ascot. Even in a Paris airport, he stood out as particularly French. "Carré? Carré, is this you?" He extended his hand, and as I reached out to shake it, he pumped my arm up and down, a bit too enthusiastically. I had just met the infamous Jacques de Nointel.

Jacques was a close associate of Gérald Marie, the president of Élite Europe. I would later learn that in that distinctive corduroy coat he carried dozens of watches that he tried to sell at every opportunity. Patek Philippe, Cartier, Tiffany, Rolex. Like a character out of an old movie, Jacques was ready and eager to throw open his coat and make every new "good friend" a special offer. He was a bit of a nut, and not necessarily the endearing kind. I would learn to steer well clear of Jacques.

Jacques informed me that "zee boss" (Gérald) wanted me to come straight to the agency. "He needs to see you immediately," I was told. I got the picture: It was not about my comfort. It didn't matter that I needed to shower, needed to sleep. How I felt was irrelevant to the "boss." I was now one of his soldiers. Elite owned my ass; I couldn't possibly say no, so I acquiesced, and we got into Jacques's car.

We passed enormous billboards on our drive into Paris. I was amazed by what I saw: The models were nearly all nude. Every American who comes to Europe notices the greater openness about nakedness in advertising, but my shock was compounded by what I was in Paris to do. I was a model—and couldn't take my eyes off the exposed nipple on the Clarins body-lotion ad and the perfectly tanned butt of another model in an advertisement for suntan lotion. This was a different world.

Jacques drove fast. Not unusual for a Frenchman. We wended our way at a breakneck pace through the small streets, still slick from rain, zipping past cars tinier than any I had ever seen. As we drove into the heart of Paris, the city seemed to wake up around us. Our tires bounced over cobblestones as café doors opened and shopkeepers set out their street-level displays of fresh produce and fish on ice. The exhaustion soon faded, and exhilaration pulsed through me. It was so new, so different, so perfectly beautiful. Everyone falls in love with Paris at first sight, and I was no exception. The difference was that I was also thinking of my career. In the fresh light of morning, I felt a wave of optimism. Perhaps everyone had been right: I just needed a new start, a new chance. That was the magic of Paris, a magic that makes anything and everything seem possible.

My reverie stopped as abruptly as the car did. We rounded one last bend and came to a sudden halt. We had arrived at 21 avenue Montaigne, Elite's glorious Paris office. Before I got out of the car, I stole a quick look in my little handheld mirror, smoothing my hair and making sure I didn't have any sleep left in my eyes. It would have been nice to have showered after the flight, but if "zee boss" wanted to see me right away, he'd just have to cope with Carré au naturel.

I climbed out of the backseat of the car and took a deep breath. I gazed at the stunning (and to my eyes, ancient) building. This was my moment. I knew I needed to make a great impression. And as I stood there, right on the sidewalk, something shifted inside. It was as if the clouds had parted and I realized all at once that my prayers were as good as anyone's; I deserved a break as much as the next girl. That sudden sense of well-being was rare and elusive when I was seventeen. I would learn, many years later, how to connect to that energy and confidence at will. But all those years ago, it was a most surprising, welcome, and needed gift. And with that gift and that sudden surge of confidence, I followed Jacques through the front gates.

With each step I took, I felt my doubts and mistrust slip away. I felt certainty rise in me; everything was about to change for the better. Upon walking into the inner courtyard of 21 avenue Montaigne, I felt almost defiant. *Come hell or high water,* I told myself, *I won't go back home defeated.* What I didn't know was that defeat wears many faces. I thought defeat would be failing to make it as a model. What I was about to discover is that our most devastating defeats sometimes come disguised in the form of success.

Walking through that door was electrifying. Even early in the morning, you could feel the energy. My exhaustion was gone; my pulse grew quicker. In the center of the room, half a dozen agents sat around a circular booking table, all on phones, all talking, smoking, laughing, and glancing intently at the model board. I moved around that table in slow motion, checking out all the model composites, the famous faces of past and present framed and hung on the walls. These photos were their trophies, I realized. These were their stars. These were their victories. It was the first time I realized how much I wanted to make it in this industry. I wanted to work. Badly. And I wanted to succeed.

I didn't have much time to linger over the portraits. When a short, stringy-haired, pug-eyed man walked briskly and deliberately toward me, I had no trouble figuring out who "zee boss" was. Gérald Marie was wearing leather pants, pulled a bit too high and cinched at the waist with a cowboy belt and oversize buckle. The look was completed with snakeskin boots and a button-down shirt and blazer, Gérald's greasy curls touching just below his shoulders. He was the walking embodiment of what Americans already called Eurotrash. He was quite a sight.

Gérald looked me up and down. He took my hand and twirled me around, studying me from my head to my toes. I was numb to this sort of thing at this point, having learned to stand back and wait for the verbal assessment to come. If you weren't numb, those candid assessments could be brutal. They could hit a girl like a punch in the gut. I had steeled myself against those words for so long already that it rarely seemed to matter what any agent or photographer said. But Gérald wasn't brutal. He nodded with a slight smile and a little wink. "You will do well here, my dear. Let's get you on the set and see what you are made of."

He turned to Jacques and told him, "Take her to Phil Stadtmiller at La Tour Eiffel. Now. Everyone is there, and you are running late!"

I stammered. "But wait. I just got here. My bags. My hair. I'm exhausted."

Gérald spun around, his voice hard. "Are you in or out, my dear?" (And this was twenty years before Heidi Klum would make a nearly identical phrase legendary on *Project Runway*!) I could barely understand what he said; Gérald's accent was particularly thick when he got annoyed. But there was no misunderstanding after what he did next: He took me by the hand once again and marched me down the hall, away from Jacques and the agents. When we were out of earshot, he hissed, "On my dime I do not want your opinion, Carré. I want your obedience." With that, he slapped my ass, a bit too hard. "Are you game?" I nodded in shock, but also in resignation. I knew that working in Paris would be different from anywhere else, and because I had no choice, I would be game for anything. As for the slap, I ought to have taken it for the bad sign that it was. Today no one smacks any part of my body without my permission. But it was a common enough thing for agents and photographers to do. Sometimes the gesture was sexual, sometimes it was meant as encouragement, and sometimes it was just a way of punctuating a conversation. But Gérald's slap was different. It felt possessive. And mean.

We rushed out of the Elite offices, Jacques whisking me over to the Eiffel Tower as fast as he could. We pulled up and saw that Gérald had been right. A small van and an entire photo crew were waiting, none too patiently. Everyone was in a rush, and I—still unrested and unshowered—was in the center of the bustle. I sat on the tiny chair in the van, the hairdresser frantically brushing and pulling, blowing and curling as the makeup artist did her thing. No one said much of anything, and none of what they did say was in English. I could see wild, colorful clothes hanging on a rack, my outfits for the day. Just as the team was finishing the task of pulling my look together, the door of the van flew open. The next voice I heard wasn't French but pure New York.

"What the fuck is taking so long?"

Enter Phil Stadtmiller, asshole extraordinaire. Really, there's no other way for me to describe this impressively belligerent human being. We were like oil and water from the moment we met. Of course, I knew he hadn't come all the way to France just to torture me, but damned if it didn't seem that way. What's worse was that Phil understood very well what it meant for a "New York model" to be sent to Paris: I hadn't been able to make it. As far as he was concerned, I was already a failure, and he was skeptical that I'd have anything to offer.

Working in the confines of this tiny van, the crew stuffed me into stockings, a frilled skirt, a corset, and go-go boots. If you've seen the Cyndi Lauper or Madonna videos of the mid-1980s, you know the look. The moment they were done, they kicked me—literally—out of the van. There was no time to complain. We were racing the light.

That first day in Paris was as terrifying as it was amazing. I climbed the base of the Eiffel Tower, at more than one point swinging from those famous metal girders like a monkey. Time and again I clambered into dangerous, seemingly impossible positions, all to get to the best angle and shot. Phil said little that was pleasant, but the other members of the photo crew were exuberant. "Genius!" they cried. "*Ça c'est très belle!*" On and on the thick French compliments came. And at last, as the sun sank toward the horizon and the light began to fade, as I began to shiver from cold and exhaustion, I realized just how good I looked. This was working. *I* was working. John Casablancas had been right, it seemed: Everything was different in Paris.

By the time the shoot was finished, I felt delirious. I hadn't slept properly in what seemed like days, not since New York. As I finished changing for the last time, Jacques sidled up to tell me that Gérald had called him and directed him to drive me to his home at 8 rue du Bac, in the seventh arrondissement—the very heart of Paris.

I had not expected to stay at Gérald's house. Alarm bells ought to have gone off again. But I was too tired, and I knew I didn't really have any other options. I was eager to collapse into sleep, and I knew that as long as I had my own room and my own bed, I'd be just fine.

As it turned out, in that house things wouldn't be fine. Not at all.

The drive to Gérald's place was mercifully quick. Jacques parked his Mercedes on the sidewalk and retrieved my bag from the trunk. I waited on the pavement, staring at yet another gorgeous building. I'd already seen so many throughout the endless day, but 8 rue du Bac was particularly striking. We went in through two enormous wooden doors and turned to the right to climb an elegant spiral staircase. Encased within that spiral was a fine but time-worn cage elevator. Jacques ignored it and took the stairs, perspiring all the way as he lugged my bag. We were only climbing two flights.

We rang the bell on the second floor and waited. Jacques sighed. With a fat paw, he fished out a handkerchief from his pocket to wipe the sweat from his face. As we stood there, he looked at me intently, almost hungrily, his eyes moving up and down. I tried not to shudder. He made me feel naked.

Fortunately, the door swung open a moment later. To my amazement the woman standing there was Linda Evangelista, wearing nothing but a silk robe. Linda was already world-famous as an up-and-coming star, though she had not yet claimed true supermodel status. That was still a year or two in the future for her. Almost comically, Linda mimicked what Jacques had been doing a moment earlier. She, too, looked me up and down, though I felt as if she did it more with evident disdain than desire.

"Oh, yes, here you are," Linda said as she stepped aside to let us in. "Gérald just informed me you were coming."

As we entered, Linda pivoted on her heel, waving one dramatic hand in the air. "Follow me," she said, the exasperation still evident in her high-pitched voice. She led us into the living room of one of the most exquisite apartments I'd ever seen. The wooden floors creaked underfoot; the curtains were pulled open next to the tall windows, revealing the bakery and café in the street below.

"Come along," Linda repeated as she took us down a narrow hallway to a large bedroom. Gérald's. The king-size bed dominated the room, but it was impossible to miss the mirrors on the ceiling. I noticed the open shower and bath, which were in plain view of the bed. Gérald was clearly a man who didn't like anything hidden from him.

We circled the flat to the wonderful, expansive kitchen. A wooden chopping-block island stood in the center, with stools at each end. Gleaming copper pots and pans hung next to braids of garlic and other herbs that I didn't recognize. The stone counters were lined with elegant little jars of honey and jams. An ornate wicker bread basket had pride of place on the counter, baguettes protruding from it. The room was what so many of us imagine when we envision a truly refined Parisian kitchen, glamorous and cozy all at once. Sadly, I would taste and experience very few of the kitchen's glorious comforts during my stay.

Linda told the cook to prepare another plate for dinner. At this point I was too tired to think about food. I only wanted to get to bed, and I tried to politely refuse the invitation to eat. Linda fixed me with a stare.

"In Gérald's house we do as we are told. You are having dinner with us."

Linda took me by the hand, her firm grip belying her childlike voice. She guided me along still another narrow hallway, to a room that I can only describe as Lilliputian. Compared to the expansive splendors of the rest of the apartment, it was tiny: a small single bed, a small chair, and a round porthole window—the sort one finds in the cheaper cabins on a cruise ship. A child's treasure chest stood at the foot of the bed, and a single lamp perched on a fragile little bedside table, providing most of the artificial light in the dim room. The ceilings were very low; if I wore heels, I wouldn't be able to stand up straight.

"This is yours," Linda said briskly. "While you're with us, that is. It's normally Roxanne's room. We call her 'Cookie.' Gérald's daughter."

His daughter's name was Cookie? Really? I bit back the question, asking another instead. "Where is she now?"

"With her mother. Do you remember Lisa Rutledge? The Australian model? She and Gérald divorced a while ago?" Three questions in rapid-fire succession.

Linda waited for a flash of recognition to cross my face. Unfortunately, I hadn't a clue who Lisa Rutledge was. I'd never been a student of the industry's history. I stifled a grim laugh, thinking that I'd been too busy Dumpster diving for dinner in Berkeley to pay much attention to top models.

"Oh, yes, of course." I willed Linda to see that flash of recognition. I was afraid that she already thought so little of me, and I had a past to hide. I didn't need to give her any reason to be suspicious of me.

"Okay, I'll let you get settled. Dinner will be at eight. If you need me, I'll be cleaning things out of the hall closets. I have to fit all my clothes there."

Curiosity won out. I had to ask. "You mean Lisa's things?"

Linda looked at me indulgently. "Oh, no, Christine's things. Christine Bolster."

I managed a nonchalant "Oh." I was very tired, and it was all too much for me to keep up with. I hadn't heard of Christine either and didn't feel like asking any questions about her. (I would hear of Christine again later. Our lives intersected in odd ways: She would soon become a headlining Guess model, as would I. Christine also briefly dated Mickey. Not long before I met him, he had introduced Christine to the man she ultimately married, character actor Robert Davi.)

Clearly, many girls had inhabited this house before me. But Linda was the new reigning queen, something I suspected she wasn't about to let me forget. What she didn't know, and what I would soon discover, is that everything changed when the queen was away.

The dinner bell rang a little before eight. Jet-lagged beyond belief, I rubbed my eyes and stumbled out of my room. As I turned a corner, I found Linda standing amid a huge, messy heap. Women's clothes were strewn from one end of the hallway to the other.

She glanced at me. "Anything here you want?" She seemed cheerful at the prospect of giving away Christine's things as rapidly as possible.

Was she serious? I had come to Paris with one bag. I had no clothes, at least nothing suitable for going to castings. I nodded at Linda, and she started handing me things. She began with a flawless pair of blue suede Kenzo shoes. I'd never owned anything so high-fashion—I just held them in my hands, staring. But they were quickly obscured by the other items Linda tossed into my arms: a Kenzo shirt, black Christian Dior pants, and an exquisite silk Valentino dress. More followed.

I was speechless. Was Linda being kind? Or was it just the sweet satisfaction of giving away a rival's belongings? It didn't matter. My wardrobe had just doubled in minutes; the retail value of what I'd scooped up in the hallway was more than that of all the other clothes I'd ever owned put together. Elated, I raced back to my little room to stash my loot. And then it really was time for dinner.

Before we sat down with Gérald, Linda pulled me aside. She had some sisterly advice, speaking model to model.

"We only drink one drink," she whispered conspiratorially to me, her voice staying remarkably high even at a low volume. "Gin. And tonic. It's full-proof and diet safe. It will fill you up and keep you skinny." Linda mixed one for each of us, and we sat down.

I had much more to learn. Warm, freshly baked bread was placed on the table; it smelled heavenly. I reached out my hand, only to have Linda slap it back.

"Ta ta," she said, shaking her head. "Bread is always a no-no. Never ever!"

The lessons were getting less pleasant.

Gérald finally came home, and with his arrival Linda's demeanor shifted completely. She was on guard, alert to every one of his needs. She doted on Gérald, sweet-talked him, and fed him his meal indulgently. She nodded at everything he said in his impenetrable accent. It would have been difficult to watch under any circumstances. As exhausted as I was, it was impossible. Before I embarrassed myself by falling asleep at the table, I made my apologies and excused myself to bed.

"Ma chère," Gérald called after me. "You need to be up at dawn. Another test shoot awaits you!"

Nodding and yawning all the way down the hall, I didn't care what tomorrow would bring, as long as I could sleep. I fell into my minuscule bed, wrapped the comforter around me, and pulled the pillow over my ears and eyes. It had been the longest day of my life. I slept like a rock.

The very first time I'd seen Paris was at dawn when I landed at Charles de Gaulle. For the rest of my time there, I never ceased to be enthralled by its early mornings. The city had a song all its own.

Long before sunrise, while I was still nestled in my tiny room, I'd hear the rumble of shop doors rolling open. The idling engines of delivery trucks would soon follow, and then—this is what I learned to wait for—the aroma of fresh bread and croissants would rise up to—and through—my little window.

The sounds and smells reminded me of the more pleasant parts of my childhood. As a little girl in Marin, I'd often wake before everyone else, roused by the thump of the furnace kicking on. I would climb out of bed in the pitch black and straddle the heating vent, letting my flannel nightgown billow around me, heat enveloping my body in delicious and comforting warmth. Back then what I heard outside was the garbage truck, its red lights twinkling in the predawn. All toasty from the heater, I'd dream of traveling around the world. Those memories came back to me almost every morning in Paris.

Most days I was up with the sun for one reason or another. Gérald had me out on test shoots and castings around the clock. Linda kept a very different schedule, often sleeping until noon. Gérald knew her preferences and scheduled her castings and shoots for later in the day. To be fair, Linda often worked until very late, frequently not returning to the apartment until the wee hours of the morning.

"Don't disturb Linda. She is resting." Gérald told me this often, his voice tender and indulgent. She lived the life of the superstar she was on the verge of becoming, emerging from her bedroom no earlier than noon, stretching like a confident lion. (She always got up early on Sunday mornings, however. Linda took her Catholic faith seriously and rarely missed Mass.) I was in awe of Linda, not only for her success but because of her willingness to dispense advice about everything I should and shouldn't do. She was only three years older than I was, but those three years seemed to me like a huge gap I needed to fill. Given how competitive the world of modeling is, this was a very generous quality.

Less than ten days after I arrived in Paris, Linda landed a major shoot. She was thrilled. She would be off to an island location for at least a week, working with one of the top photographers out of New

York. As excited as she was, Linda took the time to give me a subtle but unmistakable warning.

She told me that I needed to know just one thing.

Since I'd come to stay with her, there'd been so many things she thought I should know that I was surprised she'd narrowed it down to just one. "Yeah?"

But once she said what that one thing was, I knew why it took precedence over all others. She very clearly told me that Gérald was hers and that she would have her eye on me.

I was shocked. How could she even . . . ? Ewwww! The thought of touching Gérald was disgusting to me. Linda had nothing to worry about, or so I thought. But it appeared she was worried all the same, and I couldn't understand why. I was too young, too naïve, and too eager to grasp all the reasons for Linda's anxiety. As it turned out, her fears were justified.

The day Linda left for her island shoot turned out to be memorable for me, but for all the wrong reasons. Under Gérald's direction I'd gone on several test shoots and finally had some very good photos to use. At last I had a book to take on "go-sees" around Paris. I headed out of the house that morning armed with my new portfolio, a Métro pass, a map, and a list of castings. The first meet-and-greet was at 10:00 A.M., and the go-sees continued all day long. A native Parisian would have been challenged negotiating the underground any more rapidly than I did that day. I made it through the schedule, more or less on time, but was nearly in tears when I finally finished.

Night had already fallen when I returned to 8 rue du Bac. I let myself into the dark apartment and fumbled for the light switch. It was the first time I'd been in the apartment by myself. I called Gérald's name once, then again. No answer came.

I began to wander through the flat. Linda had always been territorial about both Gérald and what she saw as "their" home, so I hadn't had much of an opportunity to explore. I was tired, I was curious, and I was still a teenager—of course I was going to have a look around! I wandered down the hall and stood in the doorway of their bedroom. I hadn't seen it since my brief glimpse on the day I arrived, and it looked even grander than I had remembered. Living in my tiny room made everything else seem enormous. The mirrors on the walls and ceiling were dazzling. The marble in the open bathroom shimmered. And on the wall I saw a medicine cabinet. My curiosity grew much stronger. I hadn't gotten high on anything other than Linda's damn gin and tonics since I'd been in Paris. I was eager for something stronger, and after a day like the one I'd just had, I felt justified in looking for it. I assumed that Gérald had to be a partier; everyone in the industry partied. Partying meant cocaine, and I suddenly felt certain that if I searched hard enough, that's exactly what I'd find in his bizarrely luxurious bathroom.

I didn't rush to the medicine cabinet right away. I walked slowly through the bedroom first, studying the paintings and photographs on the walls. The frames themselves seemed old and glamorous. The scent of fresh flowers was thick in the air; every day the maids brought in spectacular bouquets, placing them in antique vases around the room. I thought of all the models who'd been in this room before me. And I thought of all of the models who had shared Gérald's bed. I shuddered. Fresh flowers weren't worth that.

In the bathroom I ran my fingers along the gleaming porcelain of the magnificent tub. It was cool to the touch. I moved on to the medicine cabinet. Nothing of interest, just toiletries and what looked like over-the-counter medications. But as I stepped back, I noticed a row of white jars, neatly lined up high on a shelf above the sink. I reached up and grabbed one; it felt full. I turned it upside down and unscrewed the lid, preparing to shake its contents out into my hand. I expected pills.

A second later I stood aghast in a cloud of white powder. One quick inhale and I knew that the jar had been full of cocaine. It was more than I'd ever seen in one place in my life, and I'd just spilled a fortune's worth all over the bathroom. The coke was everywhere, under the tub and settling deep into the cracks and lines of the old wooden floor.

"Shit, shit, shit, shit, shit." I muttered the same word over and over like a mantra, frantically trying to sweep up the powder using the one piece of paper I could find. "Shit, shit, shit."

I hadn't been on my hands and knees for more than two minutes when I heard the sound of the antique locks of the front door turning, echoing like gunshots through the flat. Gérald was home. There was nowhere to run—no point in running. He would know I'd been snooping no matter what I did, so I stayed down on the floor, pathetically sweeping whatever I could on to the paper and pouring it back into the jar. I could hear the floorboards creaking as he made his way down the hall. He seemed to be coming very slowly, almost as if he knew where I was and wanted to draw out my agony.

Gérald entered the bedroom, tossed his overcoat onto the chaise, and turned to exit again when he caught a glimpse of me. His eyes widened with surprise, but as he took in the scene, he began to smile and another look—one I couldn't quite place—crept onto his face.

"Well, well. What have we here?"

I stood up. I had no choice. Part of me was embarrassed beyond belief to have been discovered like this, while a bigger part of me, I realized, was excited to have found the drugs. I missed partying. I missed coke.

"I . . . I was looking for some aspirin. I'm so sorry."

Gérald's smile grew broader. He didn't buy it for a second. Who would? There I was, caught white-handed.

"Looks like we have quite a mess to clean up, you and I." With that, Gérald laughed, sat down on the floor, crossed his legs, and announced with a wink and a grin, "What we can't pick up, we'll just have to snort." Then, he plucked an American hundred-dollar bill from his wallet and neatly rolled it up.

And so it was that Gérald Marie and I shared our first lines of cocaine together, laughing on his bathroom floor. The ice was broken between us. As the evening wore on, I felt comfortable enough to divulge things I'd never shared before, and he did the same with me. We stayed up most of the night talking, smoking cigarettes, and doing lines.

Linda's career began to take off rapidly. Her travels away from Paris became more frequent, and as a result Gérald and I spent increasing amounts of time together. He wanted to push me, he said; he was sure he could make me a star as big as Linda—if not bigger. "You are a rare beauty, Carré. The only thing that could ever fuck this up would be you." He told me this over and over again, following it up with a never-ending stream of advice. Gérald was a man of strong opinions about everything: makeup, hair, posture, and social etiquette. He was very particular about how I walked—not just on a shoot but on the street and in the apartment. I was desperate for his advice, and did my best to please him. I knew that this was my last chance to make it in the business. I knew that Gérald could help me become a star. And I knew that becoming a star meant being at his beck and call.

In front of others, Gérald could be as demanding and cruel as ever. But everything changed when we were alone in the apartment, doing coke together. It was secretive, but it felt strangely safe. I liked the way Gérald would laugh with me when we snorted lines together. I liked the way he teased me gently. And even as young as I was, I could figure out how my relationship with Gérald mirrored my dynamic with my dad. I had kept the secret of my father's drinking. Now I was keeping the secret of Gérald's and my cocaine use. In an odd way, I felt like Gérald's confidante. It was a very familiar role, and as sick (and age-inappropriate) as it was, I felt comfortable with it. To keep a secret involving someone you look up to can be immensely empowering, particularly when you tend to think of yourself as a misfit. I'd felt like an awkward outsider so much of my young life that having any kind of trust bond with someone in a position of authority gave me a certainty and a place that I clung to.

But despite Gérald's endless stream of advice, my career still wasn't getting off the ground. I was still traveling around Paris on the Métro, still going to casting after casting, go-see after go-see. One particular day as I raced around the city, the rains came. The shower was torrential. I remember the shopkeepers pulling down their awnings and

bustling their wares inside. Women were leaping puddles in impossi-
bly high heels and carrying big umbrellas that protected their perfectly
coiffed hair. I hadn't brought an umbrella with me. By the time I got
back to rue du Bac, I was soaked to the bone. I could feel a cold coming
on. My inner mood matched the weather: dark and despondent. With
no friends except Gérald, no real hint of success on the horizon, and
no real option but to just keep trying, I was on the verge of depression.
I was missing the States and terribly sad.

No one was in the apartment that rainy evening when I got home.
I peeled off my wet clothes, jumped into the shower, and then crawled
naked into bed. I was too tired and sick to think about dinner. I just
wanted to be warm. I just wanted to rest. Though I tossed and turned
most nights, that evening I fell asleep in an instant.

Hours later something woke me suddenly. I heard the drunken shuffling of feet moving down the hallway toward me. Filled with alarm, I
pulled the covers tightly around me. But in a flash my safe haven was
invaded and I was exposed.

Gérald stood above me, ripping the covers from the bed. Before I
could react, his sticky body was on me and those disgusting wet ring-
lets of his were falling on my face. I pushed back, but I could barely
breathe with the weight of him pressing down on me. I cried out, a
lame attempt to shake him from what seemed like a drunken stupor.
I could smell gin on his breath as he harshly pushed his mouth onto
mine, a sharp tongue darted out, trying to open my pursed lips in a
grotesque kiss. The smell of him made me want to vomit. The fury
in me made me want to throw him off me. But in my naked, fevered
state, I couldn't seem to find the strength or the leverage to move him
aside. Gérald seemed all too expert at getting what he wanted, and
in the tangle of my naked legs and pleas and cries his hand found my
mouth and clamped down, trying to silence me. Why even bother? I
wondered. I knew we were alone. And I knew that even if I were to
fight back and scream, no one would hear me. No one would come.

Gérald proceeded to viciously penetrate my body, his grunts and groans mixed with the sound of the rain that had begun to pound the tiny window in that tiny room. My thoughts drifted to the other models who were temporarily housed in this room. I fleetingly wondered if I might not be the first girl to be violated in this strange place. I cried silently as well as out loud. I cried a river. I cried while the rains fell steadily outside. I became the rain. I became the room. I disappeared in the awful endless rocking.

I remember the horrific feeling of his penis sliding out of me, the wetness that told me he had come inside me. I remember nausea welling up, and then the involuntary gagging that began as he stood, looked down at me, then turned and stumbled out of the room.

There is nothing like lying naked and watching it storm outside while your teenage vagina is on fire because some asshole has just defiled you with all his might and power. The shame hit me like a ton of bricks; to this day the confusion as to why I'd never told a soul can still bring me to tears. If my daughters were ever to experience such horror and abuse, it would devastate me.

We hear so many stories about such events that we risk losing our sense of outrage and horror at what it really is. Some women have a hard time naming what happened to them, but I don't. Could Gérald have thought that the friendship we had forged, the fact that we did drugs together, the fact that I lived in his house, all indicated, in some way, that I was amenable to having sex with him that night? I can't say. I can only know that I never asked for it. As far as I'm concerned, the sex we had that night was not consensual. There is no way to wrap it up in a nice, pretty package, no way to say that "things just got out of hand." As I have learned well after this event, no one should tolerate—and our cultural beliefs and practices should not allow or, worse, invite—anything other than loving, safe, consensual lovemaking as the norm.

In the days that followed, it became clear to me that I couldn't do anything other than pretend. Pretend that nothing had ever happened. Pretend that Gérald hadn't forced himself on me. And so I pretended.

In my grief, shame, pain, and isolation, it was easier to keep my mouth shut and not tell a soul about the degrading event that had taken place. It was also perfectly clear to me that my future career depended on my keeping this secret deep in the archives, to be guarded with my very life. Although my relationship with Gérald changed to one of awkwardness and distance, I remained in the house, in that horrible little room. I became an obedient robot. A shell of myself. There were no more hugs or laughs. We still did coke together, but it was out of a desperate need to medicate myself for what I knew would come next. I soon found out that I was expected to let Gérald fuck me whenever Linda left town. Gérald held all the cards. The only hand I had to play was to stay and survive.

After that night Gérald's demands only grew. He still saw my "potential" and insisted I needed to drop even more weight to get the "star look" that he was convinced would send my career into the stratosphere. The look was super skinny, and if I wanted success, that would be the only way to achieve it. Before that night I had been quietly indulging in chocolate croissants and croque-monsieurs, but after that night I didn't give a shit if I ever ate again.

To keep me on schedule, I was supplied with a small brown glass vial of cocaine every other day. This was the secret to model weight management. And at that time of depression and desperation, I was happy to receive my vial along with the list of castings for the day. Cocaine became my one friend. It carried me through the times when I felt as if I were running on empty. It fueled the frenetic pace I was expected to keep. I was using around the clock. I was a mess. At just seventeen years of age, I was lucky that my baby face could conceal the stress. From the outside looking in, I was an example of the all-American model striving to get to the top.

My life was a predictable grind. And the song that was always on my Walkman, Grace Jones's "Slave to the Rhythm," summed up my predicament perfectly.

I'd usually hold off on doing a line until my second cup of espresso, just before lunch. And of course I smoked, too. Coffee, cigarettes, and cocaine—hardly a healthy diet. But it needed to be this model's diet. Whatever else Gérald was, he was an effective agent. Less than a month later, I finally got a break. One that would change everything. I'd been pounding the pavement day after day, bouncing back and forth between photographers and editors. At last I was being sent to the headquarters of *Elle* France. Louis, my booker at Elite, told me I'd be meeting with the editor in chief, Odile Sarron. Everyone knew Odile. She made careers—and broke them. (She would be credited with discovering many supermodels, including Claudia Schiffer.) This was, Louis assured me, a huge opportunity. The best I'd had since coming to Paris. But he had a warning for me as well. With a wry grin, he told me that Odile had a unique way of running her castings.

"You'll have to be nude, Carré. Odile insists on doing it that way. And you'll be alone with her."

That didn't sound very good. Part of me hoped that Louis was teasing. So I asked a few of the other girls at Elite about Odile. When they heard her name, they quietly and sympathetically wished me good luck. So I steeled myself for the meeting and hoped it was just her effective way of testing a model's confidence and mettle.

The day my big break came, the signs were promising. Rather than pouring from morning until night as it had been doing for weeks, the first rain of the day passed quickly. By the time I hit rue du Bac's Métro stop, the sun was already peeking through the clouds. I recognized this as an auspicious sign.

Although I was no expert, I had acquired a little familiarity with the subway system by now. To get to the Elle offices, I would need to change trains at my favorite station, a place I called my "musical wonderland." As I got off one train and hurried to another across the platform, I stopped, mesmerized by a group of African drummers whose rhythm echoed through the underground chamber. I tossed my extra coins into a hat, waved, and smiled my gratitude, feeling sure that their symphony of sound was the second good-luck charm of the day.

I arrived at *Elle* five minutes before my eleven o'clock appointment. With my portfolio tucked securely under my arm, I walked through the doors of the offices and announced myself.

"My name is Carré, and I'm here to see Miss Sarron."

The girls at the front desk giggled, making little effort to be discreet. *Jesus,* I thought. *What next?*

I was escorted into a large, bustling sitting room. It wasn't entirely private—assistants were snapping Polaroids of the newest designer collections before they were to be sent out to various shoot locations. As I looked on enviously, they wheeled rack after rack of clothes out into the hallway. I needed a fucking break so badly I could taste it. I got up off the couch and began to walk around. As I looked at the photos on the wall, I felt someone enter the room behind me.

My back was to the door but I knew in an instant I wasn't alone. Whoever was there was watching me. I took a deep breath, turned, and saw a slender woman with blond hair and tanned skin. As I met her eyes, she brought her cigarette to her mouth and inhaled deeply. This was Odile. She was striking in both her grace and her power.

The legendary editor exhaled.

"Well. Carré Otis. So nice to meet you at last." Her accent was thick, her voice deep. "Gérald has told me so much about you," she said with a wink, making me instantly cringe. *Great,* I thought. *What the hell has he said?* That little eye play suggested she knew far more than I wanted her to know. It made my skin crawl.

"Um . . . yes, it's . . . um, nice to meet you as well?" It came out more as a question than as a greeting. Whoops. I was screwing this up already. I held myself perfectly still and waited. I was acutely aware of how much smoke there was in the room and had to stifle an urge to cough. Sarron said nothing. She just looked at me. I had a good idea of what was coming next, but I needed to say something first. I couldn't very well start undressing right away. "So . . . you want to see my book, right?" Shit. I sounded like a hopeful twelve-year-old.

"No. I don't care about that. I have already seen your book. You wouldn't be here if I hadn't." Odile appraised me as she spoke, her eyes taking everything in.

"So you want me to try on an outfit?" I felt like an idiot. I seemed incapable of saying anything that didn't come out in the form of a question. Odile smiled. "No, my dear. I want you to get undressed. I need to see your entire body." She took another drag on her cigarette and then sent a column of smoke my way. Her eyes were locked on mine.

Well, I couldn't say I hadn't been warned. I looked around, hoping that Odile would volunteer to leave so I could take my clothes off in private. But she didn't move; she just watched me in a way that made me feel undressed already.

There was no obvious changing room nearby. The racks of clothes behind which I might have hidden had already been wheeled out. No one had told me I'd have to strip in front of her, too. I hoped she didn't expect me to do it artfully as well. I fought the urge to giggle. I was always laughing at inappropriate times, and this moment was the very definition of inappropriate.

"Um, okay. I . . . uh . . . I guess I'll just get undressed." Hey, at least I'd stopped asking questions. I turned my back to Odile, thinking it might provide at least a moment's protection from her penetrating gaze. But of course that was just plain silly. This was her thing. Clearly, she loved watching girls squirm. *Fuck it,* I thought. *Two can play at this game.* Pissed off that I'd been placed in this awkward position, I turned around and stood tall. My timidity vanished. I could feel the certainty and the confidence—more like cockiness—surge through me. I was five feet ten inches of upright, proud, seventeen-year-old attitude. If Odile wanted to see what I was made of, I would show her every last inch. I was going to get this job even if this was the way to do it.

For a moment we stood there, glowering at each other. Then she raised her eyebrows, cocking her head in surprise. I could see the wheels turning in her mind. Boldly holding her gaze with my own piercing look, I pulled my shirt over my head, removed my bra, dropped my blue jeans, and took my underpants off.

"And here you are, mademoiselle," I said brazenly, doing one professional pivot, giving *Elle*'s notorious French editor a chance to see my body from every angle. And, I thought, giving her just enough time to want to print everything she saw.

Meeting Odile's eyes once again, I smiled coyly. I reached down and in a few quick movements put my clothes back on. I picked my portfolio up off the floor and strode over toward her, extending my hand.

"Such a great pleasure to meet you, Miss Sarron. Hope to see you again soon."

Her jaw was still on the floor as I turned to leave.

By day's end I got the call. Odile wanted me. For a cover shoot: French *Elle*'s April 1986 edition. I'd broken through at last.

B ut that break, as important as it was to my career, still didn't solve the serious problems occurring in the flat in rue du Bac. My days had been passing in a blur: castings and go-sees, cocaine and espresso, frantic and usually unsuccessful efforts to avoid being alone with Gérald. And then the unthinkable: Linda and Gérald announced their engagement. I couldn't fucking believe it! While I had endured subsequent nighttime visits from Gérald, he had proposed to Linda. I wasn't jealous; I loathed the man's touch. After that first night, I was scared that if I didn't find some way to reconcile his carnal expectations and my dire need to just survive I would be done, completely washed up in Paris as well as New York. His eagerness to marry Linda made it clear how little I meant to him. I wasn't even worth the smallest degree of courtesy and respect. He had always intended to marry her. And he fucked me all the while. I was confused and furious. And I was still only seventeen. It was evident then that my youth, inexperience, and vulnerability made me such easy prey. It was devastating on so many levels.

After announcing his engagement, Gérald made one more attempt to come into my room. I remember feeling a wave of dismay as I sat there in my doll-size surroundings with an adult-size anguish over everything that had passed. I finally found my voice. I found my "No" and refused to let him touch me. There he was in that tiny room, staring at me with both lust and rage. And there I was standing my ground, prepared to fight with whatever I had left.

I said it again. "No. No. Not anymore."

Gérald's face screwed up into a hateful mask. "Do you know what it is you are saying to me?" he hissed. "Do you know who you are rejecting?" Then he asked if I understood the implications of my decision, and despite my fear and anger I almost laughed. "Yes," I said defiantly. "I understand."

Gérald, of course, didn't hold back his bitter laughter as he turned on his heel, and left the room. Not one more word was said.

The next day I was moved out. But my career was already on the rise. I knew I didn't need to let Gérald touch me anymore in order to make it. And not long after getting my own tiny flat, I received a call. I was going on location with *Elle* to the other side of the world: Tahiti. It seemed like a dream come true . . . until I heard that Phil Stadtmiller, the photographer who'd made my first day in Paris so miserable, would be shooting.

Things went wrong from the very start. While we traveled from Paris to LAX in business class, the *Elle* crew's rowdiness made the trip seem endless. By the time we landed, I was ready to scream. It didn't help that Phil, who had never spoken a nice word to me, was especially chilly and distant. We had a six-hour layover in Los Angeles before flying on to Papeete, and it was at LAX that a second model, Daria Jasari, joined our flight.

When Daria stretched her lean form to place her carry-on bag into the overhead locker, all of business class turned around to stare at her ass. Seriously, she had the best ass I'd ever seen. None of us could take our eyes off her. Phil was even more interested than the rest of us, and it didn't take long for me to figure out why. Daria plopped down in the seat next to him and rested her head on his shoulder, her hand caressing his leg. They were lovers. My slightly-less-perfect ass didn't seem to fit on this trip. I began to have a sinking feeling.

Tahiti was everything I'd imagined. A sultry humidity hung in the air as we stepped out onto the tarmac. Tall palms swayed in the warm breeze. We were greeted with gardenias and treated like royalty. We were, after all, on a shoot for *Elle*. It seemed to make us the island's newest stars.

Our hotel was a Club Med on Bora-Bora. It was extraordinary— fragrant flowers everywhere, tiki torches lighting the walkways from dusk to dawn, and a mile-long sandy beach located just steps from our rooms. As soon as we hit the lobby, sweet alcoholic drinks were pressed into our hands and we were whisked to our accommodations. A beautiful Tahitian woman with waist-length hair gave me a tour. She spoke to me in French, and I proudly responded. After several months in Paris, I spoke French fairly well.

The rooms were clustered together in a compound by the water's edge. Phil had the most remote room, perched right over the sea, accessible only by a long wooden walkway. I saw Daria carrying her bag along that walkway and breathed a sigh of relief. I'd been told I'd be sharing a room with her. The one advantage of having her in Phil 's room was that I wouldn't have anyone in mine.

I was exhausted from the two long flights, and yearned to take a bath and go to bed. The plan, however, was to wash up quickly and meet for dinner together. The welcome drink had turned out to be stronger than I'd thought. I felt woozy, but I pushed through anyhow. I needed to be with the others for our first meal on the island. Protocol.

I made my way to the outdoor dining hall. A warm, soft breeze and the sounds of Bob Marley met me as I arrived. Phil, joint in hand, was holding court around a large, rectangular table. He looked up at me as I approached. Sneering, he leaned over and made what seemed to be a snide remark to his assistant. I couldn't hear what it was over the reggae music, but I knew that it couldn't be anything good. What the hell did this guy have against me? What had I done to him? For the first time, it occurred to me that maybe he knew about Gérald and me. "Well, well, well. Look who's finally joining us," Phil declared in a much louder voice. "Please," he said with false courtesy, "do sit down." With that, he pulled Daria toward him, her tiny minidress slipping off her shoulders to reveal the swell of her young breast. She might have been a bit older than me, but not by much. Phil took a long hit off the joint and pressed his lips against Daria's, exhaling flamboyantly into her mouth. Smoke curled around their heads. Daria coughed, sputtered, and finally giggled. I realized that everyone else was already stupid high. I felt totally out of place, an outcast once more.

"Carré, Daria is a top model in New York City. Did you know that?"

Fuck. The asshole wasn't wasting any time in picking on me.

"No, Phil, I didn't." I really hadn't known much about her at all.

"Well, you should. Where the fuck are you from anyways?"

"Ummm . . . San Francisco." I wished I had some snappy retort.

Phil snorted. "Funny, I thought they made sure the models coming out from San Francisco knew what they were doing. But you don't know a fucking thing about moving in front of the camera."

I was starting to tremble. He'd been cold before, but now it was obvious he wanted to start a fight. Sure, he was drunk and stoned as could be, but still. This was getting ugly.

"Oh, wait. I know why you got this job. I think it had to do with you fucking a certain somebody . . . right? Because I sure as fuck didn't hire you." He was snarling now, his eyes red and hateful.

My bottom lip twitched, and I could feel tears welling up in my eyes. I knew I was going to blow. Just as I was about to stand up and let him have it, one of the crew members placed his hand on mine and said, "Come on, Phil. Leave her alone."

Phil stood up, his drink spilling across the table.

"Stay the fuck out of this!" he yelled. Spit spraying from his mouth, he turned and shook his finger at me. "You stupid little SF bitch. Don't you come here and think you can give me attitude! I do not like you.

Don't know why, and I don't even fucking care." He wobbled on his feet and stumbled back.

I was terrified. The tears were streaming down my face by now. I stood up and ran, ran down through the maze of torchlit walkways and kept running till I reached the water's edge. I had no idea why this explosion had occurred. Phil might not have liked me, but it didn't explain why he was filled with so much rage. What the hell had I done to him? More important, how could I ever work with him in the morning? I wanted out, off Tahiti as soon as possible. I was desperate and scared. I had no choice but to call Gérald.

Back in my room, I phoned the hotel operator and asked to place a call to Paris, France. "Madame," the operator asked, "do you know what time it is there?"

"I don't care. Please put the call through." After a long silence, I heard the ringing on the other end of the line. Fresh tears began to roll down my face. I was so homesick. And for better or worse, Paris was home. I heard someone pick up the receiver and fumble with it, as if unsure of which end to talk into. I had awakened Gérald.

"*Oui?* Hello?" I heard his familiar thick voice.

"Gérald, it's me," I sobbed into the phone. "It's Carré."

"What is wrong? Why are you calling me?"

"Something . . . something terrible happened." I could barely get the words out. "It's Phil. He was drunk and yelling at me. He hates me. Please, Gérald, get me out of here. Get me back to Paris. I can't stay. I won't stay here."

Gérald paused. I heard him take a deep breath and knew he was annoyed.

"No. Carré, this is your problem. Why would he hate you? What did you do to him? Phil is my friend, and he is a professional. I thought you were as well. You are staying on that shoot, you are not leaving, and you are going to do your job." He was lecturing me, getting more annoyed by the minute.

I began to wail. How could Gérald leave me hanging like this? But then again, what did I expect? I took a deep breath and slammed the phone back down into the cradle. I didn't have anything else to say. I didn't know where to turn. And at precisely that moment, I heard a knock on the door .

"Carré? It's Carlo. Are you all right? Open up."

Carlo. One of the crew members. The kind man who had put his hand on mine and tried to calm Phil down. What perfect timing. I wanted a friend badly. I opened the door and stood there, still crying. Carlo stepped into the room and wrapped me in his arms. "There, there. It's going to be okay." I cried harder. Damn, I needed an ally, someone to help get me through this trip. I was so grateful he had come to my door. I clung to him.

Carlo then took me by the hand and led me over to the bed. He lifted my chin and slowly started to kiss my eyes, my cheeks, my tears, and my mouth. I was stunned. I couldn't speak. He pulled back, looked me calmly in the eye, and threw me down onto the bed.

"Wait, wait a minute," I protested. "What are you doing?"

Carlo climbed on top of me, straddling me. "No, no, you're okay. This is okay, Carré. I can help you." He started to kiss me again as I tried to wriggle free. He was over six feet tall, heavy, and very drunk. Getting him off me wasn't working. I was pinned.

"Please. Please don't." I started to cry again. Carlo ignored my sobs and held me down, pressing his mouth onto mine, his hard-on thrusting angrily against my thigh. He then pulled himself up onto one hand and slid my dress aside, shoving his other hand into my underwear. I gasped. And as hard as I could, I kneed him in the balls.

With a loud groan, he flew back and staggered for a moment, nearly falling. I ran to the door.

"You asshole!" I cried. "You fucking asshole scum!"

Carlo was furious. Pointing a finger at me, his face a contorted mask of pain and rage, he said, "You bitch. You are as stupid as Phil said. They all bet me I could come in here and get in your pants. You stupid fucking little girl. Now you're really fucked."

Mortified, I ran to the bathroom and locked the door behind me as Carlo stumbled out into the night. A wave of nausea came out of nowhere, and I started retching into the sink, my body heaving. The sickness passed. And what replaced it was a scream, a scream like I'd never unleashed before, one that rumbled up from my belly and roared out of my mouth. I just stood there in the bathroom and screamed until I couldn't scream anymore. The girl that I was, the despair I felt, and the sound of those anguished cries are with me to this day. Eventually I went numb. I stumbled into bed and into a short, dreamless, restless sleep.

In makeup the next day, a redheaded artist wagged her finger at me. In her heavy French accent, she said, "So I heard you got poked last night." She began to cackle. I wanted to die.

But I didn't die. I finished the job in Tahiti and made the long trip back home to France. Just a few weeks later, I sat gazing out the window of a train traveling from Paris to Milan, watching a brilliant summer sun dip slowly across a golden sky. Whatever my next job in Italy might hold for me, at least the start of the journey there was glorious. I was captivated by the sprawling, spectacular countryside in the fading evening light. The lingering glow of dusk was reassuring. I nestled down into my seat, alone with my thoughts and the darkening landscape outside. *Good things will happen,* I told myself, *Good things will happen.*

The truth was, jobs were scarce for me in France. I had thought that the *Elle* cover would lead to near-constant work, but it hadn't turned out like that. A series of amazing photographers told me how much they loved my look, but despite their praise and encouragement I wasn't getting bookings. Gérald and I had nearly stopped speaking; he was busy with Linda, and I sensed that they both wanted me out of the way. And so it didn't come as much of a surprise when I was told that I was being sent to Milan.

Milan was—and still is—one of the world's great fashion capitals, ranking only just behind (and some say ahead of) Paris and New York. Gucci, Valentino, Versace, Prada, Armani—they were all headquartered there. And where there are major fashion labels, there are also many jobs for models. I hadn't made it in New York, nor had I caught on as I'd hoped to in Paris. Elite assured me that the third time would be the charm and that Milan would be the city in which I'd break through at last.

In Milan I'd be assigned to a different agency. I was told it was one of the biggest and the best; if anyone could get me work, they could. I was ready and willing and hopeful, even though it meant another move, another country, and another language with which to contend.

Milan is not a lovely city per se. It's huge, crowded, and industrial. Tourists looking for charm are better off in Venice or Florence. But the people I would meet there were warm and friendly. They were always eager to help. It was unlike Paris in that way, and as I walked the streets in the bright summer sun, sensing that uniquely Italian enthusiasm for life and pleasure, I couldn't help but feel optimistic.

Another difference between the two cities was the quality of model housing. My home in Milan was not like my home in Paris. The agency put me up in a small pensione filled with other models. It was cheap and close to all the main transit lines, but it was utterly devoid of any character. Compared to Gérald's gorgeous apartment, this was quite a letdown. On the other hand, there was a benefit to my tiny new digs: no Gérald! That benefit couldn't be underestimated. The view from my little room was limited to the neighboring building. There was one small bed, a scratchy but clean set of sheets, and a bathroom. It was sparse, but it was mine.

The pensione was the temporary residence for models from all around the world, most of them as young as I was (some even younger). We were kids, really— kids from everywhere. Walking through the lobby was like walking into a major casting. Everywhere you looked, tall and gangly girls and boys were pacing the floors or sprawled on couches, smoking or chewing gum. The combined smell of cigarettes, bubble gum, and perfume seemed to have soaked into the walls. The girls wore denim cutoffs, tank tops, and calf boots; the boys were all trying to look dangerous, with torn jeans, wifebeaters, and stubbly faces. We were poor—or to put it another way, not everyone who was hungry was necessarily dieting.

Although we all weren't repped by the same agency, many of us had the same list of castings to get to each day. Sometimes we took cabs together, sometimes we took the bus, but we always shared our stories. And in Milan our stories tended to center on one topic: the Italian Playboy Club.

I suspect that every country in the world has a small group of rich young boys who want to grow up and be playboys, living lives of excess and leisure and relentless womanizing. But in Italy the playboy phenomenon exists on a whole different scale. Men with money and style and fast cars are admired there as they are nowhere else, and they know it. In the 1980s these playboys had a very strong sense of entitlement, particularly when it came to women. (In Italy it was and is considered totally acceptable for a man to live with his mother well into his thirties and beyond. Many Italian mamas pamper their sons, keeping them boys forever.) And it was thanks to the influence of these playboys that I began hearing rumors. Apparently, in Milan a modeling job wasn't always a modeling job. One of the places where this different definition applied unfortunately was the agency repping me.

I found this out when I was booked for a job in Lake Como, working with photographer Marco Canipelli. My booker had given me very specific instructions. I was to take a particular bus toward Lake Como. A bus that left at exactly—*if* anything in Italy happens exactly—2:30 P.M. on Friday. When I got to my specified destination, I was to wait. The photo shoot would last all weekend, I was informed, and I might—or might not—be working with another model. As was common in those days, pay wasn't discussed. The agencies prepaid our room and board and travel expenses, then gave us a small weekly allowance. Most models, including myself, had only a vague idea of what we were actually making.

Soon after getting on the bus, I began to panic. The massive old Fiat swerved and lurched through the mountains and forest, carrying me far from the city and anybody I knew. Looking at my watch and the road signs, I realized that I would be arriving well after sundown, and I began to ask the driver what time he thought we might reach my stop. He spoke very poor English. So I kept pointing at the bus-stop name written on a piece of paper. "*Sì, sì,*" he would mutter, nodding wearily, his finger jabbing in front of us, indicating that we still had a long way to go. It was eerily dark by the time we finally reached our destination: a dusty, poorly lit parking lot in the middle of nowhere. Now it was my driver's turn to look concerned. He could see that no one was waiting for me. He began to point to my slip of paper as if to ask, *Do you really want to get off here? Alone?*

My heart was pounding. What was the agency thinking, asking me to wait in the dark, miles from civilization at this hour? I thought about staying on the bus and riding back to Milan. But I knew I'd be in trouble if I did.

Slowly and hesitantly, I pulled my suitcase down from the overhead rack and stepped off the bus. "*Buona notte,*" the driver said softly. The doors creaked shut and the bus lumbered away, engulfing me in exhaust fumes. I stood and watched the red taillights disappear. When the bus was gone, I sat down on the edge of my suitcase, took a deep breath, and began to do what I'd been told to do. I waited.

After five very long minutes, I saw a pair of headlights slow and then turn into the parking lot. A big maroon Rolls-Royce had pulled up to the dusty stop just feet from me. Coughing, I stood and backed away nervously.

The driver's-side door flew open, and a very heavy man with an enormous mustache threw himself out of the car. He bounded toward me, extending a fat, sweaty hand. "Marco Canipelli," he said with a thick Italian accent. "And you must be . . . ? I know the agency sent you. Yes?"

Great. I was nameless. I wondered if this man had even seen my portfolio. This wasn't looking very good. I peered into the car and heard the awful Euro disco blasting from the speakers and the sound of female laughter, too, which both relieved and annoyed me. At least I wasn't going to be alone with Marco. "Climb in, I'll get your bags," he said with an imperious wave. "Let's head to the house."

I was the third girl in the Rolls. Already enjoying the ride were two blond Swedish models. They were dressed, if you could call it that, in revealing miniskirts, tight tank tops, and sky-high heels. In comparison I was dressed simply and prudishly. I certainly hadn't brought anything like their outfits to wear. I tried to ask the girls and Marco questions, to get an idea of what the shoot was, when we'd start in the morning, and so on, but each of my inquiries was just met with snickers from the Swedes and unintelligible grunts from Marco. Finally he explained that we would all be staying at his villa on the lake. "What lake?" I asked naïvely. I still didn't know where we were, and though I'd heard the name, I had no idea that Lake Como was one of the wealthiest and most exclusive vacation spots between Italy and Switzerland. Marco seemed to find my ignorance amusing. I know that the miniskirted Swedes certainly did.

Marco's villa was indeed impressive. One of the largest mansions on the lake, it featured an enormous and brilliantly lit circular driveway. As we approached the house, he pulled in next to his collection of cars: another Rolls, two Lamborghinis, and a Porsche. From the lights and the sounds within the house, I could tell that a party was in full swing. My scantily clad fellow models and I were the guests. Or, as I began to suspect, my stomach churning, we weren't exactly guests. The word "escort" popped into my head. I didn't know quite what to think.

The home was undeniably grand. The entrance was lit with candles, and enormous carved wooden mirrors lined the long foyer. Huge vases of flowers were placed on small tables, and everywhere I looked, I saw light spilling from chandeliers and candelabras.

Servants in black-and-white uniforms walked around taking coats, offering trays of hors d'oeuvres, champagne. A butler tried to take my bag, but with a firm "No thank you" I clutched it closer. I wasn't entirely sure I was going to stay.

Marco took my hand and led me to the top of a staircase. We hadn't entered on the bottom floor, but rather in what seemed like the middle of the house. This staircase led into the downstairs rooms, while an even more regal sweeping staircase led to the elegant rooms upstairs.

"Go straight down," Marco said. "We'll have a perfect cocktail dress for you. And we'll get you the right shoes. Your hair and makeup can be done quickly, too."

"Oh, so I'm going to start working tonight?" I was still operating on the premise that I was there to be photographed. I'd assumed we'd start with an early call for a Saturday-morning shoot, but I knew it wasn't unheard of for certain jobs to start late in the evening.

Marco laughed, gave me the seemingly obligatory pat on my butt, and nodded for me to head down the stairs. As I took my first step, he deftly grabbed my bag away from me. "You won't need this now, my dear. I'll have Giancarlo put it in your room for you." I started to protest, but he had already turned and begun to walk away. "Hurry, there's no time to waste!"

Great. It looked like I'd be staying.

Downstairs, the gorgeous rooms were filled with equally gorgeous women. Everyone was in a frenzy of activity. Everywhere I looked, I saw tall, tanned young blondes lounging about, glasses of champagne in hand, smoking cigarettes. Some of them were half dressed. Suddenly a completely naked girl about my age darted in front of me, laughing as she disappeared into a side room. What the fuck was going on?

I followed the naked girl into what turned out to be an enormous powder room. One section of the room had been transformed into a glass-enclosed sauna; a number of nude girls were in there. I turned and noticed that one wall had dresses hanging from it; walking closer, I saw my name pinned to one of them. Just as at a fashion show, my whole look had been arranged for me. Heels, exactly the right size, were placed below each dress. I managed to find a private room in which to discard my grungy travel clothes and slip into the perfect little black cocktail dress that had been assigned to me.

As soon as I had emerged from the changing room, I was seized by the elbow and brought to the hair and makeup artists. Several of them were clustered in a single large room. With speed and efficiency and very little talking, I was pulled along, primped, and spit out the other end of the production line. The woman who finished my makeup gave me a final once-over. "Up," she said, pointing. I went.

Marco took my arm as I got to the top of the staircase. He may have been a large man, but he knew how to work a room effortlessly. Over the next few minutes, I was waltzed about as Marco introduced me to the various playboys, nobles, and Italian government officials who made up the guest list. I was given nods of approval, looked up and down, and then whisked off to meet the next guest. I couldn't help but feel as if I were a piece of meat for sale. I wondered if I were going to be auctioned off.

I eased my nerves with champagne. Every time I finished a glass, Marco placed a fresh one in my hand. After my long, strange day—the endless bus trip, those nervous moments in the parking lot, the bizarre ride in the Rolls with Marco and the half-naked Swedes—I was exhausted. And I was definitely tipsy. I really just wanted to turn in for the night. The party showed no signs of slowing, but I was done. I pulled Marco aside.

"I'm so tired. Where is my room?"

"Of course, my dearest girl. I'll have Giancarlo show you right away," he said with a smile.

I was relieved. I was worried that Marco would want me to stay up hours longer as his "arm charm." But my relief soon turned to disdain. Marco leaned in, alcohol dripping from his mustache and his breath.

"I made sure to put you on my floor, Carré. You're right next to my room," he whispered. He seemed to be drooling.

I wriggled in disgust.

He nodded to Giancarlo, and I was swiftly shown to my room. Just as Marco had promised, my bag was waiting for me. There was something else as well, an article of clothing that I hadn't brought with me. A very risqué nightgown was spread neatly on the bed. "You've got to be kidding me," I muttered, and quickly turned to close the doors. Remembering my experiences with Gérald, I was relieved to discover that my doors both locked from within. I was asleep within minutes.

Needless to say, it was a long night. As I had feared, Marco eventually arrived at my locked door. At 4:00 A.M. I awoke to the sound of his fists on the door as he banged and begged to be let in.

"Ah, my dear, so you are playing hard to get! How cute you are. I will get you before the weekend is over!" he threatened, slurring his words, laughing unkindly to himself.

What a pig. I pulled the covers over my ears, trembling with rage and a bit of fear. What the hell was I supposed to do? I had to get through another day and night here in this opulent playboy palazzo unharmed. What games would I have to play? What would happen now?

Marco was a famous photographer, but I hadn't seen a camera in his hands once. That didn't mean I wasn't photographed. That Saturday, when I emerged cautiously from my room, I found out that my day and night were scheduled right down to the minute. I was taken to lunch, then out on Marco's speedboat. As we traveled around, paparazzi appeared. They'd apparently been tipped off, as Marco made no effort to avoid them. Quite the contrary. Marco had a playboy image to maintain. Within days, photos of the two of us together appeared in local papers and magazines, just as he wanted.

The oddest and most uncomfortable moment of the weekend came when Marco arranged for me to have an intimate dinner with him—and his teenage daughter, who was only a couple of years younger than I was. Talk about awkward! One of the other models I met that weekend told me that Marco had taken a special liking to me because I resembled his daughter, which made his advances seem even more repulsive.

When the weekend was over, Marco drove me all the way back to Milan in his Rolls. "My dear," he insisted, "I don't want you traveling alone for hours. I'll take you home." I certainly didn't mind a ride, but I did quickly tire of fending off his right hand, which fell onto my thigh every few kilometers. The trip back was much faster than my Friday-night bus ride, but Marco made it seem longer.

When we pulled up to my pensione at last, Marco reached into his pocket and drew out a beautiful bejeweled gold money clip. He peeled off a few crisp American hundred-dollar bills and handed them to me. I was shocked. But I took them. I had certainly earned them, and I knew I wouldn't see a cent from the agency cut. I thanked him and then quickly climbed out of the car, knowing that if I lingered a second longer, he would perceive it as an invitation.

Marco drove off into the polluted Milanese sunset, the driver's-side window down and his left hand waving in casual farewell. As I watched the Rolls disappear, I told myself that it was time. Time for me to head home. I wasn't sure where home was anymore. But it sure as hell wasn't in Europe.

THE FIRST HOMECOMING

I was ready to get out. I'd had my fill. What success I'd had wasn't worth the price I'd been paying. And after a friend's dog bit me in the face, it seemed an obvious signal. It was time to depart back to the homeland.

There was only one person I could call from Paris. Only one place I could think of to go.

Ethan Allen (yes, his real name) had been a fellow student at John Woolman. His mother, famed midwife Nan Koehler, had a place in Sebastopol, California, called Rainbow's End. In the 1980s it was a small commune with an organic farm housing several different families, as well as a few stray kids about my age. It was also the center of a movement. Classes on Western herbology, midwifery, and general family wellness were held there. Nan's husband, Don, also had a gynecological practice there. Nan was a true mother in every sense of the word, and—much to Don's exasperation—she was notorious for taking kids in under her wing. When I'd been at Woolman, I'd felt a strange connection to Nan. She was the safest and most accepting adult I'd ever met, and I'd thought about her from time to time ever since I'd dropped out.

Nan remembered me immediately when I called from my tiny apartment in Paris. As I explained my situation, I was honest about not having a plan. I just needed to return to California soil. Her support and the promise of open arms was all I needed to hear to find the courage to book my ticket back to San Francisco.

At SFO I was met by Ethan, now a beautiful, tall teenage boy with a lion's mane of brownish gold curls that flowed halfway down his back. The last time I'd laid eyes on him, he was merely a gawky adolescent, but now he was well on his way to manhood. And I certainly was no longer the same girl who had left. I felt a stirring, a sense of relief and safety with him. I immediately knew I was in the right place and on the right path.

The drive up to the farm was magical. Black Uhuru was blasting on the cassette player as we moved through the city's foggy streets, crossed the Golden Gate Bridge, following the 101 northbound. I held my breath by the Greenbrae exit, knowing how near I was to my estranged family. My heart skipped a beat with yearning as we passed, but I knew it wasn't yet time to go to that home. Maybe someday, I told myself, but not now. Not yet. Veering off the freeway at Sebastopol, we entered the redwood forest. Paris felt a million miles away.

Frati Lane is a tiny road with a dense canopy of branches arcing overhead. Signs let us know we were drawing near: RAINBOW'S END, CHILDREN AT PLAY, and finally SLOW DOWN. In the main parking lot, Ethan came to a stop. He turned off the motor and looked at me. "Welcome back, Carré." And I couldn't help but grin.

I was anxious to see Nan. Although I didn't really know anyone at the farm all that well, if ever there were a hippie family to spread the love, I was sure it was this one. And I needed the love.

Ethan grabbed my bag—a bigger one than the one I'd left California with—and we walked up to the main house.

Nan greeted me with a warm bear hug and sat me down for some tea. Her kitchen was stocked with every drying herb imaginable. Seeds were sprouting in jars in the sunroom, and the smell of incense wafted through the air. There were crystals on windowsills and treasures like hawk and owl feathers tucked into cracks in the wooden walls. Nan was a healer, a shaman, and a bountiful woman. And she would soon show me the many facets of what it meant to be just that: a *woman*.

Nan became my first positive female role model. She was hearty, challenging, intelligent, vocal, and controversial. No matter what her opinion, there was love behind it. Nan was fearless, so unlike the women I'd known growing up (my mother included); she talked openly about weight and sex, aging and wild emotion. She was also physically demonstrative, her touch strong and safe and tremendously reassuring. I'd never met a woman so comfortable with her own body and her own raw womanhood. Meeting her was a revelation. (Nan Koehler now has a book called *Artemis Speaks: V.B.A.C. Stories and Natural Childbirth Information*.)

Ethan offered to let me stay with him in his cabin, and as Nan agreed, she looked me in the eye, holding my gaze for a long time. It was as if she were peering into my soul, seeing the past I had endured as well as the future that would be. Her eyes welled up, and she gave me another motherly hug, this time holding me close and tight.

"Sweetie pie, you can land here," she whispered encouragingly. "Come on home." I, too, had tears in my eyes. I felt as if I were being *seen* for the first time. All the hurt seemed acknowledged, and all my potential was held with assurance in her embrace. I sighed, exhausted from the trip. "Ethan," his mother said gently, "let's get this sweet girl tucked in. She needs a good rest."

We finished our tea and snacks and made our way down to the cabin. Afternoon was slipping into evening, and along the path the last few crickets of summer chirped and the sound of the evening bullfrogs croaking could be heard in the nearby pond. The air was sweet with the unmistakable smell of the damp Northern California earth. Though I'd never stayed here before, I felt more at home than I had in many years.

Ethan's cabin was a tiny shack with a loft. There was a single light but no running water. It had a wood-burning stove and mud on the floor, but after Paris it felt so right to be close to the earth and simplicity. *I could make this work*, I thought. *This is heaven.*

Nan placed my bag just inside the door, lit a candle, and pointed to the loft. "You should have all you need for warmth—there are plenty of blankets up there. And we will get a fire started for you. Now, why don't you climb in and get some rest, my dear. We'll see you when the sun is up." With that, Nan left, walking back up to the big house.

Ethan climbed up after me and cracked a window. He rolled a cigarette and sat leaning against the thin wooden wall, looking away as I pulled my shirt over my head and slipped off my blue jeans and wiggled to get under the weight of the heavy comforters. The fire crackled below. And as Ethan struck a match to light his cigarette, I looked at him behind the flame. He was different, this one. Beautiful. Open. I watched as he took a few drags and exhaled, smoke curling around his silhouette against the backdrop of dusk. And off I slipped into the sweetest, safest sleep I'd had in a year.

L ife on the farm was anything but routine. It was everything under the sun. People from all walks of life came to visit, including teachers from all different fields. There were amazing herbalists; shamans like Brant Secunda; Aryuvedic doctors like Harish Johari; women of wisdom such as Jeannine Parvati Baker (a midwife like Nan and author of *Hygieia: A Woman's Herbal*). There were Native American

elders and local hippie celebrities such as Stanley Mouse, the vision-
ary artist who created many of the Grateful Dead album covers and
sixties-era posters. Nan was very respected by everyone who knew her
work. Held in high regard for her voice and expertise in the field of delivering babies, she was something of an anomaly, enjoying praise from
both Western and alternative practitioners.

It wasn't long before Ethan and I began to enjoy a youthful, innocent, and sweet sexual relationship. It was safer and kinder than
anything I'd known before. But no matter how much love I was to receive on the farm, it was nearly impossible for me to let it sink in and
embrace it.

Although I stepped easily into the shoes of hippie girl and played
that part as well as I did the many others I had assumed before, I felt a
torturous disconnect within me. The pain of my secrets and of the vio-
lations I'd suffered on my road through Paris and Milan remained in
my consciousness. And no doubt I was not the easiest girl to be in love
with. I was complicated; my moods could turn dark and dangerous
with very little warning. It was only a matter of time before I would
begin to sabotage my chances of thriving on the farm.

Sweet moments and memories mixed with the sour: listening to
Bob Marley's *Kaya*; gardening in the rain; harvesting herbs; feeding
our ducks, Ping and Pong; watching the clouds roll by as I lay naked in
the sun. Learning to grow food planted a seed in my consciousness—it
was the first time I really began to understand that food could nurture
as well as tempt. Though my worst struggles with disordered eating
were ahead of me, plenty of damage to my physical self-image had already been done in Paris. It was a revelation to see, if not fully understand, what a healthy relationship with food might look like.

But while I was doing a great deal of inner healing at Rainbow's
End, I was also engaged in a lot of textbook acting out.

Though the farm's family gatherings always included me, I inevitably felt distant and detached during them. I couldn't ignore the

yearnings I had to reconnect with my own family, and it resulted in a terrible homesickness I was too young and too stubborn to admit or tend to. I had no idea where to begin. I felt an inexplicable alienation around large groups of loving people. Whether it was that I felt I didn't deserve that love or didn't trust it (or both), my volatile emotions kept people at bay and kept me in what I thought was the safest place possible—alone within myself. The gatherings were actually quite painful for me, a reminder of my differences from everyone else. Even after Paris and a success that some might think would put me more at ease, I only felt more unable to relate to those around me.

Christmas would be arriving soon. In early December I reconnected with Dawn, the beautiful, lithe girl who had served as Gary Loftus's assistant in San Francisco. We'd shared that strange electricity when we'd first met, and we'd talked a few times over the years as she kept tabs on my career, even after dear Gary had lost his battle with AIDS. Dawn was a lesbian—and I was curious. When we'd seen each other again after several years, we'd shared a few kisses, and there was an undeniable mutual attraction. The thought of any real sexual or emotional intimacy with her unnerved me too much to go any further at that time. I wasn't ready. Now, of course, I was in a relationship with Ethan. Nevertheless, I invited her to the farm to join us for the holidays.

Ethan wasn't entirely sure why I would invite Dawn up to celebrate with us. Neither was I. It was the beginning of a conscious betrayal, one that would drive a wedge into my relationship with innocent Ethan. Yet I couldn't seem to help myself; I was pushing every boundary, testing to see if love really could be everlasting and enduring despite provocation. But everyone has a limit. Even the innocent.

Christmas Eve began with rounds of apple cider and marijuana in one form or another. Someone had brought pot cookies. Dawn didn't smoke reefer, so how she ended up eating one of those incredibly potent treats was anyone's guess. As we all munched, we sat in front of the fire listening to Leonore, Nan's elderly German mother, read "The Night Before Christmas." I had curled up on the sheepskin rug, spooning Shayna and Sara, Ethan's youngest sisters. We were extremely close, and I knew I was like an older sibling to them. The eldest of Ethan's sisters, Jubilee, sat with him next to Nan and Don on the couch. Dawn quietly made her way in from the glow of the fire, the telltale crumbs of a cookie still on the corners of her mouth. I sat up and whispered, "Dawn, be careful . . . those cookies are reallllly strong," but it was as if what I'd just said hadn't registered at all. She just hungrily shoved another piece into her mouth.

I stretched back on the floor next to the girls while Dawn found a place on the rug nearby. And as the fire blazed and crackled, Leonore's German accent punctuating Santa's journey, I could see out of the corner of my eye that Dawn's body was beginning to tremble. A moment later a groan filled the room, escalating well above the storytelling. I held my breath, wondering if anyone else had heard her. Sara looked up at me and asked innocently, "Carré, what's wrong with her?"

"Shhhh, Sara. Listen to the story."

But all of our attention was now fixed on Dawn. Her body arched and writhed; a squeal and a hiss emanated from deep within her. *Oh, shit*, I thought. *Here we go.*

"Dear God, what is that girl doing?" Leonore begged to know, putting the book down on the couch beside her.

"For God's sake, what the fuck did you guys give her?" Don demanded.

"Good one, Carré," Ethan chimed in, a rare edge to his voice.

Oh, man, this one was on me. I leaned over toward Dawn, placing a hand on her shoulder. "Dawn. Dawn, are you okay?" I asked in as calm a voice as I could muster. But she responded as if my hand were a hot coal. She shrieked and jumped up. Wild-eyed and frightened, she looked accusatorily at each one of us.

"What have you done to me, you crazy fucking people?" She was having a serious reaction.

"Whoa, Dawn, it's fine. You just ate some pot cookies—that's all."
I tried to sound reassuring.

Reassured or not, Dawn reeled toward me, her arms sloppily falling
around my body. To my horror, she tried to kiss me on the lips, and
as I pushed her away, a silence hung in the air. Nan, Don, and Ethan
looked back and forth between Dawn and me, the same question on
each of their faces. Nan asked it.

"Just what *is* going on here, Carré?"

"Um . . . I don't know." I looked at my feet. Cat was out of the
bag. In an instant, everyone knew why Dawn was in the house. And it
wasn't exactly innocent.

"Jesus, Carré! How could you?" Ethan was furious. A look of disgust crossed his face. Not only because it was obvious Dawn and I had
something "going on" but because I was so reckless and insensitive as
to bring it to the farm. On Christmas Eve of all days.

"I'm sorry. It's not what it seems. It's . . . complicated," I stammered, trying to relieve the tension.

Nan looked aghast at first, but then the savior in her took charge.
She liked coming to the rescue. "Carré," she said, "it looks like you
and I have our work cut out for us tonight." I was only partly off the
hook. This was my mess, and I was expected to clean it up and move
it on out.

Dawn was ready to bolt out into the night, and Nan knew that
it was our responsibility to calm her down. We coaxed Dawn into
another room, lit some candles, and proceeded to assist her in purging the beast. While wild and paranoid accusations came roaring out
of Dawn, to my dismay, Nan herself began throwing up. I finally got
Dawn settled down by wrangling her into a cold shower. And bless
Ethan's heart, but he was the one who had to drive Dawn all the way
back to the city on Christmas Day. Later I found out that she'd been off
her medications—lithium, to be specific. Dawn was a bipolar paranoid
schizophrenic. Not a good mix, and not a good candidate for halluci-
nogenic home-baked goods.

. . . .

A month or so after the Dawn incident, I was shopping at the little local health-food store in Sebastopol. I would always peruse the bulletin board as I drank my fresh-pressed juice concoction, checking out what was going on in our community. Beneath the newest flyers for full-moon drum circles, there was a photograph of a woman, her sky-blue eyes contrasting with her shock of wavy brown hair. I froze in my tracks. Taking a deep breath, I reached out and pulled the picture to me for closer inspection. There was something about this face, this woman. I knew her, even if I hadn't known as much until this moment.

From deep within my body, a feeling of connection and longing steadily rose up. *"Dakini Retreat with Tsultrim Allione,"* it read; a picture of a Tibetan female deity danced off the page. I was stunned. Tsultrim's lioness face and mane of wild hair seemed to move on the flyer. *"Location: A comfortable private residence in Bodega Bay."* I had no idea what a *dakini* was, nor was I interested in going to a woman's retreat. Yet all the way back to the farm, I couldn't stop thinking about that face and those penetrating blue eyes. I knew I had to go, despite my reservations.

When I told Ethan and Nan of my finding, Nan began to fill me in on her knowledge of Tibetan Buddhism, sharing with me what she had read of the many deities that were "worshipped." *Dakini*s were like female Buddhas, the enlightened feminine aspect in what was primarily a patriarchal culture. I needed to know more, and in Nan's vast library I found the Tibetan Book of the Dead. I was blown away. Since childhood I'd been acutely aware of the suffering that surrounded me, absolutely overwhelmed with compassion as well as fear about the lack of response and conversation concerning the omnipresent pain that existed. It was as if I were all of a sudden connecting the dots. Dots I never even knew were there. I was finding answers. And as I devoured all the books I could find, I wanted more. I called the number on the flyer and got the dates and details. I would go to the retreat.

Spring had come. The earth was still cold and damp, but on one Friday as I packed a small weekend duffel bag, the rays of sunshine cascaded down around me, illuminating and warming my small cabin. Ethan was ready to give me a ride to Bodega Bay. He looked at me quizzically, wondering what changes this retreat might bring. There was much between us, and a great deal of it was resting in the unknown. I could feel a momentum, a movement, and a time of growth and wonder ahead. So, perhaps, could he.

We drove along the coast and into the small town of Bodega. Stopping at the address I had been given he leaned in to kiss me. "Call if you want to come home early," he joked. As he pulled away, I stood for a moment in the drive, collecting myself and taking a deep breath. I was nervous. This was unknown territory.

Just then a beautiful, streamlined young gal a few years older than me pulled up on a bike. Her long blond hair was caught up in a rainbow barrette. "Hi! I'm René," she greeted me with a grin.

As she dismounted, I couldn't help but stare at her unbelievably athletic body. Her arms were rippled with muscle, and she reached out to give me a hug. Again a sense of familiarity hung in the air. Together we walked into the house. Warm faces, flowing skirts, mostly grayhaired women greeted me. I removed my shoes and placed them next to the other pairs inside the door.

"Have you met Tsultrim yet?" one woman asked. I had not, I replied.

"Well, why don't you go on upstairs and say hello before everyone gets here."

In an instant I was herded through the house and up a long flight of stairs. I could smell a strange incense burning. A faint but familiar bell sounded from the room I was moving toward. As I heard it, it was as if the lights dimmed, yet everything before me became crystal clear. Quietly, I knocked. A moment of hesitation, of fear, bubbled up. *Why am I here?* I wondered. *What on earth am I doing?*

Entering the room, I could see that a beautiful altar was set out on the floor. Candles of different colors sat in each of the four directions, while a blue one flickered in the center. Flowers and crystals caught the light, and in the middle of all this there appeared to be a small cauldron. Later I would come to know that cauldron as a *kapala* skull cup, a human skull used as a ritual tool in both Buddhist and Hindu practice.

Sitting at the end of the room, holding court, seated in a cross-legged position, was Tsultrim. Her being emanated brilliance and compassion. I made my way slowly toward her, and she smiled, nodding for me to come closer. As I did, something uncontrollable happened. I burst into tears until my tears became quiet, body-racking sobs. Falling at her feet and placing my forehead on the floor before her, I just let myself cry, not entirely sure, nor even caring, why. It was as if lifetimes of longing and pain were moving through me and I was finally before someone who truly knew and loved me. I hadn't said my name, yet in a flash her arms wrapped around me, stroking my hair, and then a simple, clear greeting—"Welcome home, Carré"—came from her mouth. I was stunned. And silenced. I immediately knew I *was* home. I couldn't explain it intellectually, but I understood it emotionally. That old longing, that old heartache I had always associated with being homesick, evaporated.

That weekend was a milestone in my life. I will never forget it. How long had I been searching for this path? How long had I been waiting for my teachers? After meeting Tsultrim, I began to study and put into practice the profound elements and instructions of Tibetan Buddhism. And as I did, a wisdom awoke inside me, a wisdom that would guide me through some of the most trying times anyone could face in this life.

Returning to the farm that Sunday afternoon, I knew that things had changed. I now had something I did not before. I had found my teacher, and I had connected with my beliefs, both remembered from another time. A new chapter was beginning, and in it was more of the unknown. But I was ready. Armed with a new strength and a resilience within, I realized I was ready to return to work.

MODELING AGAIN

The farm was proving to be a smaller world than I had once thought, and I was getting antsy. Every community has its politics, and the farm was no different. Ethan and I were both in an increasingly uncomfortable position; we never had jobs, so we never had any of our own money either. It was humiliating to so constantly be dependent on Nan. A part of me craved being busy and out in the world again. I had already tasted that kind of independence. No matter how far behind I had left Paris, the yearning to be back "out there" was returning, like a beast to his feeding grounds. Whether it was for fame, money, acceptance, or just to finish off what I'd begun, the world of modeling still had its allure. And as safe and nurturing as the farm was, I still wanted an escape.

I was ready for a change. Rumor had it that there was catalog work in the city. Thinking that could be a good steady gig, I set up an appointment with a local agency called Look and drove in for a meeting. Marie-Christine Kollock was the agency owner. This petite French woman with plenty of spunk to spare met me at her office. We looked through my portfolio together; I showed her the shots from New York and France. By San Francisco standards, I was considered a star. I had a French *Elle* cover, and that counted for a lot. I went straight to work.

Slowly and steadily I began to clock my hours. And just as steadily I was able to put some coin in the bank. I would drive from the farm in the early-morning traffic, an hour into the city. By 5:00 P.M. I was making my way home. The commute was endless but necessary at first. The farm gave me the security I needed to find my way back into the industry. San Francisco proved to be tame enough, so within a few months Ethan and I decided we could handle the move. We found ourselves a sweet little apartment on Dolores Street. From our second-floor balcony, we would often hear the calls of the wild parrots of Telegraph Hill screaming through the air.

As the months passed, a basic routine began to develop. I was able to balance work, home, and a strong devotion to my Buddhist practices. My world was opening up. I was gaining strength and momentum. The daily bookings for local catalogs like Macy's and Emporium were helping me to hone my skills and boost my confidence. But soon San Francisco began to feel like a small town, too.

I continued to set my goals higher. I felt as if I could conquer the world one step at a time. I began to think that maybe success was all in the timing—and perhaps my time was coming. I knew I still needed a "big" agent, but I didn't want to go backward and be represented by a massive corporate agency where I was just a number. I wanted to hold on to my individuality. I'd seen what it was to be caught up in the great modeling machine, and I hadn't liked it, to say the least.

Los Angeles was the best bet. I did not want to return to New York. And I would rather be dead than go back to Paris. I began to ask around about agents in Southern California. One name kept coming up: Paul Fisher with It Models. From what I could gather, he was the closest thing to a New York agent—only he was close enough to familiar stomping grounds.

He and I chatted easily on the phone, and I agreed to drive down and meet him.

Paul was young. He seemed like a kid himself, or at least a big-brother type. He talked a mile a minute and was all about "possibility." Dressed in a pair of white jeans, a T-shirt, and a pair of sneakers, he was the walking antithesis of the agents I had met. I believed his rap, though, and his enthusiasm was contagious. I was very frank about what I wanted. And even clearer about what I didn't want.

I wanted to work, I wanted money. But I didn't want to sell my soul or have anyone else do so. "Groovy, sister"—he nodded as if he understood me. Time would tell whether he did or not. But we agreed to work together. And that was the beginning of a new era for me.

By the time I arrived home, I already had a call from him. Herb Ritts was shooting for German *Playboy* and wanted to see my tits.

"What? Are you serious? First of all, who is Herb Ritts? And second of all, Paul, there is no way in hell I am going to shoot for *Playboy*!" I was appalled. *Playboy* stood for everything I hated.

"Carré, baby, you gotta trust me on this one," Paul begged. "Can you please just have Ethan take some Polaroids of your tits and FedEx them to me, sweetie?"

What did I know? He was asking for my trust. I wanted to break into the big time. And this was the way he thought it would happen.

"Okay," I told Paul. And that day Ethan took a gazillion Polaroids of my tiny young breasts. Maybe two included my face, but the rest were all tits.

As it turned out, Herb loved my tits. And that was the beginning of my biggest breakthrough. At that time Herb Ritts was shooting for every magazine under the sun. And doing it beautifully. His black-and-whites, his nudes and shadows, as well as his amazing editorials were all the rage. He was on top. He turned out to be my in.

Within months I was shooting for American *Vogue, Elle, Allure,* and *Glamour.* I was booked for Revlon's "Most Unforgettable Women" campaign with Richard Avedon. It was Arthur Elgort who photographed me in the Hamptons for *Vogue.* It was awesome and exciting.

I spent a week shooting for Guess with Ellen von Unwerth in Italy, and the pictures rocked the industry. I was traveling, having fun, and beginning to develop an attitude of invincibility. I carried over the magic of the farm, the self-image of being a wild hippie girl, and I maintained my spiritual practices. But I was starting to have trouble staying grounded in such a body-oriented business. I needed to slow down. Unfortunately, my requests for a break went unanswered. There was a constant reminder that it was now or never hanging over me. That damned sense that the clock was ticking, that an expiration date loomed on the horizon, was always present. That urgent "get it while you can, get it while it's hot" mentality prevailed, and with it both the pace of the work and the round-the-world travel only increased.

Just before my burnout, I was scheduled to fly to Baja California
to shoot with Patrick Demarchelier, one of *Vogue*'s most famous photographers. I was on thin ice. Paul was pushing me past my limits. I
was a wreck. I had begged him to cancel the job in Mexico; I told him
I couldn't go on. I needed to shut down and head home. I needed to
see nature, and Nan and Ethan. But he was insistent. His rap never
changed. He always promised that every job would be the last before
I'd get some rest, but it never was.

Once I committed to Baja, Paul decided to fly in and meet me to
help me get through the shoot. I recall arriving sometime after midnight. The Hotel Twin Dolphin was the best luxury resort Cabo San
Lucas had to offer at the time, but for me it was all wrong. I was escorted to my room and proceeded to have a meltdown. There was no
TV. No minibar. It was too hot. I was too tired. I sobbed and sobbed,
and, quite frankly, I don't think Paul knew what to do with me.

"Do you really want me to go and tell Patrick you can't do this?"

"Yes!" I screamed. "Would someone finally fucking listen to me!"

I collapsed onto the bed and slept, listening to the waves crashing
below in the pitch darkness of the Mexican night.

When I awoke, it was morning and Paul had come back from a
walk. He'd found Patrick and the crew on the beach and told them I
was sick. We had to go home.

"Well, what did he say? Is it okay?" I asked Paul.

"I don't know, sister." Paul looked at his feet. Clearly I was bum-
ming him out.

I had this gnawing feeling in the pit of my stomach that the pay was
more important to him than I was. *Am I just this guy's meal ticket?
Does he care at all?* I thought. Agents are aggressive by nature and I was
one of his biggest clients at the time, so I know that leaving money on
the table was hard. But I had to draw the line somewhere. I was at my
breaking point.

Back in L.A., I decided it was time to check in with Tsultrim, my
teacher.

"Carré, I am doing this retreat in Ojai, California," she told me. "Another *dakini* retreat. You should come."

It sounded perfect. Amazing. I would just need to extract myself from my life and clear the dates. Calling Paul, I booked myself out. He was baffled and clearly disgruntled. "But, baby, we have all of these incredible jobs on hold for you."

"Paul, I have to take some time off. The jobs will wait." And without another word I hung up the phone and packed my bags for Ojai. I knew that if I were to continue on, I would have to take care of myself. No one else would.

The beginnings of spring were in the air. I made my way north out of the city and drove along the coast and then inland to Ojai. It was a beautiful drive—blossoms on the trees, a crisp blue sky. Gentle winds kicked up the dust on the lone road that wound up the mountain. At the top sat a small retreat center, the Ojai Foundation.

I parked my car in the open lot, then got out and stretched. Looking around at the 360-degree view, I drew in a long breath and exhaled. Damn, was it time to leave that storm and stress behind or what?

Making my way to the main yurt, I could see Tibetan prayer flags snapping in the wind. I sensed Tsultrim near, and an excitement bubbled up. I missed her, and I missed that sense of connectedness She was it. And I was close.

I saw her an instant later, standing in a field not far from me. "Tsultrim!" I yelled excitedly, and ran toward her, almost stumbling as I moved across the grass. She grabbed me tight and held me close. I remember breathing in her scent, so grounded and full.

"Beauty . . ." she cooed at me, holding my face in her hands. I lost myself for a moment in the sea of her sky-blue gaze.

Brimming over with joy, I followed her like a puppy to the practice hall, a beautiful wooden dome with hardwood floors. Maroon prayer cushions called *zabuton*s were set up in a circle. I made my place next to Tsultrim and her assistant, a Native American medicine woman named Sparky Shooting Star, and sat quietly watching as the other retreat participants, all women, entered. There was a silence that hovered, a quiet I hadn't felt for some time. Closing my eyes and listening to the wind stirring the pines, I relaxed.

Tsultrim began with a greeting, and we went around the circle, stating our names and setting an intention for the time we would share together. And then we began our evening practice.

When darkness descended, Tsultrim raised her bell, the sharp tinkling letting us know that our session was over.

In the cool night air, I got out my flashlight and found my way to my yurt. I placed my bag in the corner, undressed, and pulled the mosquito netting down over the small and simple bed I would rest in for the week's stay. An owl hooted in a tree overhead, and I wondered about that old tale I'd heard from Nan: The owl signifies death and change, representing the great mysteries of the night. I knew that a part of me needed to die. And to do this I needed to surrender. Death was part of the flow. It was part of life and a central piece of slaying the ego. I was back on my path and clearly had some work to do.

Our days were full of practice, outdoor meditation, and mask making. I hadn't let that creative side of me come forth since I'd left the farm. I relished the time to play and explore.

But a part of me was holding on to the outside way of life. I had become accustomed to certain foods and diets, and now in the contrast of a group of healthy, hearty women, I felt that my strange habits and neuroses seemed to stand out in the light. I was always on a diet. Always fearful of gaining weight. And even in this relaxed atmosphere, I had to micromanage everything.

One afternoon I departed from the retreat's schedule, deciding to go for a run. I blasted along the winding dirt paths up toward the top of the mountain. After an hour, still breathing heavily, I returned to the group. Tsultrim sat quietly under the shade of an old oak tree.

"Why are you running, Carré? What are you running from?" she asked in a very open and curious way. Clearly, running was not part of the curriculum.

I was speechless. I had no answer for her. I was running. I just wasn't sure from what.

During our evening practice session, the caretaker for the retreat center came in and looked around the room. She had a note in her hand. And although she'd entered discreetly, everyone stopped and noticed her presence.

Tsultrim looked up. "What do you need?" she asked.

"There was an urgent call for Carré. She needs to call this person back as soon as possible."

I was alarmed and stood to look at the piece of paper she handed me. The note simply read, *"Call Mr. Fisher as soon as possible."* What the fuck was he doing calling me here? But my concern grew, and I excused myself to go to the main house and make a phone call.

"Paul? Is everything okay?" I asked once he had picked up.

"Yeah, baby. Better than ever. I have the most exciting news!" I could hear the kid in his voice.

"Paul, I told you not to call me. Not for the week. Come on! Whatever it is can wait!"

I was pissed off. And put off. But a little part of me was curious. And jonesing for some contact with the busy outside world I was so used to.

"Baby, I'm sorry. But this can't wait. It won't wait. It's a now-or-never thing."

"What?" I demanded to know. "What?"

"It's what we've been waiting for. It's your big break. Zalman King called. Mickey Rourke wants to meet you. They're casting a movie—a big movie. They . . . want . . . you." He was beside himself, talking a million miles a minute.

"What? Are you serious? Are you kidding?" I was stunned. A movie? With Mickey Rourke? Like, from *9½ Weeks?* Oh, my God. Any kid would be over the moon with this news.

"But, Paul . . . I can't leave retreat. I really can't. I can meet them in five more days. Please." The karmic rules of retreat were clear. And I knew the fallout of breaking their boundaries could be serious.

"No, Carré. It's now. The time is now. They'll send a car. They want to meet you tomorrow."

Excitement mixed with apprehension. I needed to talk with Tsultrim. But somewhere my mind was already made up. Samsara was calling. Temptation was beckoning. I was being lured. It was unclear in that moment *what* exactly was out there calling my name, but there was a sense it was dangerous.

I told Paul I'd call him back, I had to speak to my teacher.

"Okay," he agreed. "But, Carré . . . this is your shot. You can go back to the retreat after your meeting. A few hours out of your time. That's all I am asking."

"I got it, Paul. I'll call you back." And with that, I hung up the phone and walked through the night to meet with Tsultrim.

"Carré, this isn't good," Tsultrim warned me. I knew what she was going to say. I just didn't want to hear it. "You made a commitment to be here. It is just like when a flame is ignited in the darkness, many things will flock toward that light. Not all of them good things. That is you now. A bright light. And there are forces that beckon. This is a test, my dear." I knew that what she was saying was true. I knew it in my heart and soul.

But for some reason I was unable to follow my heart. Once again I went against my gut. I called Paul back and told him to send the car.

Hollywood was calling, and I wasn't going to resist.

That moment marks a page in my history like no other. It was a turning point, one that sent me down a long, dark path. And it would take me at least ten years to find my way back into the light. Little did I know that I was about to be cast in my first movie, meet my future husband, and basically fall flat on my ass. All very publicly.

3

The Mickey Years

MEETING MICKEY ROURKE

There are moments in life that define us. Moments we know are coming. And one of those defining moments for me was the first time I met the man who would become my first husband. I walked through the door to Zalman King's house, and I changed my life.

It was a warm and sticky Los Angeles afternoon. I saw him right away. I will never forget the lone figure hunched in a corner. There at an open kitchen table, with stringy dark hair shrouding his face, trembling hands lifting a dainty saucer of coffee to his lips, sat the famed Mickey Rourke. I was curious but for some reason unimpressed. Instead of feeling any great sense of intimidation, I actually felt quite unaffected. That realization released a warm confidence within me.

My eyes rested momentarily on his hands, his pinkie finger raised as he took a sip of coffee from his cup. Mickey had unusual fingernails that seemed to curl over the ends of his nail beds, arching more like claws. A red flannel shirt, with a wifebeater underneath, didn't hide his impressive torso and biceps. He was a strong, solid man. He wore torn blue jeans and a pair of unlaced boxing shoes. His legs were crossed as he tapped his foot. In the silence he carried an attitude that said he was nobody's fool. There was an ashtray in front of him, full of cigarette butts, one still smoldering.

Mickey didn't stand or acknowledge me. I waited for a beat and then decided to enter the kitchen and look for some food. I was hungry after the drive from Ojai. Without looking at him or saying a word, I opened the large refrigerator door and rummaged for something to eat. I found leftover broccoli. I took it out and put some on a plate. Pulling out a chair, I sat down across from him and began to eat.

He lit another cigarette, and when he set it in the ashtray, I reached over, picked it up, and took a drag.

He finally looked up, his eyes meeting mine, and smiled. It was a surprisingly open smile, a playful smile, a beautiful smile. And I smiled back. I looked back down at my broccoli, finally a bit bashful. There was energy. There was chemistry. Basically we set the room on fire.

Not a word was spoken, just a long pause. It wasn't an uncomfortable one—just a pregnant silence. Zalman, the director of the movie they were casting, walked in. I already knew that the name of the film was *Wild Orchid*.

"I see you two have met." Zalman and his big nose nodded with an approving smile.

Mickey and I both kept smiling. It was rather funny, really. We hadn't met, yet we both felt so familiar to each other. I was happy to see him. Unsure of why, I felt an immediate closeness and kept smiling.

"Nah, Zalman. We haven't met." Mick looked at me, a shadow of formality crossing his face. He was changing before my very eyes. "Mickey Rourke," he said as he stood with his hand extended. And I stood as well, grabbing his hand, happy to finally be touching a part of him. I looked him in the eye, let him know through my gaze that he had met his match, and introduced myself.

"Carré Otis. Nice to meet you, Mickey." I smiled again. And although it was our formal meeting, we had already shared something in the moments before Zalman's entrance. And we both knew it.

Zalman laughed and motioned for us both to join him in his sitting room. I hadn't a clue what the film was about, nor did I have any idea what casting for a movie entailed. I wasn't an actress. Just a pretty girl. And my looks were why I was there. In that sense I was nobody's fool either.

I stared wide-eyed at the artwork and statues that dotted Zalman's enormous living room. Larger-than-life bronze figures hung about, alongside casts of oversize feet, hands, and breasts that were shaped more like missiles. Mickey watched me and laughed. He was amused by me. That much was clear.

Zalman told me a bit about the script. He said that they were casting for the part of a young lawyer named Emily Reed. The film was shooting on location for three months in Brazil.

He handed me a few pages out of a script. I had never seen one before. I looked down, confused.

"Oh," I said. "You want me to read this?" I was great at being myself. I wasn't so sure I could convincingly pull off being someone else.

Mickey sensed my apprehension. "Zalman, give me a few minutes with her, okay?"

"Sure, bro. Whatever you say." With that, Zalman left.

Again I was alone with Mickey. And for the first time, I felt nervous. He was an actor. I was not. And I was uncomfortable.

He put a hand on mine "Breathe. It's just a fucking script," he said reassuringly.

He had a "Who gives a shit?" attitude, and it immediately put me at ease. There was an element of rebel in us both. That was partly where the familiarity lay. But there was something else as well.

"Carré, why don't you lay back? Just lay down on the floor. Let me do an exercise with you." I must have looked at him suspiciously, because in an instant he justified it by saying, "No, it's safe. Really it is. I used to be an acting coach in New York."

I was in no position to question this, so I did as I was asked. I lay down, resting my head near the very large foot of a statue. Looking up at her tits, I began to laugh.

"Close your eyes and go back. . . ." And then Mickey proceeded to guide me through a sense-memory exercise. It was powerful and corny, but I wanted to impress. I was just wondering where it was all leading when he said, "Now sit up and read the lines." I did. And it worked. I was present, reading Emily, not being Carré. Mickey smiled. "That was great."

We worked on the scenes several times with Zalman in the room, and then after an hour or so we were alone again. Sitting, just the two of us on the oversize green velvet sofa.

I recall feeling the warmth from him. The heart that beat in him. Before I left Ojai, my friend Sparky Shooting Star had woven a black condor feather into a braid in my hair. "For your protection," she'd said. It hung down onto my shirt, a story of its own. Mickey watched me. His eyes studied me. He lifted a hand to feel the braid that held the feather, then leaned in as if to smell me before sitting back again with his eyes closed.

"Tell me the story of this . . . the feather in your hair."

And I did. I told him many stories that evening. As we sat so closely on that couch, an indescribable electricity moving between us, we worked our way through the past and into the present. I was the strongest I'd ever been in that moment: sound and centered. Mickey listened intently, stroking my hair with the familiarity of a long-lost lover. It was love and longing and breathtaking intensity, all at first sight.

My car had been waiting outside for me, and as night fell, I knew it was time to go. I bit back a momentary twinge of anxiety, unsure if I would ever see him again. Truth be told, I wasn't nearly as interested in getting the role in the movie as I was in him. Knowing him. Being with him. Loving him. But we didn't exchange numbers. If we were meant to see each other again, I trusted we would.

We hugged good night, locked in an extended, private, and powerful embrace, one that I think neither of us at the time could explain.

Mickey walked me out to the black Town Car, opened the door in a very gentlemanly way, and nodded his head good-bye. And for some reason when I sat down in the backseat, enveloped in the night and the silence, there were tears streaming down my face. Tears of excitement, tears of sadness. I was head over heels. I was wild and raw, filled with a yearning that had never existed in me prior to meeting this man.

The drive back to Ojai flew by. I was lost in giddiness. And although I stayed for the remainder of my retreat, only a part of me was there. The other part of me was already with Mickey. The passion and fury and confusion I could feel that first night encapsulated everything that was to come. After only a few hours with him, I knew as well as I knew anything that Mickey had a heart of gold. And I would come to know that he also had an iron fist.

WILD ORCHID

I waited, knowing he would call. I waited, knowing somehow that the movie was mine. It's not even that I was right for it. Unlike others who had tried out for the part, I wasn't an actress, nor had I ever tried to be one. But what *was* clear to me was the karma that Mickey and I had with each other. And I was certain that it would unfold.

When I heard that Cindy Crawford had been offered the role of Emily, a part of me was relieved. The other part of me was undaunted. Again I was certain that Mickey's path and mine would cross. I couldn't really explain it.

The call did come. And when I heard his voice on the other end of the phone, my heart jumped, my stomach did flips. I just wanted to be with him. We talked, and when he asked if I wanted to know about the movie, I said no. I just wanted to be close to him again.

He pulled up on his Harley, the loud motor revving outside my friend's apartment. Sharon had been on retreat with me. "I'm warning you, Carré," she said, shaking a finger at me. "He fucks anything that moves." I laughed as I slammed the front door, racing down the steps, my hair flowing behind me. I didn't care. I didn't care what they said about him. My mind was made up, and I was ready for the ride. Or so I thought.

I had never been on the back of a motorcycle, but I immediately knew what to do. I swung a long leg up and over, wrapped my arms around Mickey's middle, and pulled myself tight to his back. I held him like that for a minute as he leaned back into me. He laughed. "Aren't you even going to say hello, Otis?"

I crooked my neck around so that we were nose to nose. "Hello." I smiled. "Now drive this thing!" I was beside myself with excitement. Motorcycles, I was about to find out, are a great excuse to snuggle up and be close with someone. It's an intimate experience: A big, warm motor humming between your legs, vibrating your whole body. The sensation of letting go and surrendering to what's ahead. Rider and passenger merge in the movement of what the road brings. Words have no place. The wind just whips them away.

Our first days together were full of magic and lust. Mutual obsession grew stronger, and though it seemed settled that I wouldn't be in *Wild Orchid*, Mickey and I began to spend more and more time together. He was secretive. He was giving. He was loving and funny. We were friends. We were both completely smitten.

It was exciting and confusing to be with Mickey in those first days and weeks. I'd never wanted a man as much as I wanted Mickey, but even when we were having sex—especially when we were having sex—I was conscious of performing. As with every other man I'd been with, my lust always vanished when I felt him inside me. Once we were actually having sex, my focus was on making him come quickly and getting it over with. In that sense I was an experienced actress. I'd learned too young the power of my sexuality, and at times it felt like the only leverage I had. I wanted to be the greatest lover Mickey had ever been with, so I was focused much more on how I made him feel than on what I was experiencing. I was years away from giving myself permission to focus on what I desired, years away from having an orgasm with anyone other than myself.

Already in those early days, my craving for him was at its strongest when we weren't together. We'd be separated for a few hours, and I could think of nothing else but being with him again. We both loved the drama of it all, loved the fantasy of being head over heels in love, unable to be apart. When people ask why I would end up staying with him for so long, this is a huge part of the answer. The times we weren't together were the times I wanted him most. Not only did my lust vanish when we fucked, my mad fantasy of who he was and who we were together faded when I was around him, too.

But I wasn't thinking about that disconnect, not yet. I was thinking about other things. For one, the paparazzi were already on our asses. Mickey was still involved with another well-known model, and neither of us needed any premature exposure in the press. We were in an intense state of "like" that was bubbling over with want. But there was a lot we needed to wait and see about. The movie was just one of those things.

When it was finally announced that I had gotten the role of Emily, I was both elated and terrified. Elated that I would be with Mickey for months in Brazil—and terrified by that same fact. I didn't know what I was doing. I wasn't an actress. And I wasn't too sure if our relationship could survive, much less evolve, under the watchful eye of the public. But the thought of not being with Mickey was more upsetting.

In an instant my life changed. I was a young model on my way to Brazil to make a movie. But just because you appear in a film doesn't mean you're an actress. I would learn this very painful lesson in time. If I had different representation, maybe my experience would have been better. Paul was my modeling agent at the time and had limited prior experience with actors. I would ultimately come to think of him as someone who'd make a deal with the devil if it paid the bills and put him on top. Basically I felt that's what he did with me.

I had no protection. No support system. And no business doing a movie without rehearsing or working with an acting coach. There were very few provisions in my contract that ensured access to the things I needed in order to stay healthy and remain sane. Because the film was not a union film, I didn't have the SAG-mandated twelve-hour turn-around. I was expected to work six days a week. This might have been fine for a seasoned actor, but for me it was death by way of absolute exhaustion. I was about to learn what working around the clock really means. With such a relentless schedule and so little preparation, the climate had been set for some serious tensions and some seriously bad acting. And not just on my part.

Sadly, I didn't have a clue about any of this before signing on. When I boarded a Varig Airlines flight in Los Angeles, bound for Rio and seated in first class, I had no idea that I was flying high into the unknown, alone.

Mickey had his entourage by his side. But without agents, friends, or family members watching over me, I was just a kid playing a game of hardball with the big boys. I was out of my league. Way out. Mick, by contrast, always traveled in a pack. On this particular movie, the entourage included Bruce, Franco, and Mickey's little brother, Joe. Each of them could be sweet or a complete asshole from one moment to the next. Just like Mickey. And they were all under the spell that he cast.

They only called me by my last name. They were like a band of big brothers, joking and teasing with me—and threatening anyone who got in their way. As much as I would like to think they loved and cared about me, I knew they were just following orders. And those orders would change depending on the boss's moods. I came to learn that absolutely everything under the sun was relayed to Mickey. Even things that were totally unrelated to our relationship were dutifully reported back. It was as if the walls had ears and the mountains had eyes.

Nothing could have prepared me for what would happen when we arrived in South America. I'd been on the cover of magazines before, but I had never really been a recognizable celebrity. Clearly, things were different now. Within hours of our landing, my name was in every newspaper in the States and Brazil.

We were booked at the Intercontinental, and by the second morning of our visit the media was reporting everything from what we were having for breakfast to where we were sleeping. They said that Mickey and I were cohabiting, but the truth was that, for many reasons, we were staying in separate rooms. I was relieved to have a little private space of my own. The attention was overwhelming. The public scrutiny was incredibly intense. And on top of it all, rumor had it that the locals were not happy we were there.

The crew was mostly from California, so a certain camaraderie existed. We were all far from home, working one hell of a grinding schedule. I was getting special treatment because I was a lead, but it was nowhere near the treatment Mickey got. What really shocked me were the additional demands he'd make, despite the amenities he already had. I didn't know the tricks of the trade and what was and wasn't "standard" star behavior. All I knew was that a whole new side of him was emerging on and off the set, and it wasn't always pleasant to watch.

The night before filming began, there was a cast party in the hotel. The first week had been spent mostly working up "looks" for each character, dealing with hair, makeup, tests, and locations. What should have been a comforting process—one that could have helped familiarize me with the way things work on set—only seemed to make matters worse. My apprehension was building. Maybe it would have been better if I had just dived right in. The more time that passed, the less certain I was that I could pull off being Emily.

I threw on a tiny Azzedine Alaïa dress and a pair of Marciano half cowboy boots and made my way down the elevator and out to the pool area where the party was being thrown. Tiki torches lined the huge infinity pool; a beautiful young Brazilian boy manned a tropical floating bar. There was magic in the air, and we were all letting loose, readying ourselves for the long and grueling weeks ahead of us.

Even though our call time was 4:00 A.M., the crew was partying.

I danced my way over to the open bar and ordered a glass of white wine. Just then someone came up behind me and put his hands over my eyes. I stiffened immediately. I had always hated when people did that. It seemed to bring back some very bad memories of waiting in the unknown, in vulnerable and compromised places. I pulled the hands from my face and turned around. I was relieved to see that it was Mickey. But something was different. Something had changed between us.

"What's wrong?" I asked.

He just quietly stared at me. He was behaving oddly like Wheeler, the cold and enigmatic millionaire he would be playing in the movie.

My heart sank. My stomach roiled. All of a sudden, the magic of the evening was deflated and a new set of apprehensions filled my chest. Mickey leaned over, pausing at my neck to take in a deep breath of me. "Good night, my dear," he said sinisterly. And with that, he was gone.

I stood alone at the bar, confused. I threw my drink back, swallowing it in just a few gulps. The only person who I thought would get me through this movie had just flipped a switch. I realized I was utterly alone.

The next morning, through the darkness, I found my way to the small trailer marked EMILY. Next to it was a trailer marked WHEELER. It was triple the size of mine.

I laughed, then pulled myself up and into what would be my home away from home while filming, Thankful to smell some coffee brewing, I smiled at my makeup artist, Hiram Ortiz. He would become one of my only friends and refuges during the long and arduous adventure to come. Unfortunately, Hiram would also become the chief source of cocaine that the country prided itself upon. I wouldn't be the only one with an appetite for it and the need to escape the mounting pressures on set.

We were well into our first week of shooting when the weather turned. Monsoon season approached, and there was one scene in particular that would lend itself nicely to a downpour. We were filming outside a dilapidated hotel, and although Mickey was not in the scene, he wanted to be there to make sure I "got it right." It was a scene that required Emily to register a real sense of betrayal. After a few takes that were too flat, Mickey stepped forward from where he'd been watching. "Hey, Zalman," he said. Zalman was clearly frustrated with me. Word was that he was beginning to doubt his decision to cast me as Emily. Knowing that made me more and more anxious in the role.

"What, Mickey?" Zalman snapped. He looked at his watch and then back up at Mickey. Mickey moved closer in to whisper something in Zalman's ear. Zalman slowly smiled and shrugged, "Yeah, man. Have a go at it."

Mickey stood in front of me, and I heard Zalman give the instruction to roll camera. And in an instant Mickey slapped me across the face hard enough for it to sting. Then he grabbed my dress, pulling it up, and ripped my underwear. I pushed him away, nearly falling. I was gasping as tears of humiliation welled in my eyes.

"And . . . got it!" Zalman yelled. "Well done, kids."

I was in shock. I was in pain, but even more than that, I was furious. Throwing the books I was holding to the ground, I stomped away, Mickey close behind.

"Otis! Otis, Wait up. I just want you to be the best you can be. That was only for reaction." He looked into my eyes, a big puppy-dog expression on his face. I was totally confused. This wasn't how I did things. This wasn't how anyone I knew did things. I was hurt, feeling more and more shaken by Mickey's erratic behavior.

He wiped the tears from my eyes and threw an arm around my shoulders, pulling me to him in a friendly embrace. "Let's go, kid. You done good." And then he simply led me off set and back to the hotel.

Mickey had arranged for us to have dinner in his room that evening. We had only a little while together, since there was still a full night of shoots ahead of us. I had never maintained such long hours and was beginning to feel not at all like myself. My world had been turned upside down.

By this time the negative energy of the movie had tainted the sweetness I'd felt earlier with Mickey. And I wasn't the only one upset by the whole tenor of things. Since we'd been shooting, major flooding had destroyed thousands of homes in the favelas that dotted the mountains around Rio. We heard that the locals were blaming us for their hardship.

It was true that as filming went along, our production values appeared to stand in stark contrast to the immense poverty that existed there. It didn't seem to me that we were giving much back to the locals, and the ramifications of that neglect seemed more and more real. There were rumors that we could be poisoned. In this superstitious country where Santeria was practiced by millions, we got serious threats of retaliation through black magic. Tragically, one crew member drowned at a nearby beach, compounding the uneasy sense that a dark cloud was hovering above.

All of that was on my mind as we dined in Mickey's hotel room. Before we ate, he poured us each a glass of red wine and swallowed a small pill.

"What's that?" I asked, concerned.

"Xanax. It's for anxiety. I get really bad anxiety, Otis. Especially when I'm stressed." I believed him. I'd seen Mickey pacing around the set with a brown paper bag in his clenched fist, at times seeming to struggle for breath. We'd never spoken about his attacks before that moment.

"Oh. Would it work for me?" I had never really taken pills and didn't know there were ones to relieve stress. I'd always been into street drugs or pot.

"Sure." He shrugged. Like so many other people at the time, Mickey seemed to think that if a doctor had prescribed it, then it was all okay. He broke off a quarter of the oval-shaped pill and handed it to me. I smiled, tossed it into my mouth, and swallowed, hoping it would do the trick.

I learned to get through the filming of *Wild Orchid* with the help of one substance or another. Mickey's pills came in handy, but they didn't make the all-nighters that were increasingly required any easier. We must have been halfway through production when Hiram, my makeup artist, broke his little secret to me.

I was overtired and constipated. That's not a good combination. We had a seminude scene coming up, and . . . well, let's just say I was unbelievably uncomfortable.

"Sweetie," Hiram cooed from outside the bathroom door in my trailer. "I have something for you."

"What?" I snapped irritably from the toilet. I really just needed to take a crap.

"Open up the door, darling. It will relieve you instantly." And with that, he handed me a small dark vial and a tiny silver spoon.

"No way!" I screamed, elated. "Where did you score this?" I was no stranger to coke. But it had been years since I'd used it.

"My dear, this is the land of the coca," Hiram said with a laugh as he shut the bathroom door again. I hadn't a clue. But it seemed that just the sight of the vial in my hand remedied my problem. I stood, flushed the toilet, and walked into the living room of our humble abode.

He smiled and winked at me. "Not too much, my friend. Just on occasion. It will help us get through some of these long-assed nights." Hiram was a beautiful boy. I knew he had my back.

"But, sweetheart . . . I don't think it's good if the boys were to find out," he added, nodding toward Mickey's trailer. I stopped and thought about it for a minute. No, it wouldn't be good if the boys found out.

"Our secret, Hiram. Okay?"

"Yes, absolutely." He nodded exaggeratedly.

And just like that, cocaine came back into my life. Fast and furious. It was also the first of many secrets I had to keep from Mickey. I'd spent enough time with him at that point to know what was cool and what was not, what would fly and what wouldn't.

In the same way that he had his friends and allies, I had mine. He had secrets, and so did I. I learned from the start that even if Mickey and I were to be together, there would always be a barrier between us. There was love, but there were also lies. There was passion, and there was abuse. Everywhere you looked, there were confusing contradictions. But when it was good, it was *so* damn good. I was hooked on the drama, on the thrill. I was in thrall to the danger and to the crashes. I had become addicted to Mickey. And to all the different forms that life with him took. I didn't have a clue how to break that spell.

The grind of our schedule was wearing everyone down. The script and filming continued to take shadowy and sinister turns. Life was beginning to imitate art. There was a dark sea of confusion around this film. I was struck by how many others in the cast and crew were doing lines daily, but definitely *not* Mickey.

Although my costar Jacqueline Bisset was always cordial, I could feel her watching me from afar. One night, during the filming of the carnival scene, she came up to me, winked, and wiped her nose. "My dear, you must learn to be discreet," she said, not unkindly. I was mortified and made an effort to reel myself in. It was hard, though. Emily, in the film, was becoming wilder. And so was I.

As we neared the end, there were so many discussions about the notorious love scene that remained to be shot and about our approaching wrap date. It was at this point that Mickey told me he would be leaving early. We were watching a great black storm pass over the ocean from the window of his room when he shared the news.

"What do you mean, 'early'?" I felt shaky inside. I knew that the end of the film might potentially be the end of our relationship.

"I wanted to talk with you, Otis." He looked into my eyes, and we sank into that familiar place with one another. It was a place past secrets. A place that truly did hold love.

"I'll be leaving a week before you. I wrap early. I'm going to miss you, baby." He ran his hand through my hair. I gazed out toward the ocean.

"What does that mean, Mickey?" I asked. "Was this just a movie thing? Will I see you again?" I didn't want to appear desperate or needy. But in a way that's exactly what I was. I was young, caught up in the intensity of things, too deep into it emotionally to turn back.

"I want you to move in with me," he said out of the blue.

"What?" I was shocked. I knew there were "loose strings" at home, mostly with another model/actress he'd dated on and off. And I knew that his home in Benedict Canyon was very much under construction. Then again, I didn't really have a home. Since I left the apartment I'd shared with Ethan, I'd been living in hotels and on the couches of friends. "Move in where? When did you decide this? Are you sure?"

Was *I* sure? I was still stunned.

"I want to leave Joey here with you while I'm gone. He'll get you home safe and sound. I'll find a place for you to live . . . um . . . for us to live. Just do me one favor, Otis."

My mouth hung to the floor. He was serious. And I was as excited as I was terrified. "What's that, Mickey?"

"Just be a good girl. While you're here and I'm at home. Just be a good girl." I had a strong feeling that if I wasn't, he would know.

I mustered all the innocence and strength I could find and smiled, looking into his eyes, steady and strong. "You've got nothing to worry about, Mick. Nothing." I leaned in and gave him a kiss, my arms wrapping around his neck. I climbed into his lap, and we sat there together, quietly watching the waves, feeling each other's rhythmic heartbeats and each other's every breath. Feeling both safe and confused, I rested in the arms of the first truly adult *man* I'd ever loved. At least the first since my father.

The one scene left to shoot before Mickey's departure was the love scene between Emily and Wheeler. I had no idea what to expect. My nerves were flying high, and there was tremendous apprehension around the culmination of their relationship in the movie as well as about Mickey's and my relationship in real life.

But when I walked onto the set, the bed was surrounded by bright lights and sound guys. It was a lot like any other scene in the movie. We were not alone. As much as Mickey and I could generate chemistry, there were angles and marks to hit, and ours was a highly choreographed tumble and embrace. That's not to say we weren't able to get into the moment and lose ourselves and our bodies in genuine, rollicking passion. But we were also on a movie set. We had to break up our embraces each time the sound guy or the lighting guy or Zalman himself would quietly interject and say in an awkward tone, "Um, can we get that shot again? Sorry, guys." We would freeze for a moment, laugh uncomfortably, and get into position to repeat the take. And then Mickey and I would be lost once more in our moment.

My naïveté and lack of experience no doubt led things awry. My judgment was off. I had no frame of reference. I never realized that the way the scene was shot might suggest that more was happening than actually was. Almost immediately after we finished filming, the rumors that Mickey and I had actually had sex in the scene began to fly. Zalman King and his producing partners did nothing to squelch those rumors. Quite the contrary: When it came time to promote the film, they did everything they could to exploit the sensation around that one scene. Against my will the producers sold the footage to *Playboy* magazine, so still images of the scene could appear in the publication. This was only one of the many humiliating and maddening moments of exploitation that ensued from my role in *Wild Orchid*. It was the beginning of some very painful and public lessons for me.

This promotional tactic worked. The press seemed to go crazy when some of the footage was leaked. "They had sex!" the papers screamed. Of course, that became the inevitable and unavoidable question during every interview that followed. For better or worse, the controversy over "the scene" overshadowed questions about my poor acting. What was to have been my breakthrough role as an actress was, as one reviewer called it, "wooden at best." But at least the poor box-office showing would not be placed on my head alone. Mickey had already been in a string of films where his acting had been far from praised. He was just entering a long downward spiral.

I made it through that last lonely week of filming and boarded the Varig flight back to LAX. I was exhausted and disoriented. I knew that the life I was returning to would look immensely different from the one I was coming from. I didn't feel like a star. I didn't feel like I was on top of the world. I felt wounded and scared, and more exposed and exploited than ever.

But seeing Mickey waiting as I came through customs at LAX was a relief. He was my family. My friend and partner in the madness. And I would have to trust him. He was all I had in that moment.

But, in truth, I was more on my own than I had ever been.

BIRD IN A GILDED CAGE

We drove through Beverly Hills in the back of a limo, the air-conditioning sending a chill through my body. When I reached over to lower the window, Mickey wrapped his arms around me and pulled me close. I protested. I just wanted some fresh air, but Mickey began to smother me with kisses, telling me how much he'd missed me.

"Were you a good girl?" he asked me, playing with the button on my blouse.

I felt small and insecure. Was I good? I wasn't so sure. But I nodded yes as I watched the trees whiz by. How else could I answer a question like that?

We drove past Mickey's house in Benedict Canyon—the one that was still under construction. As impressive in size as it was, it stood lonely and perpetually unfinished. It was a money pit of indecision and would eventually be reclaimed by the bank when Mickey went broke. The limo didn't stop.

"So where are we staying?" I asked, confused.

"Not far, just up and over Mulholland, the Valley side. You've got great views, and Bruce has fixed it up real nice. We already got your stuff out of storage for you. You're all moved in."

Gulp. That was one huge decision taken care of.

The Alta Loma Terrace house sat on the top of a hill, behind iron gates at the far end of a cul-de-sac. It was huge and dark, and it couldn't have looked more remote or less inviting. Mickey was beaming, assuring me I'd be happy here. I was bewildered. He seemed much more interested in impressing me—and isolating me—than in spending time with me. That wasn't the Mickey I thought I knew.

Bruce, who was perhaps my favorite member of the entourage (and the only one who had the courage to stand up to Mickey), came bouncing out of the house as we drove up, wrapping me in a brotherly embrace as I stepped from the car. Mickey didn't follow.

"Otis, I have a meeting. Gotta run. Bruce will show you around." The limo driver shut the door, and they sped off down the hill. Bruce grabbed my bags and walked into the house. I trailed behind, stopping to linger on the doorstep. The air was warm and dusty, the view admittedly spectacular. I felt a wave of loneliness wash over me. I would never have chosen a house like this, gated and so far removed from the heart of the city. I had the strange feeling I was a little bird being put in a gilded cage.

Bruce gave me an enthusiastic tour of the kitchen, explaining that Mickey had asked him to stock the refrigerator with all my favorite things. Nice, I thought, but also necessary. I didn't have a car and was at least a mile from any store. After the kitchen Bruce took me through the rest of the house, finishing in the huge master bedroom. The place was well furnished and immaculate, but soulless. Even with Bruce beside me, I felt utterly alone.

"Otis, you cool?" Bruce had noticed my mood and was looking at me with concern. I turned away from him just in time to hide the tear that spilled down my cheek.

"Yeah, Bruce. I'm just tired." That was partly true. But there was also something else, a sense of foreboding. The house seemed more like "mine" than "ours." The complete absence of anything that was identifiably Mickey's made it hard to feel otherwise.

After giving me the number at which I could reach him whenever I needed something, Bruce said his good-byes. As he opened the front door to leave, I stopped him. "Wait . . . do you know when Mickey will be back?" Bruce grimaced, as if he'd hoped to make it out the door before I posed that question. He forced a reassuring smile. "I don't know, Otis. Not sure about that." He shrugged his shoulders and left. I listened to the fading roar of his Harley as he headed back down the hill. And then, exhausted, I went straight to bed.

Two days later Mickey finally appeared. I'd had no number at which to reach him, no idea where he was. I was hurt and angry. I felt rejected, and also humiliated. Above all I felt confused. So when I heard Mickey pull into the driveway, I came running out of the house to greet him.

"Where the fuck have you been, Mick? What the fuck's going on?" I was so enraged that I flicked my lit cigarette at him. It bounced harmlessly off his shoulder. Mickey grabbed my hand, twisting it roughly, his fingers digging into my flesh. I winced in pain.

"Otis, listen. You gotta bear with me. I told you there are loose ends to tie up."

"So that's all you're doing? Tying them up? The loose ends?" I looked hard into his eyes, willing him to tell me the truth. I was still young enough to believe I had that power.

Mickey promised that was all he was doing. He pleaded with me, telling me that he couldn't wait to be with me. "Come on, baby," he said, pressing his forehead against mine. My body ached from jet lag, from anger, and from the conflict between wanting him so badly and not trusting anything he said.

"I don't need this, Mick. We can be on hold for a while if that's what we need to do. Why don't you work your shit out and then we can see if we can be together. Maybe in a few months?" I was calling his bluff, scared that he would walk away, more afraid of being kept waiting, hidden on this hill.

Something flashed in Mickey's eyes the moment he heard the words "on hold." I'd come to call it "his crazy," because there was no other term for what seemed to happen to him when he felt he was about to lose me.

For some reason, since the day we'd first met, I could be no one else's. I was his, and that was that.

"Give me a day, Otis. That's all. And I will be back." He tried to kiss me, but I pulled away. I knew I needed to play the cards I had, and play them well. Mickey's neediness was my ace, the one thing I could rely on from this otherwise unpredictable man.

I gave him a little shove, tinged with both affection and aggression. "So go do your thing, my friend. Tie it up. And I'll see you when it's done." Mickey turned to go, heading back to Joey and Bruce, who sat on their Harleys at the bottom of the driveway, watching everything. The trio roared off down the hill, leaving me alone at the top of Los Angeles with no car, no friends to call, and nowhere to go. I'd been home from Brazil for three days, and already I was trapped.

Walking back into the house, I remembered Mickey telling me when we first met that he was still "entangled in a situation." I hadn't wanted to know the details, and he'd sworn that that would soon be over. But as I reflected on all the things I'd seen—things such as Mickey hanging up the phone too quickly when I entered the room—I wasn't so sure. There were other signs, too. It seemed that I'd come home to a part-time relationship with a man who was far more entangled than he'd admitted or I had known. I thought hard about leaving, about calling someone to get me off that hill and away from Mickey. But I wanted to believe what he said to me. I wanted to believe that soon, very soon, he would be all mine.

Mickey did come back, assuring me that the entanglements were broken and that he was free to be with me, just me. I wanted to believe him. For a while—for too long—I did.

Playing House

I was playing house. I knew that something was very wrong with this new life of mine. By everyone else's standards, I had everything I could possibly want: a big, beautiful home, a relationship with a famous actor. But I had to stop counting there. That was all there was. Something was wrong. Very wrong. As bad as things had gotten for me before, I'd always been in command of my misery. I'd always felt like I was the one in control, able to come or go as necessary, able to create and destroy opportunities and relationships at will. But while living "with" Mickey, I felt a disconcerting sense of paralysis. I was in need to a degree I hadn't ever allowed myself to be before. And I felt my power and strength slipping away.

I spent too much of my time waiting for him. Long, lonely nights were passed listening to the winds whipping through the canyons and the coyotes howling in the distance. I would lie awake wondering if or when Mickey would show up. Had I known that this was going to be my fate, I would never have moved here. I wasn't good at waiting. (I'm still not.) I'm a doer, a manifester. I like to make things happen, to initiate change, to move forward. I think a part of me just withered during that time. I was perpetually waiting for Mickey. Waiting for the verdict on *Wild Orchid*. Waiting for a new modeling job. I was also waiting for a new agent. When I came back from Brazil, I'd taken Mickey's advice and let some of his managing crew run the show for me. Later I began to suspect that Mickey was much more comfortable when there was no show of mine to run.

But just about every time I thought I couldn't take the isolation anymore, Mickey would show up and pull a rabbit out of a hat, surprising me with his generosity and momentarily reassuring me of our love.

On September 28, 1989, I turned twenty-one. I had met Mickey earlier that year and spent the spring and much of the summer filming *Wild Orchid*. My life wasn't what I thought it would be by this time. There were successes on some levels and failure on others. The movie we'd made together was due to be released in the U.S. in the spring of 1990. Press hadn't yet begun. I was in a lull.

Mickey was supposed to pick me up that day for a birthday lunch, but the hours passed and soon the sun was setting. I was furious. What's more, I was stranded. I hadn't made any other plans, because I assumed we were going to spend the day together. All I could do was pace.

I sat on the front stoop smoking cigarette after cigarette. I wanted to call my mother. My father. My sister or brother. But I couldn't bring myself to pick up the phone. We had been out of touch for so long. . . . Just then I heard the big metal gate at the end of the drive creak open. I hadn't heard Mick's Harley, so I stood to see who was driving up to the house.

There was Mickey, behind the wheel of a souped-up black Mustang convertible. A red bow was tied to the front bumper. He pulled in with a screech and stood on the seat of the car, grinning from ear to ear.

"Happy birthday, Otis!" he yelled my way.

I was stunned. I wanted to ask him where he'd been, why I was kept waiting on my birthday. But I knew it would seem ungrateful in light of his expensive birthday gift. At the same time, I didn't care about things like cars. I rarely felt worthy enough to receive gifts. There was a discomfort I felt being the recipient of such generosity. I was an odd bird.

I slowly walked over toward Mickey, touched the car with my finger, then circled it, tracing its chrome detail. I didn't know what to say. I had never had a car. Especially not a new one.

"Otis, don't you like it?" Mickey was puzzled. So was I.

"I . . . I love it, Mickey. It's amazing. The best birthday present I could ever imagine," I lied. Actually, the best birthday present would have been him showing up when he'd said he would. *The best birthday present would be getting the fuck out of this house,* I thought. But I bit my tongue.

"Let's take it for a ride. . . . What do you say?" he coaxed.

"Sure." And with that, I grabbed my purse, jumped into my new ride, and we were off tearing down the drive, back up to Mulholland, and on to Sunset Boulevard.

It was September and fall was in the air in L.A. I bundled up in my leather coat and looked over at Mickey, who had taken the wheel. Why did my heart palpitate when he was near? Why did I need him so? It was actually a terrible feeling to know how desperate I was for him.

"Otis, you're gonna have to drop me off down at Caffé Roma. I have a meeting."

I was shocked. "What? What about my birthday? Dinner?" I shook my head in confusion.

"Hey, Peanut, come on. I love you. You know that. Hey . . . don't you love the car?"

That wasn't the point. But what could I say? I didn't want my love to be bought. Gifts couldn't make up for neglect. But I couldn't articulate those feelings. I didn't know where to start. So I reflected back on the obvious and the factual; at least I now had my own car. My escape vehicle. My way out.

I pulled up to the alley behind Caffé Roma. It was a small motorcycle café run by Mickey and his brother, Joey. I never knew what went on inside and didn't trust it. For some reason I was still being kept inexplicably in hiding; Mickey still wanted our relationship to remain under wraps.

As Mick jumped out of the car, Joey stepped toward me. "Happy birthday, Otis. What's in store for ya tonight?" Mickey's brother leaned forward and gave me a kiss on the cheek. Joey had been in so many motorcycle accidents that his face had been sewn up and reconstructed a number of times. He had the look of a wounded lion. But a sweet one.

"Thanks, Joe." I shrugged. "Nothing, I guess. Mick's got a meeting." I looked past Joey and could see that inside the store Mickey was talking and standing very close to another long-legged, brown-haired girl.

"Jesus . . . bro . . ." Joey looked at me with empathy. He had seen it all. He shook his head toward his brother, sharing my obvious disappointment. "Later, Otis. You take good care of yourself, you hear?"

And just like that, I turned twenty-one. Not nearly as sweet as I had thought it would be.

CALVIN KLEIN

Wild Orchid opened to horrible reviews. I should have known what was coming, especially after the producers sold the footage of the famed sex scene to *Playboy* without my consent. There was nothing I could do about it, of course. My ass was owned by the studio. Or at least my ass as it appeared in *Wild Orchid*.

But I wasn't the only one receiving bad reviews. Mickey's "chipmunk cheeks" were in serious question. It was the first of many surgeries Mickey would have to alter his physical appearance. And not the last that would be noticed by the media.

Mickey's way of dealing with negative press was to act out in his usual ways—and to secure another film. He could move on. It wasn't so easy for me. My big break was actually turning into my breaking point. I wasn't sure which way to go. Mickey and I both endured embarrassment and scrutiny, but he was more accustomed to that kind of attention than I was.

The thought of anyone I knew going to see *Wild Orchid* was beyond disturbing. Until I saw it, I hadn't a clue how it would look on film. I sat through it only once. I've never seen it since, and I have no plans ever to see it again. For me it represented abuse, darkness, exploitation, and the beginning of my long walk of shame. I was so gun-shy afterward that the thought of doing another film was the furthest thing from my mind. (Much to Mickey's relief, I think.) I just wanted to get back to modeling. Thankfully, I scored a major campaign for Calvin Klein at just the right moment. It would be shot in my hometown, San Francisco.

Mickey assigned Joey and Bruce to stick by my side during the shoot. If I was going to work, Mickey was going to have me watched. I argued about it with him endlessly. "Mickey, no one has a watcher. Why me? That's so silly."

I was more embarrassed than anything. Modeling was my world, not Mickey's. It was what *I* did. He didn't know a thing about how it worked. I was also concerned that having handlers would be problematic in my industry. No photographer wanted to be told what to do or feel as if someone was looking over his shoulder.

"Just think of them as your bodyguards," Mickey said.

"I don't need bodyguards," I argued.

"Then think of them as your assistants, damn it. They *are* going, Otis. That's that."

I was furious. But more than that, I felt belittled. Not trusted. I mean, shit, who went and watched Mickey when he was away from me? The double standard drove me nuts. Yet I felt as though the only way I could do anything that interested me was to do it Mickey's way. My freedom was slipping away. My voice was falling silent. I was becoming Mickey's bitch.

Not long before I left for the Calvin Klein campaign, Mickey had me meet him in the parking lot of the high school below my house. He wanted to show me something. Joe had picked me up on the back of his bike and driven me there.

"This is for you, Peanut." Mickey grinned. Another gift? I wondered. He was standing next to a purple Harley-Davidson Springer. A damned heavy bike.

"What? Serious?" I was beside myself. A motorcycle was definitely up my alley. But I figured that Mickey would forever keep me on the back of his. I knew in that moment that he was sending me a message. He was having me watched and handled, but he was also the one offering me my freedom. My fate was in his hands. We both knew it. And the motorcycle was a clever peace offering.

I walked over to it. Etched into the chrome was a feather and the nickname I'd gone by ever since the movie, "Wyoming Outlaw" (as in W.O. for *Wild Orchid*). The bike was awesome and impressive. There was just one problem: I didn't know how to ride.

"Show me, Mickey!" I begged. I swung a leg over and straddled the bike.

Mickey patiently showed me how to start the ignition and work the brakes and clutch. And when I took a spill almost immediately after tearing off for a test ride, he forced me to pull the bike up on my own.

"Help!" I pleaded under the weight of it. I was struggling with all my might.

"No, baby. You gotta be able to lift this on your own. No woman of mine is gonna let any man help her out if she goes down."

Somehow I found the strength to stand the bike upright. It was incentive enough to never go down again. Every time I rode, I remembered Wyoming Outlaw's tremendous mass.

Mickey had done me an unexpected favor by teaching me to ride a Harley, as I found out while shooting the Calvin Klein campaign in San Francisco. My entourage was there at every turn. Although I was getting used to them, the embarrassment never ceased. At least one of them was always present, overseeing my every move. They'd disguise their reason for being there by delivering cups of coffee to the set, but you couldn't mistake the reproachful looks I'd get from either Joey or Bruce whenever I shot with a male model who looked too steamy. The photographer was the legendary Bruce Weber, who had certainly photographed his fair share of celebrities before. Fortunately, he tolerated the entourage's presence. Maybe even more than I did.

Every single thing that happened was reported back to Mickey. When I'd talk to him on the phone at the end of the day, it was apparent that he knew every last detail, right down to the color of the clothes and who was in them. But the shoot produced one photograph that was groundbreaking and iconic and, in part, influenced by Mickey: the image was of me riding a Harley. It felt great to be that strong, free woman—if only in a photograph.

In another scenario for the campaign, we created a replica of a concert and I was supposed to be a rocker along with the great Marcus Schenkenberg, the world's top male model at the time. There were photos of us onstage, pretending to rock out before a packed theater of fans. It was all ridiculous and fun, and Marcus and I became good friends in the midst of the madness.

The crew took over an entire floor of one hotel, including a block of rooms for the talent, for the hair, makeup, and wardrobe people, and yes, Joey Rourke. I was getting tired of it. Tired of answering questions. Tired of feeling like I was being spied on. I just wanted to be like any other young model on a shoot, having a blast. One day I was told there was going to be a party in Marcus's room. There'd be a few models and a bottle of tequila. . . . I desperately wanted to let my hair down and just have fun. I asked Marcus to keep it quiet, promising that I would be there after I said my good-nights to the "boys."

When dinner was over, I told Joey I was going to bed.

"Otis, do me a favor and call Mick to say good night, okay?"

"Sure, Joe. Got it covered," I answered, giving him a peck on the cheek. I felt like a kid getting ready to sneak out of my bedroom, thinking ahead about all the things I needed to do to cover my tracks.

I couldn't reach Mickey, but I left him a message. "Babe, I'm tired. Talk in the morning. Love ya!" I said, maybe a bit too cheerily. And with that, I snuck out of my room and down the hall to meet my friends. I hadn't had friends my own age in so long. The only people I ever hung out with now were Mickey and his group. Most of them were twenty years my senior. It just wasn't the same level of escape and enjoyment I craved.

Marcus's room was a whirlwind of activity, filled with folks from the shoot. Jimi Hendrix was playing on the stereo, and we were all chasing tequila shots with bites of lime. I was laughing like crazy, watching Marcus stand on the bed playing air guitar. We were kids gone wild. And then there was a loud bang on the door.

"Shit!" I yelled. I dove between the beds, my hair falling into my face. "Please! Don't say I'm in here!" I begged. I knew who was at the door—and who had sent him to look for me. Even worse, I knew that someone, one of the guys I was with, would get his ass kicked if I were discovered.

Marcus looked at me, confused. I put a finger to my lips. "Shhhh . . ." I pleaded in silence for him to cover me. He nodded carefully, turned down the music, and opened the door.

"Hey, Joey, what's up?" he asked innocently. There was another model on the bed. She crossed her legs seductively and looked Marcus up and down. Thankfully, she had my back, too.

Joey was both apologetic and suspicious. "Hate to bother you, bro, but . . . uh . . . I can't find Carré. Mickey is freaking out, been calling her room, my room. It's my ass if I can't find her. And someone else's ass if I find her with them." I could hear him pause, inhaling and exhaling smoke from his cigarette. He was waiting.

"Sorry, man," Marcus responded nonchalantly. "Um, as you can see, I have some company." He nodded toward the blonde on the bed.

"Okay. My bad. Just had to check. Umm . . . if you hear from her . . . tell her Mick's looking for her. She's up shit creek." With that, Joey left and Marcus closed the door behind him.

I started laughing from my place under the bed.

"Shit, Carré. Shut up! What are you doing?" Marcus said. He was serious. The blonde just looked at us both, stood up, and said, "I'm out of here, guys."

I lay down on the bed next to Marcus and sighed. I was so tired of this.

He looked into my eyes, swept the hair off my face with his perfect hand, and placed a kiss on my lips. Whoa.

"Why are you doing this?" Marcus asked. "With him, I mean?" He seemed genuinely concerned. "You're going to get hurt, Carré." I looked away, not sure how to answer or how to explain.

"I'm sorry. I don't want to drag you into this." A part of me was in total longing for Marcus. I just needed to be held. *Quiet,* I told myself.

No games. I wrapped my arms around him and gave him a hug. I knew I had to leave. Or one way or another, Marcus would be hurt.

He lay on the bed watching me as I stood. I stared back at him, for a moment suspended in time. I knew I could lie back down, make love, and let myself be warmed by this boy's beauty. It would be so simple and, I was sure, so sweet. But it wasn't worth it. He was right. I was going to get hurt. I just didn't yet know how or when.

I left the room, quietly made my way back down the hall and into my suite. Shit, shit, shit. I sighed. And then I picked up the phone and lied as best I could.

It wasn't even that I was doing anything so wrong or dishonest. But the pressures of being under constant watch, every day and every night, had me wanting desperately to wander. I knew I would have to keep myself in check. I knew Mickey's temper. And it wasn't just me who would incur his wrath.

The Calvin Klein campaign was a success. It was a beautiful 116-page insert in every *Vanity Fair* magazine that came out. Despite *Wild Orchid*, my star was still very much on the rise. I had so much to look forward to. If only Mickey and his boys could stay out of it.

I would come to find out that this was impossible.

CHRISTMAS WITH JOHN GOTTI

The cold December wind that blew through New York City was familiar to me. Just five years earlier, I'd been battling the elements as a teenage model with not much more than a borrowed trench coat to get me by. And now Mickey and I had a suite at the Plaza Hotel. It was the end of 1990, and it would be our first Christmas together. Although my childhood hadn't been ideal, Christmas was always a magical time, and I looked forward to it every year. Unfortunately, I had no idea about the dread the holidays evoked for Mickey. They simply rubbed him the wrong way. Since I was young and just getting into my full-fledged codependence, I somehow thought that being in love meant I should follow suit.

I spent my first Christmas week with Mickey pretending it wasn't Christmas at all. The end result was some depressed and disturbing behavior on both our parts.

While the rest of Manhattan was scurrying around doing last-minute shopping, I was holed up in a hotel room drinking cup after cup of coffee, watching the snowflakes fall, and obsessively reading Ann Rice's *Interview with the Vampire*. I needed an escape, and the dark and mysterious story effectively lured me into a fantasy world. Its distraction helped me to survive the loneliness.

Despite our efforts to ignore the holiday cheer all around us, the Plaza stood regal and aglow. An enormous Christmas tree towered in the lobby, presents piled high under its branches. Carolers sang outside while Santa rang his bell and hollered, "Ho, ho, ho!" I missed my family. It was two days before Christmas. "Come on, Mick!" I said, jumping on his back as he slept. It was 1:00 P.M., and he was still snoring away. "Get up! This is ridiculous!" I tried to tickle him, but there was no response.

I altered my approach, sliding under the covers beside him and purring, "Sleepyhead, wake up!" But he just groaned and pushed me aside. I wasn't yet sure how to move around Mickey's dark spells. I recognized the mood shifts but didn't entirely know if he wanted me to leave him alone or if he wanted me to try to rescue him.

"Mickey. Really. It's daytime. You can't sleep all day. . . ."

I wanted to go out and do what I might normally do with my days, but I didn't want to leave him like this.

"Okay. I'm going downstairs to work out, Mickey," I said, hoping that it might rouse him. But all I got was a grunt as he pulled the covers tighter over his head.

We'd been at the Plaza for a week. Day in and day out, Mickey had just slept. He was on his medications and would rise only for room service or late-night TV shows. After that, he'd disappear again into the darkness. It scared me. It reminded me of my father, and up until this point Mickey had been so different from my dad, so vital and intense. But now he was in a downward spiral, and I couldn't seem to help him back up, no matter how hard I tried.

Not knowing what to do and getting increasingly concerned, I decided to call Bruce. Quietly, in the next room, I lifted up the receiver and dialed his number.

Bruce picked up. "Hello?"

"Bruce!" I said with a sigh of relief. He was also staying in Manhattan with family, having been given time off for Hanukkah.

"Otis, how are ya?" he asked cheerfully.

"It's Mick, Bruce. I don't know what to do. . . ." My voice trailed away. I needed help. I wasn't sure if I still knew the man in the next room.

"What's going on?" he asked. Bruce had known Mickey a lot longer than I had. If anyone would have some insight, he'd be the one.

"He won't get out of bed. He's been in a funk for a week straight. I think he's taking his sleeping pills in the day—and then he complains that he can't sleep at night. What do I do? I'm going nuts in here. . . ." I started to cry. I was worried. I loved him. I wanted to be with him. But this wasn't really being together.

"Ah, shit, Otis, this happens every year. He hates Christmas. Shit went down when he was a kid—so now he can't stand this time of year."

"What do I do?" I demanded, exasperated.

"Hang tight. I'm coming over." I was relieved beyond words. I thanked him and gently placed the receiver on the hook.

Within an hour there was a knock at the door. Mickey didn't even stir. Bruce came in and took charge. "Turn on the shower," he instructed me, nodding in the direction of the bathroom. A moment later I could hear Bruce's booming voice from the bedroom: "Okay, Mick. Time to get up. You have a dinner date. Into the shower with your ass!" And he flung Mickey's covers off him and hauled his naked body up and out of bed, dragging him down the hall to the shower I had just turned on.

"Goddamn it, Bruce! Motherfucker! Just leave me alone!" Mickey roared. I flattened myself against the hallway wall as the two men passed by.

"Oh, Mick. You know you love me, brother." Bruce was invariably unfazed by Mickey's temper. "Let's just get you moving, my friend."

Mickey continued to shout in protest until he was settled in beneath the warm water of the shower. The shrieks gradually subsided. All the while I stood motionless against the wall just outside the bathroom, listening and praying. Bruce closed the lid of the toilet and sat down, crossed his legs, and waited. It was clear he'd done this before.

"All right, you guys. I am up. I am *up*!" Mickey said from under the water. It was like listening to a bear come out of hibernation. "So, asshole . . . what's the plan? What's this dinner date?"

"I knew you'd come around, Mick." Bruce sighed, then smiled and winked at me. "*Il capo di tutti capi* wants to have dinner with you tonight—Da Noi at nine P.M. All the men are joining. And they want Otis there," Bruce explained.

"Oh, yeah!" Mick shouted enthusiastically. This dinner he was up for. It was just the news he needed to hear to get his ass moving. I, on the other hand, was completely in the dark.

"Who is this Capo Dee? Is that his name?" I asked naïvely, stepping fully into the bathroom.

The boys laughed at me. "Let's just keep it a surprise, Otis." Mickey chuckled under the suds of shampoo that were streaming down his face. "Just doll yourself up. I mean, really doll yourself up." So I went into my bedroom and got dressed. I was happy to have any kind of dinner out, regardless of the company.

We left the Plaza hand in hand, me in a black Azzedine Alaïa minidress, a black floor-length Armani coat, and sky-high heels. Heads turned, and once again we were the glamorous couple the public was accustomed to seeing.

This is one of my favorite photos of my parents in the early stages of their marriage.

My mother, channeling her hippie spirit at our annual visit to the renaissance fair.

My father, sporting some style in 1972.

I love this photo of my sister, Chrisse, and me sharing sweet dreams.

We had our own fashion style and loved making faces for the camera even then.

The only one who really looked happy by the time this photo was taken was my brother, Jordan, pictured here between me (left) and Chrisse (right). I was steadily drifting from friends and family, as life had already thrown me a few serious curves.

Here I am with my mom on the day of my eighth-grade graduation. As you can see, I was growing up very fast.

(These photos are from the pages of my modeling scrapbook.)

I ran away from home by the time I was sixteen . . . did some catalog work in San Francisco . . .

tried modeling in New York . . .

was photographed in Paris for French *Vogue* . . .

and in Greece with Linda Evangelista. Peter Lindbergh took this of us during a shoot for one of the first American *Vogue* covers to feature two girls.

I was styled by some of the best people in the business—this time by Manuela Pavesi . . .

and even went without clothes in this picture taken by Antoine Verglas for Italian *Playboy*.

It was fun to travel to Puerto Vallarta to shoot with Sante D'Orazio . . .

But it wasn't long before I burned out. I desperately needed a break.

After a hiatus of several months, I starting working again, hoping for a better run in Los Angeles.

I was photographed by Herb Ritts in Hawaii . . .

Matthew Ralston in the California desert . . .

and I did more work for *Vogue* . . .

and *Allure* magazine.

I also shot some great campaigns. This one is for Blumarine, with my bird Oddiyana on my shoulder.

By age twenty-one, I'd made the controversial film *Wild Orchid* with Mickey Rourke. Two years later we were married.

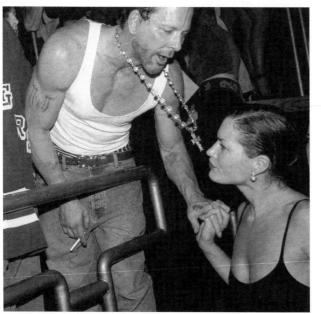

Sadly, our tumultuous relationship frequently made the news. In this moment, caught on camera by the media, we were seeing each other for the first time in months. It was during New York Fashion week in 1994, after I'd fled California to avoid testifying against him on charges of domestic violence.

Somewhere between celebrating a cakeless twentieth birthday and the time I resolved to end my troubled marriage, my long battle with an eating disorder spiraled out of control.

This is me at the height of my anorexia, just before I began obsessively training for the *Sports Illustrated* Swimsuit Edition, working with my therapist, and preparing to leave Mickey.

Years earlier, during my break from modeling, I lived on "The Farm," a co-op community in Sebastopol, California. That's me, second from the right, sitting next to my boyfriend, Ethan, in the hat and leather jacket.

It was then that I met t first of several profoun spiritual teachers in my life, Lama Tsultrim Alione. Tsultrim is on the left and her daught Aloka is in the center.

...resumed the healing journey I began in those days during a later trip
...Nepal. Here I am in the Himalayas near a "mani" rock (a formation
...scribed with the prayer of the Buddha of Compassion) . . .

and in Dharamsala, India,
on a visit to see HH
Karmapa and HH the
Dalai Lama.

I am at peace here visiting with my sister . . .

and with my mom and maternal grandmother. I have been fortunate enough to reconcile with all of my family members . . .

to have married a wonderful man . . .

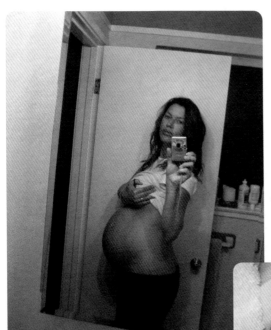

to have given life to two beautiful girls . . .

Jade and . . .

Kaya . . .

and now to tell my story in the hope of inspiring others along the path.

Da Noi was an old-school Italian restaurant and, at that time, a notorious meeting place for the New York Mafia. As Mickey and I entered, we were met by the maître d', who graciously helped us out of our coats and led us down the stairs to a private table in a dark, candlelit room. We could hear the ruckus before we entered. At least eight men were sitting around a large circular wooden table, smoking cigars and talking loudly.

"Mickey! My man!" said a gray-haired and exceptionally dapper gentleman. At once the table was silent, and all stood.

Mickey moved around the table, and the two hugged in a big embrace. "This must be your lovely lady." The man smiled at me. Mickey stepped aside.

"Indeed it is. John, meet Carré. Carré, this is Mr. John Gotti."

"Hello, Mr. Gotti," I said, smiling and extending my hand in a formal greeting. He shook it and then pulled me in, kissing me on both cheeks before letting me stand back so that he could admire me from head to toe.

"Wow. You are stunning, my dear," he said with a nod, and he slapped Mickey on the back as if he were the luckiest dog alive. The room broke into laughter, and then everyone was introduced before we sat down.

It took me a while—until maybe halfway through our dinner—to understand who we were seated with. This was the Mafia king and his entire team. I wasn't so much worried as intrigued. They were an impressive and boisterous bunch. And they clearly felt that Mickey was part of the family. I didn't realize until later, years down the road, that this wasn't necessarily a good thing.

"Carré, what year were you born?" John asked me, leaning in.

"In 1968, Mr. Gotti," I answered.

"Then let's bring up a few bottles from '68!" he said with a laugh, signaling the waiter. Bottles were opened and wine poured as if it were water. The evening ran on, and on, and on. It wasn't until well after 1:00 A.M. that we finished dessert and said our good-byes.

"We'll be seeing you all soon," John said to Mickey and me. "And you two, have yourselves a merry Christmas."

I thanked the men at the table. "Merry Christmas, guys!" I laughed, a little too tipsy. Mickey grabbed my arm and led me back up the stairs and out into the limo, where Bruce was waiting.

"Tell me! How did it go?" Bruce was full of excitement and anticipation; I knew he wished, of all the dinners Mickey could have taken him to over the years, that this had been the one.

"Okay . . . um, was that . . . the entire New York Mafia?" I laughed. "Were we just having dinner with the Godfather?"

Then I stopped. That's when the full power of that question hit me.

"Why?" I asked quietly.

"Why what?" Mickey looked at me, puzzled.

"Well, why would you bring me there, to have dinner with them?" I wanted to stay calm, but questions were forming in my mind all too quickly.

"What the hell do you mean, Otis? Wasn't that an amazing meal? Good company?"

"I mean . . . why, Mickey, why would you put me in that situation? Isn't John Gotti a known murderer?" I was starting to feel uneasy. I wanted to know the answer, but I didn't want to start a fight. We were finally out of the hotel. The spell of the past week had been broken. Yet I couldn't stop myself from ruining it all.

I could see Bruce staring at me in the rearview mirror. His look was warning me, *Don't go there, Otis.*

"Jesus Christ. What's up your ass?" Mickey's temper was spiking. I could feel the heat rise in the car. I shrugged my shoulders and sank back in the seat. I certainly didn't want to be a buzzkill.

"You know what? Just drop her at the hotel," Mickey said angrily.

"No, wait. I'm sorry. I shouldn't have said anything." I looked down at my purse.

"No, really. Just drop her at the hotel. Bruce, you and I, we're going out. Alone." His tone was flat and final. I was dismissed.

The night before Christmas Eve, I was dropped at the Plaza's entrance. Furiously wiping tears from my eyes, I made my way back to our suite, grabbed the chocolates off my turned-down bed, and climbed in. Picking up my Anne Rice novel, I read until the sun came up.

Though Mickey still wasn't back, I finally fell asleep. Now I was the one who didn't want to wake up. How ironic.

SHOT IN SANTA FE

Although the Calvin Klein campaign was a huge success, work had started to dwindle by the summer of 1991. Mickey had seen a naked photo of me, shot by the famously gay photographer Steven Meisel, for *Vanity Fair*. He was furious.

"Everyone can see your ass! That's *my* ass. And no one else's." To prove his point, Mickey sent two thugs to hunt down Meisel, and when they found him in a New York City elevator, they stole his signature floppy hat and took Polaroids of the terrified photographer. Word quickly got out that I was a liability to work with. The repercussions of dealing with Mickey Rourke and his iron fist just were not worth it for many of my clients.

While he was doing all that he could to derail my career, Mickey was also in Santa Fe, New Mexico, filming *White Sands* with Willem Dafoe. The increasingly frantic phone calls I received from Mickey begging me to come visit him indicated that things were not going as well as expected. There was constant conflict on the set. No one could make heads or tails of which way the production was going. After a series of flops, Mickey desperately needed a hit. His whole team was getting nervous.

I decided to fly out and spend a weekend with him. Santa Fe was a place I remembered fondly from childhood. I recalled more than one summer visiting there with my family. My sister and I enjoyed the afternoon thundershowers, washing our hair in the warm downpour, then walking to get fresh watermelon juice under the late-afternoon sun. I was excited to go back and explore.

Bruce picked me up at the Albuquerque airport and filled me in as we drove to the set. Mickey was in quite a state. His entourage had too much influence over him. And, worse, the Hells Angels had also come to hang out. Everything was going wrong, very wrong. Somehow the boys thought that my presence would put Mickey in a better mood. A lot was riding on my visit.

The crew was just wrapping for the day when I arrived. I left my bag in the car and ran over to Mickey, flinging my arms around him, kissing his face.

"Hey, Peanut!" he greeted me with a laugh. "Damn, it's good to see you!"

And it was. Those moments of sheer joy and desire enveloped us at times. "Come on, let's go back to the house," he said. "You'll love it. Up in the hills."

I smiled at him. I had missed him and our forever-on-the-road long-distance relationship.

"Bruce, we're gonna take the bike. Bring Otis's stuff up to the house, okay?"

And with that, we climbed onto Mickey's Harley and sped off, with Bruce, Franco, and Joey trailing behind. I held Mickey tight as we drove through the dry desert air. The sun was still high in the sky, and Santa Fe's distinct smells came rushing back at me. We raced up Canyon Road and into the hills overlooking the town. It took about thirty minutes to get to our destination, at some point leaving paved roads for gravel and finally leaving gravel for sagebrush.

The house was gorgeous: a classic Santa Fe adobe with breathtaking views through floor-to-ceiling windows, huge fireplaces, and a grand kitchen and living room. *I could get used to this,* I thought. I loved everything about it.

The boys pulled up behind us and unloaded groceries into the kitchen. Franco was going to cook dinner. Italian bliss: spaghetti, breast of chicken, and broccoli in garlic and olive oil.

Mickey grabbed my hand and led me through a maze of hallways. "Here's our room," he told me, laughing, slamming the door behind us, and pushing me onto the king-size bed. He fell onto me, kicking off his cowboy boots, looking earnestly into my eyes. "I love you, Otis." He smiled gently.

"Me, too, Mick." I sighed, burying my head in his chest. He was my everything in that moment. I closed my eyes and listened. "That sound. Isn't that amazing?" I asked.

He laid his body next to mine and listened too. "It's the wind in the pines. It's beautiful. Like you."

I turned my face toward him, but something farther away caught my attention. On the low mantel of the fireplace lay a gun. Mickey's .357 Magnum.

"Mick, why do you guys have to have guns? Especially here in the middle of nowhere? And so out in the open? They make me nervous." I was irritated. It was like living with a bunch of kids. Their recklessness with weapons drove me nuts and was the subject of ongoing and always heated discussions. I'd faced down a .357 Magnum with Elliott and lost my sweet Scott to a gun, too. I had good reason to dislike firearms.

"Come on, baby," he said, trying to kiss me and draw me back into our moment. But the moment was already lost.

I rolled off the bed and walked over to the fireplace. I lifted the gun carefully, checked to see if it was loaded—which it was—then checked the safety to make sure it was on. But there was no safety switch on this gun. Mick had taught me the basics of how to handle a gun, so I knew what I was doing. I sighed, placed the gun back on the mantel, and shook my finger at him. Then I turned and left the room. It was dinnertime.

The next day the boys got up early to get to the set. I was left to sleep in and was told that Bruce would return sometime later to pick me up. I awoke at around seven and quietly walked through the house. There was a hush, a silence I hadn't experienced for some time. The mountains, the desert, the wilderness—all lent themselves to a sense of tranquillity that I relished. I was enjoying the empty house.

And then I saw the gun again, resting alone on a table. Stopping midway down the long hall, I felt a shudder come over me. Goose bumps rose on my flesh, and I tentatively stepped closer to it. But in that moment something strange happened. I thought I saw the gun move. *It couldn't have,* I said to myself. *It's just a gun.* Yet now there was an energy in the air, a threatening electricity. I shuddered again. I could have sworn I'd just seen that gun move, all on its own.

I shook my head and quickly rushed down the hall, past the menacing firearm. In the kitchen I reached for the phone. "Bruce . . . it's Carré. Can you pick me up?" I asked brusquely.

"Yeah, of course. You okay, Otis?" Bruce sensed something in my voice.

"Yeah. Sure. Fine. Just ready to come and hang out." I couldn't explain what I was feeling or what I thought I'd seen. It was nuts. It made no sense. There was just an ominous feeling in the house. And I didn't want to be alone with it. Shaking my head and grabbing a cup of coffee, I tried to laugh it off. *Don't be ridiculous, Otis,* I said to myself, almost channeling Mick's voice. I jumped into the shower and got ready for the long day.

Waiting on sets was usually an endless and boring chore. It was the boys' club. But on occasion I was made to feel that I belonged, too. I met everyone in Mickey's trailer. They were playing cards, smoking cigarettes, and drinking coffee.

"What's up, guys?" I asked. "How's it going on set?" I was hoping things were mellowing and that Mickey was behaving himself.

"Mickey has an early wrap today. They fell behind on someone else's scenes." In his thick Italian accent, Franco brought me up to date on what was happening. "We are thinking to go to the county fair." He smiled, flashing his brilliant sea-green eyes at me. Franco was a real character. Rumored to be a hit man from Sicily, he traveled and acted as Mick's bodyguard on most movies, leaving his wife and kids at home near Rome.

"Great. Let's do it," I said, relieved that we had an outdoor activity planned for us.

I looked out the window of the motor home. Mickey was standing next to George Christie, president of the Ventura chapter of Hells Angels. It wasn't unusual for George or Chuck Zito, another legendary Hells Angel, to visit Mickey on the sets of his films. The press was frequently right behind, reporting widely on Mickey's unsavory relationships.

I opened the door and leaned out. "Hey, George." I smiled and waved. I wasn't entirely sure who or what the Hells Angels were—I just knew they were heavies of some sort.

"My dear," George said, smiling and pretending to tip his hat to me. "How are you?"

George and his crew were always cool with me. But that's not to say I was fooled or that I liked them. I just tried to blend in wherever I went.

"Mick, you ready to go?" I asked. And with that, we were off in a caravan of bikes, followed by the car that Franco drove. The day at the fair was hot and dusty and filled with lots of games, rides, and souvenirs. Soon enough Mickey and I decided to head back toward base camp, where we could have a romantic dinner somewhere on Canyon Avenue near all the art galleries.

"I heard about a great Italian restaurant—let's hit it, Otis." Mickey jumped behind the wheel of the rental car, ready to drive. I laughed. It was rare to see him in the driver's seat. Sliding in next to him, I grabbed his hand, holding it close, tracing the thick veins that ran up his arm. He smiled and nodded at me.

"What's up?" he asked, sensing that I had something to say.

"Nothing. It's just . . . something weird happened this morning." I was going to try to explain the oddity in the house with the gun, but I couldn't put it into words. Mickey waited for me to say more, then began to drive. I looked out the window, trying to collect my thoughts.

We were almost at the restaurant when I looked down and saw the .357 Magnum on the floor near my feet.

"Damn it, Mickey!" I moaned, pointing to it. "What the hell?" I was furious. "Can't you guys practice some safety with these things?"

Mickey parked the car and leaned toward me, his voice soft but firm. "Otis, remember, it's for our protection. I am sorry, though. I'll talk to the guys about putting these things away."

"Good idea," I responded curtly. I stepped out of the car and turned around to grab my purse.

"Go ahead, I got it. I'll bring it in," Mick said. What I didn't know was that he thought it would be a good idea to stash the gun inside my bag.

Dinner was uneventful. My large purse sat next to Mickey's chair while we ate. When we were through, we decided to drive the bike home and let Franco drive the car. I grabbed my bag and threw it over my shoulder, climbed onto the back of Mick's bike, and held on tight. The air was just starting to cool, the sun just beginning to set.

"Meet ya out the house," Mick instructed Franco. Then we sped off into the dusk, heading up Canyon Road.

"Brrr . . . it's cold, Mick!" I shivered as we got off the bike in front of the house. The boys were already there; I could smell a fire in the fireplace. A beautiful glow emanated from within, so I knew that candles were lit.

"Come on, Otis. Let's get into a bath!" Mickey laughed and chased me into the house. I screeched with delight and ran as fast as I could through the front door and toward the kitchen. "Grab some wine! Let's go soak!" I giggled, skidding to a halt as my black cowboy boots hit the tiled floor. Mickey ran to the fridge, searching for a bottle of white, while I slung my bag off my shoulder and tossed it onto the counter.

Boom! A tremendous noise reverberated through the kitchen. And then silence. I looked around curiously. Franco ran into the room. Bruce was just behind him.

"What the fuck was that?" the boys yelled.

"Gunshot!" Mickey screamed in a panic. "A bullet—it just whizzed past me!"

"What the fuck are you guys doing firing guns in the fucking house?" I yelled, stunned. And just then I noticed that everyone was staring at me, their eyes widening.

I stood there, suspended in time. My head reeled. I began to sway slowly from side to side. "Whoa," I said numbly as I crumpled to the floor. "What the fu—"

I looked down at my blue jeans, my white shirt, and my black leather jacket. What was this strange red puddle flowing out around me in an eerily perfect circle? I looked back up at the guys, confused and bewildered. An instant later the message from the gunpowder reached my brain. I felt as if I were on fire, head to toe. I gasped, and then a wild scream erupted from me. I couldn't speak, I couldn't move. I'd been shot. The gun in my purse, the one without a safety, had discharged the second I'd slung my bag onto the counter.

"Otis! Holy shit! Bruce, help! Franco . . . do something!" Mickey ran toward me. "Where is the gun? Where did that come from?" No one was sure what was going on. The kitchen erupted in a frenzy as the guys scurried around looking for the gun.

"Wait! Help me!" I finally cried out, forcing the words to come. "You gotta help me. . . . I'm bleeding. I'm bleeding really bad." I held my hand in front of me, watching as the blood dripped down from it. It poured out from my chest, my arm, and my shoulder. A wave of wooziness came over me. I started to gag. And then realized I still wasn't being helped. *Okay,* I thought. *I have to get their attention. They're looking for the gun. But I need to get to a hospital. Now.* "Call an ambulance," I could hear my voice say. I sounded very far away.

Franco came to my side. His eyes were wide with fear. "Carré, we don't have time to wait. I need to help you into the car." And a moment later he swept me in his big arms. "Ow! Franco! No! Don't touch me!" I wailed. It hurt so much to move.

For the first time, I heard Franco shout orders at his boss. "Mickey, get the keys! Now!"

Mickey looked around in shock. And in slow motion he grabbed the car keys, fumbling with them in his hands.

"Bruce. You need to . . . you need to find the gun. This is a nightmare. Clean this up!" Mickey was agitated. I could tell he had grave concerns that the press would get wind of the incident. I panicked, wondering which was more important: my life or covering up the fact that I'd been shot with Mickey Rourke's gun? But Franco was with me, holding me firmly, carrying me out the door and into the night.

"Mickey, front seat! You must drive this car. Fast!" Franco was in complete control, and somehow I knew he knew what he was doing. Thank God someone did.

As Mickey slid behind the wheel, I could see that his hands were shaking. Franco's weren't. He held me as if I were a baby, first sitting down in the backseat, then pulling my body onto his lap.

"Please don't squeeze me so tight, Franco!" I cried.

He looked at me levelly and said, "I must, Carré. I must try to stop the blood flow."

I vaguely remember the drive, Mickey stopping at a red light and me begging him to run the damn thing, "Just *go!*" It felt as though the three of us were in some surrealist film. Instinctively, just as I had seen in the movies, I knew that despite the tremendous drowsiness coming over me, I could not let myself sleep. I fought to keep my eyes open. *If I close them,* I thought, *I might not wake up.*

Someone had called ahead to alert the hospital, and medics were waiting as soon as we pulled up. Under intensely bright lights, Franco lifted me out of the car and laid me gently on a stretcher. I was bleary-eyed, dopey from adrenaline and the loss of so much blood. I was rushed into the ER.

Later I learned that gunshot wounds must heal from the inside out, so no stitches could be used. A large drain was placed into my left armpit. I was told it would have to stay there for several weeks. I was also told repeatedly how lucky I was. "A .357 Magnum is a hefty gun," the doctor remarked, shaking his head in disbelief at my luck. I had been hit with a hollow-point bullet. It was a miracle I was alive—never mind alive with my arm still attached to my body! The bullet had entered just two inches from my heart. The police questioned me, but no charges were filed. Despite our best efforts to keep things quiet, the story did make the news worldwide.

My mother came to see me in Santa Fe as I recuperated. I was having terrible nightmares, typical post-traumatic-stress stuff. "Carré, oh, Carré." She sat by my bedside and cried. She was confused. And suspicious about what had really happened.

"Do you know . . . do you know you can come home, Carré?" she said, looking me in the eyes. I turned away from her. My hands shook, and tears streamed down my face.

"No, Mom, I can't," I said quietly. "It's too late for that." And it was. Way too late.

BOXING AND A BIG SUR PROPOSAL

A tremendous amount of unspoken guilt settled over Mickey and me for some time after the gun incident. In some ways we bonded, in others we fell apart. I was wounded physically. And the incident was emotionally devastating for me as well. It blew me away on levels I couldn't yet articulate. The shooting brought about a greater understanding of impermanence. It also raised my awareness of the tremendously violent vortex I was living in while I shared Mickey's life. My ability to speak up, already so compromised, was more damaged than my shoulder. People who've been shot often take longer to recover emotionally than physically. That was certainly true in my case.

The silence between us hung heavy in the air. So, too, did the reality of Mickey's decline as an actor. He wasn't the box-office hit he'd once been. Rather than reflect on his own responsibility for his diminishing film prospects, Mickey began to scorn acting, dubbing it a "career for sissies." He was blackballing himself and couldn't be talked out of doing so. His mind had shifted elsewhere. Mickey wanted to box.

I remember the day that he sat down with me and Jane Kachmer, his manager at the time, to tell us of his decision to get back into the ring. It was early 1991, just as Mickey was wrapping *Harley Davidson and the Marlboro Man,* a buddy movie that would be another commercial flop. Mickey may have sensed that the film would not do well, and that played a part in his need to find something else to do outside the movie business.

He had toyed with boxing as a kid growing up in a violent household in Miami. Whether or not his stories were true—he said that he had briefly met and trained with Muhammad Ali—I never knew. He definitely had had some amateur fights when he was a teenager. I saw it all as a death wish. His new obsession with fighting struck me as both egotistical and a cop-out, something easier than working through the system to resurrect his acting career. But Mickey saw it differently, and again I was faced with an ultimatum. It was his way or the highway. And, as he told Jane and me, his way now meant fighting.

It would be years before I'd realize that his obsession with boxing, with guns, and with the Mafia was less about an attraction to violence than it was about his fear. It seemed to me that at his core Mickey was a very fearful person. By surrounding himself with tough guys, by acting like a tough guy and carrying a gun, he imagined he could keep himself safe. As I'd found out in New Mexico, the things that made Mickey feel safe had a way of hurting the people who loved him most.

Mickey wanted to have his first professional fight in his hometown. But I didn't want to be there. Miami had always been hellish for me. Whenever we were in South Florida, Mickey's demons came forth. Every unresolved issue from his childhood bubbled to the surface in a dark and menacing way. There, in particular, he was all about "the boys." I was never included. When he was out at night, it was with Miami girls. And there were plenty of them from all over the world. It was the modeling mecca of its day. The white sand beaches, art deco structures and blue skies lent themselves perfectly to the hundreds of catalog jobs shot there every year. Having been told by Mickey that my career should be put on hold if I loved him, I felt unbelievably alienated in that city—on the outs not just with him but with the entire world.

I was usually left behind in a hotel room when Mickey and his posse would hit the town. Why it was so hard for me to walk away, one can only guess. I was under his sway, seemingly unable to let go of the hope that our love would rise out of the wreckage we'd created together instead of die there on the beaches and in the late-night clubs.

Through a boxing promoter, Mickey arranged for his return to the sport. He began an intensive training schedule. He went so far as to turn our Los Angeles loft into a workout space, complete with a ring and punching bags. On any given day, there were several trainers and boxers in the place, wrapping their fists, spitting in buckets, and jump-roping endlessly to INXS. It was insane. There wasn't a single room with a door in the entire loft. I had no privacy. Our lives, especially mine, took another surreal turn.

I somehow managed to beg off of going to Mickey's first fight, in Fort Lauderdale in May 1991. I wasn't up to watching my lover's ass get kicked six ways till Sunday. Mickey didn't fight again for nearly a year, thanks to a hectic shooting schedule that included *White Sands*. But in the spring of 1992, another fight was arranged. This one would be at the Miami Beach Convention Center. Right in the heart of Mickey's hometown. And it was made very clear to me that he expected me to be there for him. After all we'd been through, I felt obligated to go. Enduring the predictable madness and fanfare, we traveled to Miami Beach for Mickey's big night.

It was every bit the hell I thought it would be.

Boxing, for me, is actually a weak man's sport. Who the fuck needs to get into the ring to prove his machismo? I had little respect for it, and even less for the men who were the stars of that profession. Yet on that April night, I found myself playing the role Mickey wanted me to play, sitting quietly ringside, listening to the savage sounds of gloves meeting flesh, the grunts and groans and unbridled Neanderthal behavior of the man I lived with. The fight, against Francisco Harris, ended in a draw.

After the big event, we were supposed to head out to the clubs. But something had come over me. I'd had enough. I needed a break. Mickey was on a tear, on a high that couldn't be brought down. He wanted to go out celebrating. With the training and the fight finally over, I just wanted to be with him. I begged him to come back to the hotel with me, to have a moment alone, just the two of us.

"Come on, Mickey, please. . . ." I pleaded.

"Fuck you, Otis. I ain't goin' back to the room with you. I'm going out!"

I knew what "out" meant, what was included in "out." And I was sick of it. The partying. The girls. The flirtations. The nights he never even came back to our room. I was sick of hiding the blow I was doing just to keep myself busy while I waited endlessly for his return. I felt a desperation that I was ashamed of. I felt pathetic.

"Then I'm leaving," I said matter-of-factly. I was scared shitless as I said it. I knew I would have to stick to my guns. I knew that for any change to occur, for there to be any real hope for us, I would have to leave him.

"Then get the fuck out, you cunt." He looked at me with testosterone and fury in his eyes. I was stung. I was shocked. But I tried one more time.

"Mickey, please don't do this . . . please. You're going to regret it." A tear tumbled down my cheek.

He didn't budge. My temper rose.

"Then you know what, Mick? Fuck you! Fuck this!" I spit at him. I was furious. In an instant, Mickey pushed me with all his might toward the door of the limo we were in. My head slammed back against the seat. But I wasn't ready to give in. All of my passivity shifted into defiant fury.

"Oh, no you don't, motherfucker!" I shrieked, lifting a hand to slap him. It was too late; the boxer moved too quickly. One hand hit me upside the head, while his other expertly backhanded me across my cheek.

"No, baby, fuck *you*." And with that, he swung the limo door open and pushed me out into the darkness of the Miami night. I staggered to get up, crying out as the limo drove off, its red taillights disappearing down Ocean Avenue. I was on my own. It was over.

Numb, I made my way back to the Betsy Ross Hotel and got on the phone, booking my return flight to Los Angeles first thing in the morning. My heart was broken, my face stung, but in another way I was ready: ready to get the fuck out.

I waited up all night, just to see if Mickey would come to his senses, if he'd come back to me. As the sun rose with no sign of him, I knew I had my answer. It was a new day, a new dawning, and it was time for me to leave. For good.

I cried the entire flight from Miami to LAX. Sitting in first class with a pillow over my face, I wept harder than I had in years. So much had happened; there was so much water under the bridge. It was terribly confusing to be so in love yet in such profound pain. *This can't be right, can it?* I wondered in despair. *This can't be love.*

Back in Los Angeles, I found a little tree house of a place up in Laurel Canyon. It was well off the beaten path. And it was all mine. I had gathered my belongings from the loft and set up camp. It was the perfect place to get my feet back under me and to heal. One room was dedicated to my Buddhist practice again; that was also something I'd had to give up under Mickey's roof.

Slowly, I began to work again: Blumarine with Albert Watson, Italian *Vogue* with Herb Ritts. Clients were reassured that Mickey was a thing of the past. And for the moment he was.

One day in late spring 1992, I got a call from Marie-Christine at the Look Model Agency in San Francisco. The makeup company

Helena Rubinstein wanted to meet with me. They were interested in having me represent them.

"Do you realize, Carré, that this is what we've worked for? This is the big time!" Marie-Christine whooped over the phone.

Within days we were on a plane bound for Paris to meet with the Rubinstein CEO. It was an exciting trip, in such stark contrast to the struggles I had endured there years before. Now I was at the top of my game, resurrected and ready to work.

When I returned from what had been a successful meeting in Paris, it appeared that summer had arrived in Los Angeles, too. The May gloom had lifted, and the city streets were already sweltering. From my little house in the canyon, I could hear the coyotes howling in the night, reminding me of the wildness and unpredictability of the course I was on. Word had it that Mickey had accepted another boxing match in Tokyo. I read about him in the tabloids, and it seemed everyone I knew had news as to his whereabouts.

Word also had it that he was missing me. Profoundly. It tugged at my heartstrings, yet somehow I knew that he hadn't changed. He couldn't change. The man I'd been with was not a man I could be with going forward. Yet the longing remained. And as I began to hear more and more about him, that old homesickness returned. There was still a huge soft spot in my heart for him.

So I wasn't really surprised to get a call from Bruce in early June.

"Yo, Otis! What's up?" he asked.

I laughed hearing his voice. Bruce was a central part of Mickey's boys' club. I was happy to hear from him. Like hearing from a long-lost brother.

"Hey there! How are you?" I asked, smiling. I knew who was behind the call, and despite my reservations my heart raced, just as it had done the first time I'd been in close contact with Mickey. The rush of him, the adrenaline our relationship churned—it was unbeatable.

"All's good. But forget about me. What about you?"

I played it cool. Played it happy. "I'm great, Bruce. Really, really good. Working and happy." It was mostly true.

"Yeah? That's fantastic." I could feel him waiting, pausing. He had called for a reason.

"What, Bruce?" I pressed. He was loyal to Mickey, but he also cared. Bruce was a good guy. One of the few in the crowd that Mickey hung with.

"Well, Mickey wants to see you. He wants to meet you—in Big Sur." He waited, but I could hear him nervously drawing on a cigarette.

"Oh, yeah?" I asked coyly. "I thought Mick was fighting in Japan?"

"Yeah, he's there. But, Christ, Otis, he's . . . he's going nuts. He needs to see you."

I swallowed. I could feel the fear come over me. I looked around my sweet little home, the oaks swaying gently in the warm, early-summer breeze. I took a deep breath. "Yeah. I'm sure he does, Bruce. I just don't know if . . . if I want to see him." I was holding firm. There had to be some reason that would motivate me to go. "I mean, come on, Bruce. Mick is fucked up. I can't see him—be with him—if he hasn't changed."

Bruce was silent for a moment. "But he has, Otis. He really has. It messed him up, you leaving him." He was pleading.

I interjected angrily, "He didn't seem to give a shit in Miami, Bruce. Come on. Be real."

It was a stupid conversation. And why I bought any of it, I'm still not sure.

"Carré, please. Just give him a chance. One chance. He said to tell you if what he has to say, what he has to ask you . . . if you don't buy it, you can both walk." Bruce was desperate. It was his job to get me to go.

So my trip was planned. I gave in. Just like that. My longing, my loneliness, everything that remained unresolved, had me buying into the hope that we could still set ourselves on the right course.

On June 25, 1992, a limo picked me up in Los Angeles and drove me north up the coast to my old stomping grounds. I had always loved

Big Sur. It held the wonderful, magical beginnings of Northern California. For as long as I could remember, I had marveled at the drama of its ocean, its craggy cliffs, and the humpback whales that migrated through its waters. Big Sur was more inviting to me than L.A. had ever been.

I was driven to the then-brand-new Post Ranch Inn and at check-in was handed a note: *"Wait for me in the Ocean House."* I looked around as if there might be cameras following me. Some sort of covert operation was seemingly under way. Obediently, I followed a silent concierge along the impressive path and down to an amazing suite that looked out over the crashing waves. Stunning views and the deep blue sea extended endlessly into space in front of me. It was breathtaking. The concierge placed my bag on the floor and poured me a glass of champagne.

"Wait?" I asked, a question rather than a command. But she handed my glass to me and winked, then left me alone in the room. I walked to the terrace, opening the sliding glass doors to the ocean breeze. But before I could step outside, the phone rang. Picking it up, I could hear Bruce's voice. "Otis, you there?"

"Yeah, Bruce. What's up? What's going on?" I was confused. Why wasn't Mickey here?

"Mickey's here. He's waiting for you in the parking lot. Go out and meet him."

"What?" But Bruce had already hung up.

Jesus, the drama! I thought.

I slugged my glass of champagne and wandered back up the path I had come down. Sure enough, there he was, sitting on the hood of a tricked-out '69 Road Runner hot rod. Periwinkle blue with a white stripe up the center. The top was down.

"Hey," Mickey said quietly. He seemed apprehensive, unwilling to look at me, gazing at his boxing shoes, one unlaced.

"Hey, Mickey," I said carefully. I was trying to conceal my own nervousness. We were like two teenagers, tangled in emotion, unable to move or speak.

I stood my ground, waiting. I was holding firm to my insistence that I couldn't be with him if he hadn't changed. But in my naïve young heart, I truly thought or hoped that change could happen overnight. It's not news that love is often both blind and foolish.

"Otis . . . I . . . I don't know what to say. I love you. I miss you. I need you. I . . . I want you." He was stammering.

"Mickey, you really fucking hurt me. I don't even know why I'm here. Other than that I love you, too. But love . . . it shouldn't hurt like this." I was emotional. My lip was trembling. I was trying not to cry.

"I've changed. I really have. Being without you, it's like death. I don't want to be alive if I can't be with you." He was putting on an impressive show. Mickey was a genius. He was brilliant. Above all he was an actor. I knew he loved me, but I was wary of all these things.

Before I knew what he was doing, he got down on one knee. "Marry me, Carré," he said.

I was silent. I was shocked. I hadn't seen that coming. Yet it was the one thing that he hadn't asked before, or committed to. Hope surged through me. *Is this proof of "the change"?* I wondered to myself.

I took a deep breath, summoning all my strength. "How do I know, Mick? How do I know you've changed?" I couldn't answer his question until he could answer mine.

"Marry me or I'll die!" he cried.

"Jesus, Mickey. Wait. I haven't seen you in months!" I was starting to feel panicked. "I need time, some time to think about this." A swirl of anxiety wrapped itself around me. That familiar pressure was back: to answer, to do, to say, to obey. . . .

"No. You answer me now," he said firmly. Standing up, he went to the back of the car and opened the trunk. "I can't live without you," he said again, pulling out a long sword wrapped in beautiful Japanese cloth.

"What's that?" I asked.

"It's a hari-kari knife," he replied, unwrapping it. The long metal sword caught the afternoon light. Mickey stared into my eyes. "Answer me or I will die."

Was he serious? I wasn't sure. I was terrified. I waited a beat. I wanted to ask, *Mickey, why can't I have time to think about this?* I recognized his standard my-way-or the-highway ultimatum in all this, but it was tinged with a threat of a different kind this time. Numbness was descending on me quickly, and I couldn't find the words to tell him as much.

I was under such pressure. I felt as if I were about to implode. And as the dread washed over me, I heard myself say, "Yes, Mickey. I will marry you." I wept, rushing into his arms.

He covered me with kisses, wiping away my tears. But I don't think to this day that he knew why I was crying. I'd been pushed to the brink, been forced to make an impulsive decision. If I'd given him the wrong answer, I would have lost him—and he might have followed through on his threat with the sword. So once again it was *his* relationship, with *his* rules and *his* timing. I didn't feel confident enough in my own strength to say no.

As far as I could see, my only option was to stay with him or lose him forever. The caretaker in me really thought he would die if I didn't choose him. My paralysis was monumental, but also painfully familiar. It was one of the oldest themes of my life.

I don't know if I would have said yes to Mickey—I don't know if I would even have been with him at that time—if it hadn't been for what happened with my ninth-grade boyfriend, Scott. I hadn't been able to save Scott from his demons—the ones that drove him to take his own life—because I'd been too young. Our relationship was too new. Even though he'd come to me for help just an hour before he shot himself, I'd had no idea of what he was planning to do. I had felt responsible for his death ever since. Now another man was coming to me in need, making it clear that I could save him. The difference between Mickey and Scott was that Mickey was telling me in no uncertain terms what he would do if I said no. I simply couldn't lose another lover to suicide. Not when it was so obvious to me that I had the power to prevent it.

Though I wasn't aware of it at the time, I now see the great paradox in my relationship with Mickey. It's a paradox I see in other women's relationships with abusive and simultaneously self-destructive men. On the one hand, I felt powerless. I was so much less certain than he was. I was afraid of his violence. On the other hand, I felt a responsibility to save him. I can now see that I'd protected men from themselves all my life. I kept Elliott from certain death when I stepped between him and that seriously pissed-off, gun-toting trucker. It was something I knew how to do even then. Something I felt I *could* do. In this case something I *had* to do.

Mickey and I were married the next day, June 26, in my hometown of San Francisco. A justice of the peace oversaw our vows as we stood several feet from a Dumpster in Golden Gate Park.

Mickey's anxiety attack that morning should have made it clear to me that he, too, was doing it for the wrong reasons. He also must have thought that if he didn't propose to me, he would lose me. Lose me to someone else, lose his chance, lose his family. We were married in the hope that our love would fulfill all that our lives up until that point had not. In the hope that somehow a piece of paper would magically heal the wounds we'd suffered at the hands of others and had inflicted on ourselves and each other.

We were wrong. Sadly and predictably, so very, very wrong.

Honeymoon to Hell

So who *do* you call when you're twenty-three years old and you've just married Mickey Rourke?

I wasn't entirely sure, but I desperately wanted someone to be happy for me. If I could find just one person, I thought it might convince me to be happy for myself. It might convince me that my decision was the right one. Yet somewhere deep inside me, an anxiety was brewing. Try as I might to push it further and further down during the weeks to come, I simply couldn't. I really wanted to believe I was on the right path, that all along it had been Mickey's inability to commit that had caused us such problems. I wanted to believe that now, married, it would be just the two of us—no more entourage, no more boys' club, no more lies and deceit.

We found ourselves trying to catch the tiger's tail of the fantasy we had just bought into. The truth was, neither of us could run hard enough or fast enough to grab it. But damn, we tried.

Before leaving San Francisco on our honeymoon, I made two phone calls at Mickey's insistence. The first was to my sister to share the news; the second was to Marie-Christine to tell her not only that I was married but that I was quitting modeling, too.

"But, Mickey, that is so ridiculous," I argued. "Why should I do that? I'm about to sign a million-dollar contract!" I was frustrated and angry. I didn't entirely understand what Mickey meant when he said I now had "wifely duties." Yet in his mind it was perfectly clear. I was to give up everything else—my modeling career especially—because my new occupation was to be utterly devoted to him.

"Otis, baby, that's the way it goes. Now more than ever. I will always take care of you." It was a line in keeping with the fantasy we were both trying to create. And sustaining that fantasy required certain rules. Unknown until created, then law once Mickey spoke them.

"I can't. I don't want to," I protested. "Marie-Christine worked so hard to put this together." I was shaking, but I couldn't find the courage to tell him I was going to do otherwise.

He picked up the phone, dialed my agent's number, and placed the receiver in my hand. I was filled with dread and shame. This wasn't my wish. But it was now the law of the land, the one I was to abide by.

"M.C.?" I whispered into the phone.

"*Oui.* Yes? Carré?"

She knew me well. She knew that something was up.

"Oh, no. *Merde,*" she said quietly in her thick French accent. "You are back together with him, yes?" I didn't have to say much. She already knew.

"Yes, M.C.," I replied quickly. I looked toward Mickey, who was pacing and waiting, smoking a cigarette. He wanted her to know I was his. Not hers.

"I'm married, M.C. We just got married," I said, trying to sound happy, but I knew she could hear the concern in my voice.

A big sigh on the other end. "Well, my dear . . . I had to know this was coming. Are congratulations in order?" she asked, a bit coolly. Mickey pointed at his watch and mouthed, *Wrap it up, Otis.* I looked down at my Converse sneakers, crossed and uncrossed my legs.

"I'm turning down Helena Rubinstein, M.C.," I said flatly.

"Why on earth would you do that, Carré? There is no need. You can have both. Don't be foolish! Don't throw it all away. . . ." Her voice trailed off. I could hear her disappointment, sense her desperation.

"I . . . I . . . I can't, M.C. It's done. It's over." I was near weeping, and Mickey wasn't liking the tone I was taking. He came over and silently placed his hand on the phone, indicating to me that I needed to end my call. We stood for a moment eye to eye.

"Now call your family. At least *they* should be happy for you," he said, trying to sound bold as well as reassuring.

But that call was even worse. There was sadness when I announced my news. A disappointment all around. Looking back, I realize that everyone was concerned, gravely worried that I had just signed away my life. It would be a while before I fully acknowledged the truth in that.

Our honeymoon was to be a road trip. We packed into the car and drove through the night, heading north up toward Eureka. We didn't know where or how far we were going. We just knew that our life together depended on the speed of our escape. It was actually the first time since I'd met Mickey that it was just the two of us, adventuring and exploring together. For a short while, it was heaven. To have him all to myself, with the top down and the early-summer sun shining on us, was bliss. We had entered into the realm of make-believe. Mickey left behind his agents, his entourage, his movies, and the paparazzi.

For that brief time, we were like the two people we'd been when we met and fell in mad, crazy love.

We laughed and took turns at the wheel. We listened to U2's "One" over and over again, tearing up, holding hands, our hair whipping in the wind. We confessed our desires, our concerns, our love and respect for each other. It felt like the first time we'd met, at Zalman King's house. I thought the moment would last forever. I was more and more convinced that Mickey was a changed man and able to leave it all behind.

From California we headed toward Montana. We drove until the sun set and stayed in whatever place we found along the way. We laughed and shared bottles of beer in cheap hotel-room beds. One night near Bozeman, we were almost out of gas, clearly at the end of the line. The only place available to spend the night was above a bar in a dilapidated old house. The walls were paper thin. Our neighbor vomited endlessly till morning. Reality was starting to seep into our fantasy. But we pressed on anyway. Our lives depended on it. It was as if we were on the run from something. And in a sense we were. Ourselves. The truth. The world that, sooner or later, we'd have to return to.

After Montana and Wyoming, we veered toward Utah. Just before Salt Lake City, our car broke down.

"Shit!" Mickey screamed. "What now?" He acted like a kid whose ice-cream cone had just hit the ground.

"It's okay, Mickey. We can just call AAA." But in that moment the reality we'd been dodging caught up with us. He had lost control. We had lost momentum. We'd come to a screeching halt. Mind you, a delay in Salt Lake City might put anyone over the edge, but it was here that the gears really shifted.

We sat together in the cab of the tow truck. There were few places with the resources to fix the Road Runner we'd been driving. It was an old hot rod that needed special parts. Mickey wasn't used to handling details or dealing with mishaps. That was someone else's job. Usually one of the boys.

"I can deal with it, Mickey," I tried to convince him. "It's going to be fine." But Mickey wanted to call the boys. And just like that, the world, the entourage, and the whole scene crowded in on us again.

Five days later the car was fixed, but during those five days we had begun to doubt the course we'd taken. Metaphorically, this road trip represented our life and the choices that were to come. Mick had already called his agents in a fit of insecurity. I could hear him arguing and could see the old Mickey resurfacing.

"What did that motherfucker have to say?" he yelled into the phone. "They don't wanna work with me? Well, fuck them!" He slammed the phone down. Another job shelved. Another producer who wouldn't touch him. I wondered secretly about calling M.C. back to see if it was too late to take the makeup job. When I even hinted at the prospect, he seethed, "No way, Otis. Not my wife. You won't be working with that fucking bitch again."

"Why? What did she ever do to you?" I asked. He was looking ugly in his anger.

"Let's just say I sent her a farewell present," he replied sinisterly.

"What the fuck does that mean, Mickey?"

"A funeral wreath. She got it a few days ago. Now she knows not to fuck with me. That's over, Otis. Over."

"Why would you do such a thing?" I cried. I was mortified. Horribly embarrassed. His behavior shamed me. I couldn't stand all the ways he found to be violent and cruel.

Just then there was a knock at the door. It was Bruce. I flung the door open, gave Bruce a look, and left, slamming it behind me. This was going badly. Really badly.

We never spoke about M.C. again. Somehow I knew if I were to stay with Mickey, I would have to surrender hope, make sacrifices, and just move on. It was defeat on my part. But I had chosen my path, so I had to be a big girl and deal with it, as gracefully as possible.

We got back on the road with only a week left of our honeymoon. "Let's head to New Orleans," Mickey suggested. So off we tore into the desert heat. But things continued to go awry. By this point it was mostly me at the wheel. Mickey's anxiety attacks had increased to such a point that he could no longer drive. We kept paper bags in the glove compartment and frequently had to pull over. He would leap out of the car, pace back and forth crying, "Otis, I can't breathe! I'm dying!" It was heartbreaking. I learned to help him through these horribly debilitating attacks by calling upon all the grounding measures that had been taught to me in my Buddhist practices. We would find a patch of grass, and I would make him sit down. "Mickey, feel the earth beneath you," I'd say. "Ground yourself into it. Inhale and exhale . . . slowly. . . . That's it. You're okay." Sometimes it would take ten minutes, sometimes an hour. I would have to convince Mickey he wasn't dying. Eventually it was only his meds that helped when these anxiety attacks hit, though I wished for his peace of mind that he'd find more sustainable measures of self-soothing.

Back on the road once more, we would drive as far as we could manage each day between anxiety attacks and the oppressive heat. Summer was at its peak, and it didn't help that the Road Runner had no A/C. We would stop at convenience stores and get packs of cigarettes and blocks of ice. We'd drive down the highway with those blocks of ice melting in Mickey's lap, hoping they would alleviate some of the suffocation he felt from the heat.

New Orleans was just one stop on the way back to hell. As we got closer, I began to notice the direction we were traveling in—we were headed toward Miami.

"Mick . . . you're not thinking of going to Miami, are you?" I asked quietly. He had promised me we wouldn't return there.

"Come on, Otis. Things have changed," he replied defensively.

"No. Not about Miami. Nothing's changed. You promised." I was furious. He was beginning to slip on his word again. Promises meant nothing to him, I was beginning to see that.

"Let's not talk about it, Carré. We'll end up wherever I say. If it's

Miami, it's fucking Miami." He slammed his fist onto the dashboard. I fell silent.

New Orleans was a blur. A hot, humid blur. The days were closing in fast. The press was calling. The reports were out that we were married. And Mickey's agents had a movie lined up for him. The world was beckoning us back, and our fantasy was crashing in violently before our eyes.

I knew where we would end up. I was becoming more and more certain that Mickey had always had a plan. Part of that plan was to "get" me, have me, conquer me, and then move on. My instincts were right. I soon found myself driving us to Miami Beach, amid a sea of tears and despair. Right back to the Betsy Ross Hotel, right back to where it had all nearly ended before.

I was now a married woman, but the security that marriage once seemed to have promised turned out to be a lie. A lie I was trying to live and uphold. The honeymoon was coming to an end. And with it went the hope that we could escape old patterns and live a new life.

"Baby, don't worry. Please don't worry. When we get back to L.A., we're gonna move into the Benedict house." Mickey was pleading with me. He wanted my smiles, my love, and my approval.

"Is it finished? Finally?" The Benedict Canyon house had been his and his alone. He hadn't been willing to open it up to me, to us, to a shared life. But now he was. Was this what married life meant? We could finally live in his dream home? His treasure?

"Not finished yet—but finished enough for us to go home to. A home, Otis . . . our home."

It sounded good. It was a step in the right direction

But Miami was just as it had always been. Within a day Mickey was back with his boys. His entourage had flown there to be by his side. They had taken their usual places in between us. We were set to be there for five days. "Just five days, Otis. Come on . . . let's celebrate. Let's party," Mickey coaxed.

That was the last thing I wanted to do. I was ready to get back to L.A., to make a home, find some routine and figure out what being a married twenty-three-year-old really meant.

Our suite at the Betsy Ross overlooked the Strand—a strip of white-sand beach—and the rolling blue ocean beyond it. We had done nothing but eat and drink and sleep on our road trip, and I felt like hell, overweight and depressed. (I wasn't really overweight. But after the honeymoon I was heavier than the ruthless standard that was on display on the streets and beaches of Miami. There were lots of models in South Beach, and Mickey's wandering eye didn't let me forget that.) I didn't want to go to the clubs. I wanted to work out. I wanted to look good and feel better. But that's not what Miami was about.

"I'm going out," Mickey announced as the sun sank into the horizon line.

"What? No way, Mickey." I was appalled. Hadn't we talked about this? Wasn't this time going to be different?

"Don't fucking tell me 'no way,'" he said angrily as he proceeded to put on his tank top and gold chains.

"Mickey, you promised."

"Promised what? To marry you? I did. And I'm going out." He spun around, challenging me. "What? You going to fucking leave me this time, Otis? Guess what, bitch? You can't!"

He was raging. I should have backed off. But the betrayal I felt was inciting me to rage back with equal force.

"Fuck you!" I screamed, tears welling up. I was hoping he would hear the hurt in my voice, see the open wounds from before, and stop himself. But he didn't. Mickey threw me onto the bed and slapped me across the face. Instinctively, I brought my knees up. My feet caught him in the gut, and I pushed him as hard as I could. Then I scrambled off the bed and tried frantically to make my way to the door. He tackled me, forcing me to the floor, shoving my face down into the carpet. A second later I felt something cold against my cheek. It was his gun.

"No you won't, Otis. Or you're fucking dead."

I froze. I could hear my heart pounding in my ears, feel the adrenaline surge through my body. I was stilled, as if some higher force had come down and spread itself over me. I was in complete surrender. *I give up*, I thought. *I give up*.

Mickey left me there, in a clump on the floor. I didn't move for some time. The numbness that had come over me settled deep down in my bones. He was right. I wouldn't leave him. Not then, not yet. But I would find a way to make it bearable to be with him.

I went to the manager's room and knocked on his door. "Nouvelle... are you there?" and when he opened it up, I simply extended my hand and asked, "Got any blow?"

And that's how I got by. For years that's how I deadened my senses and survived the insanity.

Falling for Aileen

Any remaining hope I had about our lives changing for the better now that Mickey and I were married ended when we returned to L.A. The Benedict Canyon residence was in an utter state of disrepair. Construction had been under way for years; completion was always delayed. The house had been gutted and the theme of its decor changed countless times depending on Mickey's mood. When I moved in, only the office and the upstairs bedroom were finished; the other rooms were uninhabitable. It was chaos.

The pool stood cracked and empty in the otherwise extravagant backyard. There was a muralist who had been hired to paint the walls of the grand entrance and the living room in a southwestern theme. An eerie portrait of Chief Joseph appeared on one wall, Geronimo on another. A seven-foot bronze statue of Crazy Horse by the famed sculptor Dave McGary stood guard at the front door. Besides these definitive choices, the house was a shell. Large sums of money had been poured sporadically into the place, but the results were bizarrely incomplete.

The kitchen ceiling was made of a gorgeous pounded copper, but there was no oven. There were cracked windows throughout the upstairs, but the finest luxury towels hung in the bathroom. The random and disconnected nature of the renovation mirrored our lives with their inconsistencies and absurdities.

I was the kid, but Mickey acted like one. With his strangely outdated view of marriage, he would repeatedly tell me it was his wife's job to "run the place." I still hadn't a clue as to what that meant.

If I thought the house on the hill seemed isolated at first glance, the Benedict Canyon mansion was worse. It was cold and damp, since the heat rarely worked. It was a spooky place, especially for a young woman on her own. Mickey was gone most of the time. He'd be away filming for months, and even when he returned, he'd usually hang out down at Caffé Roma or at Giuseppe Franco's hair salon. Little had changed since we got married.

I lived for the moments when Mickey was home. I waited again and again for his return. I longed for his undivided attention. I never got it. When he was in town, our dinners out always included his boys. We were never alone in the house; someone from the entourage was always with us, crashing on the couch, staying in an extra bedroom. They were there to drive Mickey's cars and even to dial the phone for him. It was incredible how little Mickey did for himself.

I got along with the boys because I had to. And when Mickey was away, the boys became an extension of him. Mickey could be anywhere in the world, but at least one of them would be with me. Protecting me. Watching me. As far as I was concerned, none of these stand-ins, these security guards, could fill the void that Mickey's absence left. I pushed to be alone, to be there without the extra help. But that never flew with Mickey. That was against his rules. In his mind I needed a chaperone. From what I could see, though, it was his own behavior that warranted watching—that's what was really making him so neurotic and jealous.

I had a hunch about his infidelities. The papers frequently reported the names of the girls he would escort about. It nearly drove me crazy.

Naturally, I fell back on the one thing I could control: my weight. Diet-ing, my old habit, took on a new and starring role in my life. Obsessing about food numbed the pain and loneliness. Night after night I would order the same meal from the same local Chinese restaurant: soup, soup, soup, and more soup.

I had plenty of time to focus on my body. I wasn't working. Mickey had insisted I stop modeling and concentrate on acting instead. What I didn't see then was that this was just another of his ruses to control me. Another strategy to dominate me. I was a successful model. I was *not* a trained actress. Once again Mickey had demanded that I fire my modeling agent and hire his manager, who he promised would find me the right jobs. What this effectively did was cut me off from a world I thrived in and from any resource I could rely on. I was in an endless holding pattern, waiting for any sort of work. None came. Or at least none that I was ever told about. I was in my early twenties and, seem-ingly, unemployable.

Stuck in the Benedict Canyon mansion, alone except for my mind-ers, I was desperate to do something, desperate for community and connection. I had no idea what that entailed, but I was willing to clean carpets if it would get me out of the house. I decided to volunteer at an AIDS center in West Hollywood. There I met Aileen Getty, the first-born daughter of John Paul Getty.

Aileen was a force to be reckoned with. She was larger than life. And she had AIDS. Her story was riveting. I learned that she had been disinherited when she publicly announced that she had contracted the disease. She was ten years my senior, someone I would really open up with. I saw her as a hero. I put her on a pedestal. And yes, there was a time when I even thought I was falling in love with her.

I'd had feelings for women before. And I certainly hadn't grown up with prejudices about homosexuality. Quite the contrary—on my wild life journey, anything went. Yet every time I'd come close to being sexual with a woman, a lack of fundamental physical interest would intervene. Basically, I wasn't into pussy. But I was into exploration. I

liked having the freedom that came with that—the chance to feel powerful. It was something I didn't feel with men. And even when I took on
a submissive role with women, it felt safer than it did with men.

Aileen and I became fast friends. We had a lot in common. We
were both rebels. Unfortunately, we both also had a fierce appetite for
cocaine. That propelled us. And instead of working at the AIDS center,
I became deeply involved in Aileen's life. We held hands, we shared,
we kissed, and we embraced each other. There was no need to go any
further. She met my deep emotional needs in a way that they simply
hadn't been met in my relationship with Mickey.

Aileen and I spent our days and nights together. I met her sons by
Chris Wilding, who was Elizabeth Taylor's son. She hid her cocaine
use from them all, and in my naïveté and need for the closeness we enjoyed, I never really stopped to consider what was so wrong with this
picture. Looking back, I realize that in Aileen's mind she had already
been served a death sentence, so she could party with abandon. I on
the other hand didn't have AIDS. I wasn't dying. To party with equal
abandon was not necessarily a wise thing for me to do.

Aileen's home in Los Feliz was cluttered with the eclectic treasures
reflective of her impressive past. Priceless original artwork hung from
her walls. Pictures of several generations of Gettys stood out on the
shelves: her older brother, John Paul III, who had been kidnapped and
so famously had had his ear cut off; her parents in their Moroccan
home; her legendary grandfather, who had become one of the first
American billionaires. I'd never seen another place like it.

We did a lot of partying in that house. But on one particular evening, things really took a turn for the worse.

A group of friends were arriving for a party. Aileen and I had
picked out matching black dresses and applied makeup between the
lines of cocaine we snorted off the marble vanity in her bathroom. I
had a glass of champagne in one hand and a cigarette in the other as I
descended the winding staircase to meet the guests. Aileen and I were
both high and wild that night. We worked the room hand in hand,

flaunting our girl-on-girl relationship, shadowed of course by the reality that one of us had AIDS.

I wondered just how obvious the daredevil in me was. Could I really have been the most unbridled one at the party? The truth is that my recklessness was simple foolishness. We all partied the night away, out under the stars. Harry Dean Stanton was there playing guitar. I sat on his lap for a minute and kissed his cheek before I moved on. Timothy Leary was holding court near a giant candelabra, leading a heavy discussion about the relationship between hallucinogens and death.

"Carré, come with me." Aileen smiled and winked. I followed her like a puppy through the courtyard and into the downstairs powder room.

"What's up?" I asked. I knew she had something up her sleeve.

She pulled out a little bag of white powder, a glass pipe, and a lighter.

"You gotta try a hit of this." She nodded, a smile turning the corners of her red lips upward. I placed my mouth on hers with a kiss.

"Yum," I said. "Do me up."

And before I knew it, I'd taken a hit of what I thought was cocaine. I had never smoked it but was willing at that point to try anything. What I didn't expect was what came next.

I choked, staggered back, and instantly panicked. At once my heart was pumping furiously. A surge of nausea overwhelmed me.

As I began to sputter, drool started to stream from my mouth. I clutched my chest.

"Hhhh . . . hel . . . help me. . . ." I could barely choke out the words. I was dying. I was sure I was dying. I couldn't breathe. The room was going black. "Aileen! Help me!" I could hear my voice cry. It sounded so far away.

Aileen grabbed my arm and held me to her frail body. "Hang on, Carré. You're okay. Just breathe. Breathe. In and out." She started banging on the door with one hand as she held me up. "Hey! Someone out there! Help!"

In rushed Stevie, her nurse. "What the hell is going on, Aileen?" he demanded. His hand quickly grasped my wrist and found my pulse. "Jesus Christ . . . You must get her to walk, Aileen. Come on, baby," I could hear him say. "Come on. Let's just walk around the block, Carré. Get a breath of fresh air."

One of my arms was slung over Stevie's shoulders and one over the very petite Aileen. Although I was taller than her by almost a foot, we were at that point equally light on our feet. Featherweights—a bit over a hundred pounds each.

Concerned faces turned to look at me as Stevie and Aileen got me out the front door. By this point the drool had turned to foam, and it felt as if my tongue was swelling and obstructing my breathing. Out in the fresh air, painfully slowly, I felt my breath return, my heart quiet, and a welcome exhaustion flow through me.

"Damn, Carré. That was fucked up. I mean really scary. You okay?" Aileen looked hard into my eyes.

"No. I'm not. What the hell happened?" I asked.

"It was crack. It wasn't coke. I thought . . . you'd like it," she whispered apologetically.

"I didn't like it, A. I hate it. Why would someone want to get high on that shit?" I demanded. I was frightened. That was way too close a call for me. Our partying was getting out of hand. We both knew it.

I was never entirely sure how Aileen managed to ravish drugs the way she did in light of her diagnosis. When questioned, all she would say was that sometimes that was the only thing that got her through the day, through the fatigue, through the endless medications she had to take to stay alive. It occurred to me at that moment that we were not a good influence on each other.

But Aileen and I were more than partners in crime. We were lovers who guarded each other's secrets. We held each other's lies as tightly as we held each other's hand. Together we were able to soothe the profound abandonment we felt from our families and from the long line of boys and men who had come and gone in our lives. We were both misfits, misfits who held court together and kept each other company.

I had suspected that Mickey might be tapping the phones. Even when he was away, he always seemed to know too much. His questions were pointed and demanding, his interrogations endless. One evening, standing in the kitchen drinking my soup, I was on the phone with my sister.

"Chrisse," I confided, "I think I'm in love."

"Of course you are, silly!" she said, assuming I was talking about Mickey.

"No, I mean I think I'm in love . . . with a woman."

Silence hung in the air. Her shock was disguised in her desire to be open, but I knew she was concerned.

"With who?" she asked quietly.

"Aileen. Aileen Getty," I answered. And that was that. The damage was done.

The very next day, Mickey arrived at Benedict Canyon. His return home was unexpected, and he was cold and curt. He grabbed my hand and led me into the office, sat me down on the couch, and walked over to the stereo system. I had a hunch there was a problem, but I was still shocked when he pressed "play" and I heard my conversation with my sister repeated. The cat was out of the bag.

Mickey paced back and forth. "How could you, Otis?" he screamed. He was furious. And no doubt confused. How could *a woman* have won my love? Was I a dyke? Was I stupid? His rant went on and on, and in my humiliation and despair I could only sit and weep.

"I'm sorry. I'm so sorry!" I wailed. "I don't know how this happened. You're gone! Always gone!" I cried. "I'm alone! Always alone!" I tried to make my case, I pleaded, and I agonized. I was desperate.

"Do you love her? Do you really love her? Did you fuck her? Does she kiss your pussy?" Mickey was seething.

I sat silent for a moment, then tried to gather up all my will and all my strength.

"No. She does none of that. We have never . . . fucked," I said simply.

"Then *what*? What the fuck is it? What does she have that I don't? What does she give you that I don't?"

"Love. Friendship." My answer was that simple, but it was still beyond him, the macho hetero male that he was.

His hand came down across my face. Hard. An open palm, then a backhand. I went flying across the room. Blood trickled from my nose. *I must deserve this,* I thought.

"Oh, Otis. What have you done? *What have you made me do?*" He wiped a tear from his face. He was crushed. And so was I.

I made a move to hold him. But he pushed me back again. I could see in that moment he despised me. I was everything he thought I might turn out to be.

"Don't you see? That's why I have to tap the fucking phones. That's why I have to keep my bros with you always."

I couldn't be trusted. I never could. And never would be again.

"So these are the new rules, you little cunt," he hissed at me. "You are never, ever, ever to see Aileen again. You will obey me. You will be here. You will do as I say."

"But . . . but," I stammered. I wasn't sure I wanted this. Any of this, any more of his rules. I was at a breaking point. I couldn't stay. But I couldn't go either. I was in hell.

"My way or the highway, Carré. You got it?"

He stood to leave. And as I heard his Harley revving up outside, I realized I was being left again. Alone in that big fucking house. Quietly, I walked up the stairs to our bathroom and retrieved a bottle of sleeping pills. The blood from my nose had dried on my cheeks. My eye was swelling from the force of his fist. "I can't stay, and I can't go," I said out loud. But maybe there was another way.

Grabbing a bottle of beer from the night table, I counted out the small white pills: One, two, three, four . . . swallow. Five, six, seven, eight . . . swallow. I cried as I counted. I cried as I swallowed. I just wanted it all to be gone. I wanted to be home. I wanted to call Aileen.

But instead I swallowed every pill in the bottle, finished the beer, and lay down on the bed.

I guess I'm taking the highway, Mick, I thought. And with that, I closed my eyes.

On the Psych Ward

I awoke at the Cedars-Sinai emergency room in Beverly Hills as a tube was being pulled out of my throat. In the distance I could hear nurses whispering in excited tones. As I strained to regain consciousness, I still couldn't hear exactly what they were saying. I lifted my hand to wipe my face but was stopped by the IV that was in my arm. Panic set in as I looked around, realizing that I wasn't at home, I wasn't alone, and I wasn't dead either. My head pounded, my body ached. I was terrified.

"That's Carré Otis," one nurse said behind the thin curtain that had been drawn for privacy. "Mickey Rourke's wife."

"Why the hell would she be so stupid?" another voice chimed in. "These young models . . . Christ, they've got no idea what they have!"

Even as sedated as I was, I could feel my blood begin to boil.

"I know! Can you imagine? Married to an actor . . ." the first voice continued. "She has it all. Stupid, stupid girl."

I was fuming. How could these bitches possibly know what I had? What I felt? What my life was like? I stood up, planted my bare feet on the cold linoleum floor, and staggered toward the curtain, steadying myself on the metal pole from which a bag of fluid hung. Throwing the curtain open, I shrieked, "Fuck you! Say it to my face if you think I'm a stupid bitch!"

I knew I was going too far, but I couldn't stop myself. I was at my most desperate point, I was totally vulnerable, and complete strangers were judging me. I'd been silenced for too long. A primal scream was building in my diaphragm.

"Get the doctors!" one of them yelled. "We need to sedate her! Another crazy . . ."

The nurse's look made it clear how pathetic she thought I was. If I'd had the strength, I would have lunged at her. But I was weak beyond words. And defeated in more ways than one. I didn't have any fight left in me.

As a fresh syringe of medication was pushed into my IV, I collapsed back onto the hospital bed. I was cold, so very cold.

Just then Mickey and his manager walked in. I thought I would never see him again. Mickey pulled up a chair and sat next to me, gingerly picking up my hand, curling his fingers around mine. "Otis, what have you done?" He was as confused as I was. It was a fucked-up situation. We were both living in our own dark movies. And we were both in total despair.

The nurses hovered. The monitors beeped. We waited under the harsh fluorescent lights, both of us wanting to say so much but neither of us finding the words.

A gray-haired woman with a clipboard entered and in a nasal voice began to ask me questions: "For purposes of last rites in case of possible death, what is your religion, ma'am?"

Mickey, a devout Catholic, quickly responded, "Catholic."

Enraged, I challenged him. "Buddhist," I replied.

He swallowed hard, shaking his head at me. But I had had it. Since we met, I'd been separated from everything that made me *me*. The very essence of me, what had attracted Mickey to me in the first place—my strength and spirituality—had all been torn away. He was forever in competition with that power: It felt as if I was like a bird to him. A free bird that needed to be caught and tamed. But as it was turning out, I would rather be dead than tamed.

"The doctor will be with you in a moment," the woman said, nodding sympathetically toward Mickey. Then, after scribbling some notes, she pushed her pen behind her ear and left the partitioned room we were in.

Mickey's disappointment in me was palpable. I realized that he was ashamed. He wanted to keep this out of the papers for several reasons, not the least of which was that he had a movie opening. This would certainly put a damper on things.

A young doctor arrived. Clearly smitten with Mickey, he stumbled for a moment before regaining his composure and sense of protocol. "Well, Ms. Otis. We're concerned about you." He spoke in a grave tone.

I nodded, beginning to sense the seriousness of my actions. "I know. Umm . . . it's just been a really hard time. But I'm sure . . . sure I'll be fine. I just need to rest." Tears started to roll down my cheeks. I was scared. And I actually *wasn't* so sure I was going to be okay.

"We want to keep you for observation. I'm going to place a mandatory seventy-two-hour hold on you."

"What? No. I mean I *am* fine. I just want to go home. I'm going to be fine," I declared, doing my best to gather my wits and try to convince him. Mickey looked on quietly. I had the distinct feeling it would be a relief for him if they didn't let me go.

The doctor switched to my first name. "Carré, excuse me, but you just swallowed an entire prescription of sleeping pills. You have had your stomach pumped. You are in an emergency room. And right now I believe that the best place for you to recover is in our mental ward. It will give you the time you need to quiet down and rest and us the time we need to monitor you while your body tries to rid itself of the excess of drugs in your system."

The decision was final. It would be useless to try to talk him out of it.

I looked at Mickey, staring into his eyes, pleading with him to help, but he also recognized that the deal was done. I was devastated. Terrified. Washed up and unsure of what would come next.

Mickey gave me a look, a tear welling in his eye, but just like that it was gone. He wouldn't, couldn't, let himself feel this one. It was too fucked up. Too big. Too off the charts for him to even attempt to deal with. It felt a lot like the dismissal I'd received from my parents every time I tried to get their attention. My actions were not appropriate. *I was not appropriate.* And again I was left.

Mickey excused himself to go have a smoke, and I was wheeled upstairs to Thalians Mental Health Center.

The elevator doors parted on the third floor, and it was as if I had entered another world. I was mesmerized by the patients and awed by the sheer fact that I was now one of them. *Is this where I really belong?* I wondered. And for that moment in time, I knew the answer. *Yes. It is.*

All I could do was lie in that small bed, curled up in a fetal position under the covers. Shivering and weeping, in and out of sweats and nausea, I relived those last moments at home when the despair was so heavy and I thought all I wanted was to die. Or did I? Perhaps I just didn't have the tools to live *or* die. I was sad for myself. Sad for the little girl in me who was still so fucking wounded. I wanted my mom. I wanted my dad. I wanted to call someone, but there was no one I could call. I moved in and out of dreams and nightmares during that long, restless sleep.

Around 2:00 A.M. my hospital roommate, Grace, was delivered back into the room. She was the sweetest little old lady. She hadn't said much before they wheeled her away. I wasn't sure where they were taking her. Everything was kept covert on the ward. But when she returned, she was left on the bed in a slump. She didn't move. She just cried softly for the daughter who she said had passed away. She, too, was utterly alone.

Together Grace and I wept through the night, strangers in the dark, back to back, just feet from one another, hearing each other's cries. Sadness and sorrow all around. When I asked the nurse what had happened, she quietly answered that Grace had had another round of shock treatments.

By day two I was beginning to emerge from my fog. My eyes were seeing again. My nose smelling. My hands working. My heart feeling. It was clear to me that I did not belong in the mental ward. I knew I needed to do whatever it took to get through the seventy-two-hour hold so I could move on. I didn't want to live my life like this.

As I looked around from my perch on a couch in the sunroom, I saw a woman about forty years old who called herself Butch. She walked back and forth talking to herself, farting loudly and frequently into the diaper she wore. Butch was a stone lesbian and had an eye for me. I kept my distance.

Just like Grace and Butch, every patient had a story, a fascinating and disturbing story. To be part of their reality, if only for a moment, was a profound and painful lesson. There was no special treatment for me. Diva behavior was not allowed. I had to be part of the group's activities: the random story times, the meals, the mandatory arts-and-crafts hour. Deviating from the rules was seen as a sign of disobedience. I did my best to check my attitude at the door and behave. I had incentive. And I was lucid enough to have a plan.

I came to know the stiff, shambling movement of the patients on the ward as the "Thorazine shuffle." Thorazine was the standard medication administered to patients in an effort to keep the unit quiet and tame.

During those seventy-two hours, I had time to think about the mentors and teachers who had so far touched my life. For all my misfortune, I had also been very lucky. There were several women who stood out as powerhouses, great archetypal mothers. Nan was one. Tsultrim was another. They had imparted their teachings to me, and they had shared lessons I'd needed to learn.

The passion to live was in my heart. To thrive—not to die, here, now, like this. I consciously breathed that in and out, trying to fill myself with that intention. I had come this far, I thought. *I can do this,* I repeated to myself. And somewhere inside me a conviction ripened. I knew with certainty I would survive.

That night I sat by my window looking down onto the traffic below. I knew that Mickey's premiere party was being held just across the street at Chaya Brasserie on Alden Drive. As luck would have it, I could see the photographers and the snaps of light exploding as Mickey entered his party. It was both devastating and telling to be a prisoner by my own hand, unable to be part of that unfolding scene. And in that stark contrast between the grimness of the locked ward and the celebration going on just a few stories down, I gained a profound perspective on my life. It is a moment I will never forget, a feeling I will hold with me always.

As bad as things would get in the future, I would never be back in a place like this. Somewhere in that hospital ward, the warrior woman in me began her resurrection. I would never attempt suicide again. But having the courage to live didn't necessarily mean that I had the courage to leave my husband. I still had years to go with Mickey.

THE SIMPSON SUMMER, CASES OF SPOUSAL ABUSE

On June 12, 1994, Nicole Brown Simpson was brutally murdered. The news shocked the world. A few days later, millions of us stayed glued to the TV, watching her ex-husband, O. J. Simpson, flee down the 405 freeway with what seemed like every cop in L.A. trailing behind. As the truth came out about O.J.'s long history of violence toward his ex-wife, the extraordinary events of that week marked a moment when we learned that domestic abuse can happen to anyone, anywhere. Often where we least expected it.

By this time my world was upside down. Not even I could keep up with the twists and turns in our on-again, off-again relationship. It had all become such a chore. Every time I thought it was over, there would be another round to endure. I was exhausted. Our marriage was fueled by fire and lies, passion and dependence. We were both acting out, alone with each other as well as publicly. As the days and months passed, our addictive behavior grew even worse. I wasn't suicidal. But I wasn't really living either.

Just weeks after the Simpson murders, we reached another moment we thought would surely be our final breaking point. At least I did.

Mickey and I were "off." Again. I was living in a little place of my own on Orlando Avenue, but we were still in contact. Even in those moments of separation, I was not free from him. I was addicted to him, obsessed with reports of who he was with and where he was going. It was painful to be married yet estranged. Painful to try putting my career back together again while teetering on the brink of obscurity. I had become, in my illness, as unreliable as my husband had forced me to be.

One night in the summer, after I'd returned from dinner and a few margaritas at a local Tex-Mex place, I received a call from him. "Otis . . . Let's talk. We gotta try and work this out. . . . We gotta figure this out. You're my wife," he pleaded into the phone.

I agreed. We were both in trouble—heartbroken and unable to repair ourselves. We were under the influence and not yet willing to take a look at that huge piece of our puzzle. Most troublesome of all was that we were unable to see the repeat pattern we'd fallen into. We would meet to talk; passion would take over; we'd give in to our hope; then we would reawaken to all that was wrong in the first place and the fights would ensue. It was how it always went. As regular as clockwork.

It was bewildering that we hadn't gotten over each other sooner.

That July evening was no different. The arguments began. And then things turned physical. How it would start, and how bad things would become, varied. Either the fights were instigated by *my* relentless questions as to whom he'd been seeing or sleeping with—or the reverse. The only problem was, Mickey was stronger than me physically. I could never win a fight. That night Mickey chased me through the loft. He slapped me. And when I fell, he kicked me in the back.

Again I ran. I headed back to my Orlando house, back to my dogs, and back to hiding in my "other" world. That's when I finally admitted to myself that this was abuse—especially the physical stuff—and that it was not okay. Whether it was because of the fear aroused by Nicole's Simpson's death or just my time to see it all in a new way, I did something I'd never done before. With the coaxing of a friend, two days later I went to the police department and asked to speak in private with an officer.

I had wanted to understand what it would take to get a restraining order on Mickey. I was scared of the volatility of our life together but also deeply concerned about protecting his anonymity. In addition, I was terrified by the story surrounding the Simpson murders. I didn't entirely believe I was in actual danger of being killed, but I wanted to have some sort of plan if I were ever to need it. The officer asked if I was in an abusive relationship, and I answered yes, maybe. I was asked if I had any injury marks on my body, and I responded that I did. I was told that for me to be taken seriously if and when I called for help in the future, they would need to have something on file. After a few Polaroids were taken of my bruises, I was informed that the police would have to intervene.

I was shocked. I hadn't wanted to press charges. I wanted help and support, but I didn't yet know what that meant for me. In my naïveté and in light of the new warnings regarding spousal abuse, I was unable to dissuade the police. The situation was out of my hands. The law was stepping in, whether I liked it or not. I was devastated. And of course my husband was as well. Looking back, I see that there was a perfect storm that had manifested. And the LAPD wanted to make a point. They took domestic abuse seriously. They were not going to let another potential O.J. escape.

Mickey was arrested. His mug shot was taken and leaked to every newspaper across the country. The police and the D.A. saw the celebrity aspect as an opportunity. And I couldn't help but feel as if I, not Mickey, were the one to blame. I regretted going to the police and asking for guidance. I ended up being the one who felt ashamed. *I should have known better,* I thought; *I should never have said a word.* I was a wreck.

The press went wild. I was quickly on the defensive. Yes, I was in an abusive marriage, but in my mind that was a private matter. I wanted to find ways to stop the violence, but it certainly wasn't by publicly lynching my husband. I felt betrayed. When I finally had sought help, it seemed as if everything were wrenched out of my hands. Truth be told, the arrest made matters much worse. It had me in a tailspin, worrying again how I could protect Mickey. Helping him became my obsession. The guilt was overwhelming, as was the fear of what Mickey might do to me. Or to himself.

I hired the same lawyer who was handling the abuse case between fellow model Stephanie Seymour and Mickey's friend, musician Axl Rose. It was explained to me that if I was sure I did not want to press charges, the best course of action was to simply not show up on the trial date. The only challenge was that if I were subpoenaed and was present in the state of California and didn't show up to the trial, then I, too, would be arrested. I was baffled by the legal system, furious that the tables were turning on me. So I made a decision. I would leave California and go to New York, staying away for as long as it took.

Not only did I feel let down by the police department, but I was terrified of Mickey's wrath. No doubt that in his mind this was the biggest betrayal he'd ever suffered. I had been disloyal to him. Mickey often said he "lived and died by the sword." I thought about that phrase quite a bit.

Textbook domestic-abuse cases often evidence the victim's tendency to protect the perpetrators. And in many ways this was true in my case. Is there ever an acceptable level of abuse? Now, of course I know that there isn't. Did I fuel some of the fires between us? Absolutely. Did I have the power to combat Mickey's iron fist? No, I was no match for it. That was just the reality.

And so I fled. In New York City, I vowed to keep quiet and protect what was left of our marriage. I was determined to remain silent. Later the guilt would have me return to him, to undo what had been done and prove that I was a woman who could protect my husband and change my ways. For the time being, all I knew was that I had disobeyed Mickey. And that was a bad, bad thing. In my mind I was convinced of my own culpability and resolved to somehow make it right.

In the interim I went back to work. I tried to leave California as far behind as I could. I walked the runway at New York Fashion Week in October 1994. Unfortunately, our drama erupted there as well. It was an absolute fucking disaster.

NEW YORK FASHION WEEK, 1994

New York City was abuzz. It was the great fashion extravaganza, and it occurred only twice a year, for the spring-summer and fall-winter collections. Models, photographers, editors, and fashionistas as well as rock stars and actors flocked to the events, all angling for front-row seats facing the lithe beauties who stomped down the catwalks. Most of us had just flown in from the Milan shows that preceded New York Fashion Week. Although we were utterly exhausted, the electricity of the city and the full-on theatrical productions the designers staged did wonders to lift everyone's energy and spirit.

Runways were never my forte. I didn't have the walk down, and I hated being part of the mob scene backstage, which always felt to me like I was one in a herd of cattle. Although I didn't have a practiced turn or pirouette, once I reached the end of the catwalk, I would always pause there for a moment, exuding my best fuck-you attitude while millions of flashbulbs went off. It was usually a blinding journey on the way back. I always felt as if my biggest achievement on the runway was to have just gotten myself up and down the length of it safely, without tripping over anyone or falling into the audience. The F-you stance was my attempt to cover up my nervousness. On occasion the anxiety showed right through anyway.

I'd been on the run since the summer. I had traveled to New York and Europe and now back again. Having made the decision not to testify against Mickey, I risked arrest for contempt of court if I returned to California too soon. I was steadfast in my commitment to keep my husband from being put behind bars. But my inability to go home, and the reasons I couldn't, had me running on empty. The tabloids were still reporting on Mickey's comings and goings, as well as mine. And Los Angeles was still gripped by the O. J. Simpson case, which was now headed to trial. I wasn't entirely sure I could continue indefinitely to outrun the law's requests for me to testify.

The stresses of the court case and my relationship just added to the stress of the shows themselves. By 1994 I was no longer the "it" girl. There was a new crop of models that had emerged: the waifs. Kate Moss had entered the picture, defying the previous law that said a top model had to be tall. The other new emerging faces included Amber Valletta, Beri Smither, and Shalom Harlow. All were inhumanly lean creatures. And then there was the new star that really ruled the scene: heroin.

The drug had quite visibly taken the industry by storm. The year before, Calvin Klein's campaign featuring Kate Moss had led to the coining of the new term "heroin chic." It was how a certain waif-like look was described—one that celebrated a wasted, skin-and-bones aesthetic. This term was often an accurate one; a lot of the models were on the drug. But little did most of us know that there was no playing around with it. Heroin was really an all-or-nothing drug. You didn't use it recreationally. And if that's what you were proclaiming (as many people in the industry were at the time), you were full of shit.

It dawned on me in Milan that the other girls might be using it, but I hadn't quite put two and two together. I was still hooked on pills and wasn't yet on the prowl for my next high. But I do recall a new walk that manifested itself on the runways that season, as well as the grunge makeup and painfully obvious protruding hip bones. Comparatively, Cindy Crawford, Claudia Schiffer, Stephanie Seymour, and I were rounder than this lot. And just like that, I felt as if I didn't quite fit in again. At least in my mind. The need to curb my appetite, suppress my individuality, and be like everyone else returned with a vengeance.

It didn't help that when I was in Milan, racing through outfit changes backstage at the Versace show, famed fashion editor Polly Mellen had come up to me and said in her deep-voiced, upper-crust manner, "My dear, you simply must do something about your profuse sweating." She nodded for emphasis as she said the last word, then looked around furtively as if someone might have heard her say it.

"What?" I asked innocently, wiping beads of sweat from my forehead.

"And you must control your face, Carré," she continued. "You need to relax, my dear. If you aren't relaxed, then for heaven's sake fake it." And with that, she was gone.

Keeping that note of advice in mind, I arrived in New York and checked into the Lowell hotel. I was to have one day of fittings for the Donna Karan show before Fashion Week began. The tents were already pitched in Bryant Park. Hotel rooms were sold out. There seemed to be models on every corner of the city.

My limo was waiting for me outside, but just as I was leaving my room, the bedside phone rang. "Hello?" I answered.

"Carré, my dear." It was Marie-Christine. I was happily working with her again. She had traveled with me to New York and was also staying at the Lowell. "We may have a small problem," she said.

"Oh, God. What now?" I had an idea of what the problem might be.

"It appears that your husband is here, in the city. He wants to get into the shows."

"What?" I shrieked. "Fuck him! That's not fair. That's not cool at all. . . ." My voice trailed off. My heart was pounding out of my chest. "Why can't the man just leave me alone for a minute? This is *my* work. This is what *I* do!" I was fuming, but also frightened. Mickey had already done so much to derail my modeling career. I was working again, out of his sight and out of his control. I knew how much that bothered him, and I knew what he was capable of doing to reassert that control.

"*Ma chère*, there is nothing we can do." M.C.'s voice was sympathetic but she was still delivering news I didn't want to hear. "Unless you have a restraining order, he can be at whatever show he likes."

"I understand that, but . . . but isn't there some alternative?" I persisted. The last thing I want to do is get to the end of a runway and stand face-to-face with him. Why does he have to do this?" Panic was setting in. As was the feeling that a scathing injustice was taking place. I felt like I was being stalked. I just wanted to be left alone so that I could do my job; I didn't need any more drama.

"We can do our best to find out what shows he will go to and avoid him. As well, we can make a request that he does not attend the shows you are in." I wasn't terribly assured by the solution, but I knew that was the best anyone could do.

"Okay. But please, please, M.C., get on the phone and try to sort this out before we go to the tents?" I begged.

I hung up the phone and took a deep breath. *It's going to be fine. I'm going to be fine,* I soothed myself. So what if I was walking into a fucking circus?!

My driver circled Bryant Park a few times as we determined which was the most secure way to enter the shows. The press had gathered at the main entrance, and I could already feel them descending like vultures. No doubt the story was out, and all I needed was a public run-in with Mickey.

"Here. Drop me here. I'll walk," I said, hoping that the paparazzi would have their eyes focused solely on the stretch limos that were pulling up in front of the main entrance. I stepped out of the car and into the gray fall afternoon, my Prada boots hitting the ground, my body ready to make a run for it.

"I'll see you after the show," the driver said. I nodded my thanks and hurried off through the gates, escaping the cameras that were still trained on the long line of limos. I wanted to avoid them at all costs.

A young guy with a walkie-talkie grabbed me by the arm and whisked me toward my first scheduled show. "Well, aren't you causing a stir!" he exclaimed in an expression of mock surprise, his tone and his eyes showing both amusement and sympathy.

"I know . . . can you believe it?" I laughed. "I just want the night to be over with."

He winked at me. "You'll be fine. Let's get you into hair and makeup."

Backstage was a blur of familiar madness. Half-naked models were being frantically swept through a production line, emerging at the other end coiffed and powdered. Wardrobe racks had been used to create temporary "dressing rooms," and each model's name, Polaroid, and list of outfit changes were hanging up. Their dressers were standing by, waiting for the green light that indicated the show had begun. Each show was the same. The same mayhem. The same setup. The same frenzy. And once the show began, the models would all line up and wait for someone to clap his or her hands and say, "Go!" or simply push them forward into the bright lights of the endless catwalk.

Some of the girls were great walkers. Totally confident. Some were not. It was hard for me to keep a straight face and harder still for me to walk a straight line. After all my experience, I simply wasn't good in heels. But I managed to get through the shows without a hitch. Outside, a media cyclone was brewing.

By now everyone knew that Mickey was at Fashion Week. Apparently I wasn't the only one to think that was nuts. Although he didn't get into the Donna Karan show, he was at many others, engaged in his usual front-row note taking, focusing not on the outfits that were paraded past him but on the girls who wore them. Typical Mickey style.

Just as I was exiting the tents to get back into my limo, I saw him. And he saw me. He stopped in his tracks, and looks of both pain and fury moved across his face. Neither of us wanted a public scene. I turned on my heel and began to walk quickly in another direction. I had no problem backing away. But a photographer spotted the perfect lineup and signaled to the other paparazzi. Through blinding camera flashes, I dashed down the block, frantically looking around to see where my car was parked. Out of the corner of my eye, I could see Mickey duck into his long white stretch limo, making his own escape from the madness. As soon as I could, I did the same. My car sped off, returning me to the Lowell in record time.

The next day the photos of our near encounter were all over the papers, eclipsing the coverage of the shows themselves. It was a nightmare. Whatever it did or didn't do for Mickey's career, I knew it wouldn't help mine. It was the shows and designers that should have been the stars of the day, not our stormy and scandalous marriage. No one in the industry liked headlines such as these. Least of all me.

As Fashion Week drew to a close, I stayed close to my Lowell hotel room, doing my best to avoid the spotlight. And then Saturday night rolled around, the last night of the shows. Marie-Christine called me.

"There is a big party at Club Expo. You should be there," she said.

"Why?" I asked. I was nearing the end of my rope. I was exhausted, out of sorts, and I just wanted to escape it all.

"Because it is the last night of our week, my dear. Let's send you off with style!" she said emphatically.

That was the great thing about M.C. I absolutely loved working with her because we always found ways to have fun together, even under the most adverse circumstances. I figured what the fuck—it's just another party. And she was right, it was important to have my face out there.

I pulled on my Manolo Blahnik patent-leather zip-up boots, black see-through tights, my signature black miniskirt, and a tiny camisole that barely covered my breasts. It was my usual club-going outfit. Teetering down the hallway, I rang at M.C.'s door and entered. She was still getting ready. She was in Chanel from head to toe. Unmistakably French.

Our first stop was a party at Café Tabac, stopping to chat with photographer Sante D'Orazio, who was dining with the model Georgina Grenville. We wandered over to where Patrick Demarchelier sat cross-legged and holding court at another smoky table.

Out of the blue, I heard a voice call, "Otis. Hey, Otis." It was Pinky, Mickey's assistant. "How's it going?" I didn't trust him. I looked around quickly to make sure Mickey wasn't somewhere in the restaurant.

"Fine, Pinky," I said coldly. "What do you want?" I took a long drag on my cigarette and blew the smoke toward him. Experience had taught me that however friendly and kind they might seem, every one of these boys had Mickey's back, and I needed to keep myself far, far from the enemy.

"Not to worry. Just passing through. Mick's not here—in case you were wondering," he said, looking at his feet and coughing through the cloud of smoke he tried vainly to wave away.

"I wasn't wondering, Pinky," I said smugly. And turned toward Marie-Christine.

"Where are you all going tonight?" Pinky pressed. Before I could answer, Marie-Christine let it slip. "Club Expo," she said without thinking.

I jabbed her sharply in the side and gave her an annoyed look.

"Now, why would you want to know that?" I turned again to Pinky, pulling myself up tall, standing well over six feet in my heels.

He shrank back and shrugged his shoulders. "No offense, Otis. Have a good night." And with that he was gone.

When I entered the pounding Club Expo it seemed like a million gorgeous models were on the dance floor, bumping and grinding to the loud music. Spotlights arced over the crowd, zooming from floor to ceiling, highlighting a sea of writhing bodies. And then I froze. One of the floodlights had found me. I stood there pinned in place, isolated and stone-still in the midst of the frenzy. Marie-Christine moved me toward the burly arms of one of the bouncers.

"Hey, Carré!" he shouted. "Let me show you to your table." Gratefully, I grabbed his arm and let myself be led through the crowd, up the stairs, and to a booth that was sectioned off with a red velvet rope. *This is ridiculous*, I told myself. I didn't need a VIP table. But somehow we had scored one, and M.C., who loved the good life, languished back in a chair and proceeded to order us drinks.

The club was like an amphitheater, with several different levels. The dance floor was below, and each tier had a view of it as well as a view of large screens projecting images onto the wall above. Getting my bearings and holding a fresh drink in my hand, I swayed from side to side, trying to find a rhythm in the maddening cacophony. The music was too loud to let us hold a conversation, so I looked over at M.C. and smiled. But I was uncomfortable. I felt as if I were on display. Every now and then, people looked up at me from the dance floor and held out their drinks in a toast of some sort. I couldn't shake the feeling that a plan of some kind was unfolding and that I was somehow in the dark. With Mickey in town, I felt as if trouble was always looming.

Moments later a ruckus broke out. There was a tussle in the crowd below, and then a group of men started to make their way up the steps, past the tier I was on. An argument ensued. I looked toward Marie-Christine but her eyes were locked on the cause of the commotion.

Just then, I spotted Tupac Shakur, the rapper and a longtime friend of Mickey's. He was followed by the whole gang. Mickey was in the center. My heart stopped. As the boys sat down, a bouncer came over to me. "Excuse me, Carré. I apologize, but it appears you are in Mickey's seat," he said nervously, half shouting into my ear over the din.

"What? Are you fucking serious?" I asked. This was too much. Who would have made a mistake like that? Flashbulbs were going off. I could barely see. I looked to M.C. for an explanation. Full-blown paranoia began setting in. I had been betrayed by so many people in this godforsaken industry already that in an instant I started to think the worst of everyone around me. Marie-Christine included. I had known her for years. *She couldn't have helped arrange this, could she?* I wondered. The Helena Rubinstein deal Mickey foiled had cost us both a lot of money, but I prayed she wasn't still upset with me for that. *Or was it my earlier run-in with Pinky?* Nothing with Mickey and his boys was ever coincidental. I put my drink down on the table and still confused, I muttered, "No problem. I'm ready to get the hell out of here anyway."

M.C. had come here ready to party, but she quickly gathered her things to follow me.

Before we could stand to leave, though, Tupac was hovering over me, extending a hand in a friendly manner.

"Yo, Otis," he said, smiling with his molasses eyes.

"Tupac, hey." I grabbed his hand and shook it, smiling back. He was an impressive artist, and it was a pleasure to meet him, regardless of the circumstances. "Otis, Mickey misses you!" he yelled over the roar of music.

"Yeah, Tupac . . . come on. You don't need to get into the middle of this. If Mick needs to talk to me, he's a big boy," I said. Then I stood up and began to make my way along the tier toward the exit sign, grasping the red rope to help me navigate my way. Unfortunately, I had to pass Mickey to get to the stairs. I kept my eyes on the floor to avoid any contact.

But then I felt a hand on mine. A warm, familiar hand. I looked up, and my eyes met Mickey's. Everything in the club faded away. The lights, the sounds, the frenzy—all seemed to quiet as we stood there in our own bubble. I held my breath. I wanted to hug him. I wanted to cry. But in an instant the rush of the club came back at me, flashbulbs going off again. Mickey leaned toward me, and in my ear, loud enough for only me to hear, he said, "I miss you so much." I leaned my forehead into his, a private moment in a public place. It was just like a kiss. A kiss of the spirit.

"I miss you, too, Mick," and with that I forced myself away, turning my back on the club and stepping into the cool October night. What a rush. A soul-breaking rush. My heart pounded with sorrow, my breath was quick with longing. I wanted to go home. I needed to go home.

Thankfully, I soon got what I needed. Less than twenty-four hours later, on a Sunday afternoon, I got a call from my lawyer informing me that the case had been dropped. The D.A. could do nothing without my help. They had decided not to prosecute me if I failed to testify. I could come back to L.A. Back to my dogs. Back to my own reality.

I had one or two more jobs booked before I could leave New York. Early the next morning I showed up for the first shoot and met the only other model booked for that day: Myka Summers. We couldn't have been more different, but those differences seemed to work.

As the rain poured down outside, Myka and I hung around in the makeup room, cracking jokes, comparing our tastes in music, and smoking cigarettes. There was something about her I liked, and I usually didn't get along well with other models. But Myka wasn't just any model. She was a rebel. And she was gay. I had a thing for boyish-looking girls, but I was particularly drawn to her unique brand of androgyny. She had a ripped, muscular body, angular cheekbones, voluptuously full lips, shaggy blond hair, dark eyes—and I don't just mean in color. But what intrigued me most was the way she wore her jeans slung low enough to reveal her men's briefs underneath, Marky Mark style. She seemed infinitely beddable and her mischievous air just added to the allure.

"Let's hang out tonight," she suggested. "My girlfriend, Heather, is in town. We can come to your place?" I liked the idea. A little New York farewell party was definitely in order.

"Cool. Come on over," I answered with a wink. Who knew what was in store? I was up for it.

And that was my first intro to the heroin so many other people seemed to be doing. Myka and her girlfriend arrived at the Lowell, and they soon pulled out their bag of tricks. As she lit up the foil and inhaled through her metal straw, she offered a few warnings that sounded more like a disclaimer from a doctor's office. "This is addictive, okay, Otis?" she said, coughing as she exhaled the drug. Rolling over backward and laughing hysterically, she handed me the hookup. "And you simply have to try this."

What can I say? It was better than any sex I'd had at that point in my life. It was absolutely awesome. It was exactly what I'd been looking for. I was tired of running. Tired of trying to get high enough to leave my hardships behind. But now, thanks to heroin, a new world seemed to open up to me. I didn't know yet that nothing would be as good as the first hit. I didn't know yet the true meaning of the phrase "chasing the dragon."

I awoke in the morning with two naked women sprawled next to me, both of whom were passed out. But I had a flight to catch. I climbed my way over their gorgeous bare asses and laid myself on top of Myka.

"Yum," I said in her ear.

"I know, Carré, yum," she said in a sleepy voice. I kissed her ear, and she turned to face me. After blinking a few times, she broke out into laughter.

"Dude! Look at your nose! Rug burn, baby!" She chuckled, kissing the end of it. I frowned, not having a clue what she was talking about. "Go look in the mirror. Your cherry was popped, baaabbbby!" She laughed again. I rolled off her and stood up, and as I walked toward the mirror, she slapped my naked butt.

"Oh, shit! What the fuck?" I vaguely recalled needing to scratch all night and rubbing my nose to relieve what seemed like the great primordial itch. I had apparently rubbed it raw. "Damn it, Myka!" But I started laughing, too.

"Catch your flight, babe," Myka said. "We'll see you in L.A."

I jumped into the shower, got dressed, and grabbed my bag. I was finally heading home.

HITTING BOTTOM, HEADING SOUTH

Ask anyone who has struggled with addiction and then recovered: There's always a moment when you realize you've finally hit your bottom. For me that moment came in early 1995. It was the year that everything I'd been trying to deny finally came out into the open. It was the year that all the tricks I'd used to fill the void inside me finally stopped working.

After being allowed to return to L.A. at last, I couldn't wait to be back in my little place on Orlando, in the heart of Los Angeles. I wasn't entirely alone. I now had our six Chihuahuas by my side: Angel, Beau Jack, Chocolate, Monkey, Romi, and Loki were my constant and loving companions. I loved my small house because it was mine. Mickey didn't call the shots there. I did. I needed a safe place to regroup, and it seemed

I had found it. I came back from New York with something else that made me feel safe, at least for a while. Heroin.

Myka Summers and her girlfriend followed me from the East Coast. Within a few weeks, they were crashing at my place. It wasn't always pretty. Heather was submissive, while Myka, as it turns out, was prone to violence. There was more than one physical battle I had to break up during their stay.

A few days after their arrival, Myka and I were sitting on the living-room floor of the Orlando house, listening to music and hanging out with the pups. She pulled out a small dark leather purse. It was her "kit," and in it was some tinfoil, a straw, a lighter, and a dab of white powder. The powder was China White. I'd been hoping she would get me high again, as we'd done in New York. I was hugely relieved I wouldn't have to ask.

That first inhalation was almost indescribably good, better than I remembered. I thought I was dying, and I didn't care. No fear. Just total surrender. It's somewhere on the edge between orgasm and death. In an instant the pain, the fear, and the constant crushing loneliness I'd felt for so long vanished. I was riding that dragon, and it was sweeter than anything I'd ever felt. And as soon as it was gone, I wanted it back.

I fell fast. After Myka and her girlfriend left, my life was all about the score. My days became very focused. Everything I did during my waking hours was about getting my hands on more heroin and staying high. I fell in love with the ritual of using. I loved the sound of the tinfoil in my hand, the smell of the China White or the Black Tar cooking, the feel of the straw between my lips. All else went by the wayside. I ignored friends, agents, bills, phone calls, and the ever-growing number of answering-machine messages. The one responsibility I didn't neglect was caring for the dogs: No matter how high I got, no matter how desperate for a hit I became, I never let my babies go unfed or ignored. (Years after we divorced, Mickey would tell Barbara Walters that our dogs saved his life. As bad as he got, he, too, never fell so low as to let these small and loving creatures suffer. It was one thing we had in common.)

I was slipping down, and slipping down fast. In one sense it was hard to notice. Because of Mickey I had been so walled off from the rest of the world that I'd lost my sense of connection with most other people. Since depression and loneliness had become familiar to me before I ever started using heroin, I didn't notice how much worse those feelings had gotten after I was hooked. But on the other hand, I was lucky: I fell so far and so fast that it would quickly become impossible to deny that I had a serious problem. My life was out of control.

As Los Angeles slipped into what seemed to be a particularly cold and wet winter, something shifted in me. My days had become like the weather, a gray and depressing blur. My body ached, and my bones felt cold. A weariness permeated every high and the spaces in between. I wasn't riding the dragon anymore, I was chasing it—and falling farther behind. Rather than give me that ecstatic sense of freedom and bliss I craved, the drug left me in a near-constant state of oppressive despair. Each high was now only a few frantic, scrambling seconds long, and filled with struggle as I tried to escape the darkness that would quickly envelop me afterward. The heroin had stopped working. And I was ready to quit.

I realized that my body was addicted, but I was completely unaware of how tough it would be to withdraw. Myka had already warned me that I was past the point where quitting would be easy. I didn't listen. I knew I could handle a lot, and I was convinced I could kick the drug in one hard weekend. How wrong I was. Opiate addiction (heroin is an opiate) is widely considered one of the toughest addictions to overcome. Once hooked, the body becomes so dependent on the drug that withdrawal is not only prolonged and painful but also very dangerous. It's not unheard of for addicts to die of the consequences of going through a medically unsupervised withdrawal. I didn't know this at the time, and even if I had been cautioned, I'm not sure I would have listened. I was confident in my ability to accomplish anything, including ridding my body of this addiction on my own.

I started the withdrawal on a Friday, figuring it might take me until Sunday to finish the detox. Rain poured down, flooding my little patio, which I watched silently from beneath a pile of blankets on my king-size bed. The dogs stayed close, sensing something ominous. It was one of the few times I heard thunder overhead from my home in L.A. I was expecting a range of symptoms, like headaches, perhaps some nausea, and general discomfort. But nothing could have prepared me for what I faced that weekend. By late Friday night, I was in real pain, and I was terrified, scared shitless that it would only get worse. It was an ugly situation, getting uglier by the hour. And there was no way around it, no way but straight through the fire. By Saturday morning I was like a caged animal—sweating, vomiting, shaking, unable to stand. In my agony it was the first time I realized just how much trouble I'd gotten myself into. I couldn't do this, not alone.

Saturday afternoon I threw in the towel. I was done. Defeated. It was one of the worst moments of my life, as I realized how helpless I was in the face of this addiction.

Myka was back in town crashing at my place again between jobs. Exhausted and ashamed, I went into the room where she was staying. "I can't do it," I cried to her. "I can't take any more." Beads of sweat were on my brow, my hands trembling. As my desperate gaze lifted to meet Myka's, I watched her smile slyly. It was as if she had known all along that I wouldn't make it out. Without a word she handed me her kit, straw and all. And seconds later I was high again.

I knew I needed to do something. Convinced now that I couldn't kick it on my own, I searched my mind for the name of someone, anyone who might be able to help. Not knowing whom I could turn to and feeling completely defeated as a result of my first failed detox, I put off reaching out for help. I kept using, slipping further into a dark abyss. I was truly fucked.

A few weeks slipped by, and then Mickey called. It was out of the blue, but we all knew that Mick kept tabs on me. He had heard rumors that I was strung out, and he was worried. I was so beat up by the drug that by the time he came around, I couldn't turn him away. At that point he seemed like a welcome old friend, which in a sense he was. It was clear to me that we still cared for each other, and after a fair amount of time apart from him I wanted to believe that he was coming to me less as a lover and more as someone who was concerned enough to help. For all the drama in his life, Mickey had never been hooked on street drugs. Mickey had, however, helped his own brother, Joey, quit drugs. He knew firsthand what was involved in getting clean.

As it turned out, Mickey did genuinely want to help me, but he also wanted me back in his life, by his side as his wife. Even in the throes of my addiction, I was conflicted about that. I'd had a lot of time to reflect in our months apart. As so often happens during a separation, I'd gotten a chance to heal a bit from my dependency on Mickey, even as I'd become dependent on something else. I had also begun to see someone new, a man closer to my own age, a guy with a regular job and the capacity to be present on a regular basis. Seeing him was giving me a new perspective on what I could possibly have in my life. But I also knew that until I was clean and sober, I couldn't weigh anything out. As normal as this guy was, he also had an addiction. The fact that I considered that to be normal is a pretty good indication of how distorted my sense of reality was at that point.

Mickey and I had a long discussion. He wanted me back, yes, but he also wanted me clean. He told me about a treatment center in Ensenada, Mexico, where they offered a cure for opiate addiction called Rapid Detox. Invented by a remarkable Israeli doctor named Andre Waismann, Rapid Detox is a radical procedure that reverses addiction to heroin and other opiates. Done under general anesthesia, Rapid Detox accomplishes in less than twenty-four hours what normally requires up to two weeks of agonizing and dangerous withdrawal. Today Rapid Detox is approved for use in the United States, and Dr. Waismann himself operates a world-famous medical center in Israel. But in the mid-1990s, this cutting-edge treatment was not yet available in the United States. If I wanted help, I would need to go south of the border.

I was excited by the possibilities. The idea of kicking drugs under anesthesia seemed almost too good to be true. I knew damned well that if I kept using, I was going to die. And I sure as hell didn't want that. I was in a prison, one that I had built around myself, and I was willing to do just about anything to get out. Rapid Detox sounded like a promising solution.

But I was scared for another reason. I didn't want this recovery to be about Mickey. I knew that if he was the one who made it possible for me to be free from drugs, then I wouldn't be truly free. I would be indebted to him again. Mickey has always been marvelous at playing the part of the knight in shining armor coming to the rescue of the damsel in distress. It was one of the qualities that had first drawn me to him. Mickey truly "got" me in a way that few others did, and I felt very early on that he could help me in a way no one else could. After all we'd been through together, here I was back where he wanted me—dependent upon him, needing his help once more.

I almost refused Mickey's offer. But I knew that I couldn't afford to. I was running out of time and options. I needed his help to help me save myself. And so, knowing that it was a risk, I told Mickey yes. Yes, I would let him take me to Mexico. Yes, I would let him pay for my treatment. And Mickey did pay—ten thousand dollars in cash. But even as I said yes, I knew in my gut that I wanted this for myself. Somehow, whatever Mickey's role was, I was going to own my sobriety. It would be mine and mine alone.

While Mickey made some calls to plan our trip, I phoned my dealer and got my last stash: eight colored balloons, tightly wound and knotted. Inside them was enough heroin to get me through the next twenty-four hours, across the border and into treatment. I packed a small bag and made arrangements for my six Chihuahuas to be cared for by a friend. I also told Myka she needed to leave my home before I returned. No arguments. I knew that Myka wasn't the only one to blame for my addiction, but I also knew that if I was going to get clean, it was time to cut that particular cord once and for all.

Mickey and I loaded up our old '69 Road Runner hot rod. It was the same car we'd driven cross-country on our honeymoon less than two years earlier. Damn, that time seemed far away. Who would have guessed that Mickey and I would end up where we were now, packing for another trip down the interstate? What mattered to Mickey was that we were together again on another adventure. What mattered to me was that I got a chance, maybe my last chance, to take my life back.

We took off from L.A. in the early morning. And as the sun rose, I got high. We blasted U2, told stories, smoked cigarettes, and Mick did his best not to scowl every time I lit up my straw. I remember that I couldn't really get high. The game was over. I was actually done, and I knew it. But what I didn't yet know was exactly how to stop and stay stopped.

We crossed the border uneventfully, the sun high in the sky. As we headed down to Ensenada, the Pacific stretched out to the right of our car, a vast expanse of the deepest blue for as far as the eye could see. I could feel how tired I was, tired of the life I'd been living, tired of running. I felt like I'd been running all my life. I was ready to be still. I was ready to rest.

We reached Ensenada. Following the directions, we pulled into a cobblestone driveway lined with swaying palm trees. This was the hotel we would be in before and after I underwent the treatment. As we approached, I swallowed hard—and realized that my hands were clammy. I didn't feel well at all. Our arrival could not have come a minute too soon.

A petite woman emerged from the hotel and cheerfully waved us to a stop. She had a strong yet slender body, dark wavy hair, a pleasant face, and piercing blue eyes. Laughing, she remarked that only we could have arrived in a "car like that." I suppose our periwinkle hot rod was a bit out of place.

The woman was Clare Waismann, sister of Andre and director of the treatment center. The moment she spoke, I knew she would become a friend. Her manner was soft and safe but also very firm and certain. Clare had seen it all, done it all, and at one point had gone through the Rapid Detox treatment herself. Despite her tiny frame, I wanted to crawl into her lap and cry. Clare seemed to notice my vulnerability and made a point of directing Mickey to his room while taking me aside so we could "chat."

The hotel was an extension of the hospital. It was by no means beautiful, but it was comfortable. Clare led me to her office, a converted bedroom with a breathtaking view of the ocean, the sky, and the crashing waves below. She knew I was scared. She acknowledged my fear. And in her gentle yet strong manner, Clare dove right into answering my questions. She explained that it was her brother, the famed Dr. Waismann, who would oversee my treatment. Andre, she told me, had performed this Rapid Detox procedure on hundreds of people— from babies born addicted to drugs and their addict mothers to other doctors, and of course, celebrities.

This was the first time that I realized how widespread opiate addiction was—and still is. Opiates include not only street drugs like heroin but medications like morphine and codeine. True opiates are derived from the opium poppy plant, but in the treatment community the term "opiate" is widely used to refer to other synthetic drugs that work the same way in the body. In this sense, opiates include prescription drugs as diverse as Valium, OxyContin, Dilaudid, and Vicodin. A lot of suburban housewives are hooked on these drugs, as are millions of other people around the world. One thing that all the opiates have in common: They're hard drugs to kick. Detoxing from a prescription-pill addiction can be as tough and dangerous as detoxing from heroin.

Clare also wanted to talk with me about Mickey. She was concerned that his presence would put me under greater stress and would jeopardize my recovery process. Almost as important, she was worried that he might take advantage of my vulnerability and pressure me to recommit to our marriage. I agreed with her; I was worried about that myself. But Mickey had driven me down from Los Angeles, and Mickey was paying the tab for my treatment. The whole trip had been Mickey's idea.

Talking to Clare, looking out at the serene sky and the sea from her office window, I realized that this had always been part of Mickey's pattern with me. On the one hand, I really believed he wanted to be my rescuer—and on the other hand, I couldn't help but think that he wanted to crush any sign of independence in me. I remembered how strong I'd been when we first met. I had just come off that retreat in Ojai, and though I was only nineteen, I was so sure of myself and my place in the world. Mickey had been instantly attracted to those qualities, to how centered I was. As time went on I think he grew to love and hate that strength. He seemed to take it as a challenge until somewhere along the way, it became a sport for him to try to break me, to make me dependent upon him. If I was right and that was his aim, consciously or unconsciously, he had succeeded, at least for a period of time. But we had both paid a price for that. Sitting there in Ensenada, I could feel again just how high that price had been.

At that particular moment, I didn't doubt that Mickey wanted me well, though his fear that I might leave him once I was healed was palpable.

What was interesting was that Clare didn't give a shit who Mickey was. She had a lioness's heart and would not be intimidated by him or anyone else. She saw me as an individual separate from him. She cared about my recovery and my growth. And she was determined to see me overcome every challenge. She saw the dynamic that lay behind Mickey's decision to bring me down to Ensenada. And she wasn't going to let him do anything to interfere with my detox and the healing process that would follow it.

Everything happened quickly, smoothly, and efficiently under Clare's watch. The cash was handed over, and I entered the hospital. I was led down a long hallway to the room I would occupy. It was clean and bright; like her office, it had a spectacular view of the ocean. I dropped my bag and went over to the window. Looking out at the vast expanse of sky and water, I took a deep breath and said a prayer, letting my mind drift and merge with the infinite. *To all the Buddhas*

out there, may I be protected and may I return soon to you. A big tear
slid down my cheek. I longed for my parents. I wanted to be with my
family. To go back in time, to be held and reassured. I was so far from
home.

Clare and Andre came in while the nurses prepped me. They told
me I would be under anesthesia for up to eight hours while they administered the drug that produced the Rapid Detox. During those eight
hours, my body would go through what it would in any detox—sneez-
ing, vomiting, convulsing, and so on—but I would be monitored medically the entire time. I could expect to wake up and feel like hell, but I
could also expect to be free of any physical symptoms of withdrawal.
That was the first step.

The next step would be getting my energy back and dealing with
my mind. I would need to face all the reasons I'd gotten myself into this
situation in the first place. Even before I went under, that was the part
I was most scared about. Andre told me that many addicts come out of
this treatment and keep their eyes shut for a long time. He wanted to
remind me that when I awoke, it would be time to truly open my eyes.
"Get ready to see a new world, my dear," he said with a reassuring hug.

I do remember counting backward and the room fading to black.
And although they say you really can't remember anything from the
treatment, I do recall something—the sounds. As powerful as the anesthesia was, it couldn't stop me from hearing those otherworldly sounds
emanating from my body. The memory of those unforgettable sounds
brings tears to my eyes today.

Clare and Andre hadn't been joking when they said I would wake
up and feel as if I'd been hit by a train. It was horrible. Every muscle
in my body was sore. Every hair follicle hurt. My skin, my eyes, my
joints, my limbs—it all seemed to be one throbbing ache. Andre and
Clare were there to greet me when I came to. Their smiles were encouraging. They informed me that I had done very well. "Rest," they
said gently. The next twenty-four hours passed in a daze. I floated in
and out of an uncomfortable sleep. I was cold and then hot, sweating

and then freezing. As I was told, these symptoms were all part of the flushing process.

I was moved back into the hotel to regain my strength. It was a very emotional time. I was flooded with uncertainty, overwhelmed with emotions. So much had been blocked while I was addicted, and now those blockages had been removed. I was overcome with fear. I was on the border of a black depression. But at the same time, I felt something wonderful. I knew I was on my way back to health, to being myself again. I knew that I had taken a huge step on my way toward a life of balance. During those first few days, I spent what seemed like endless hours watching the surf on the beach. With a sea of emotions let loose inside me, I felt as if I were made of ocean, nothing but the pounding waves, the endless ebb and flow. I felt a sense of total surrender. A big part of me was gone, but another part of me was becoming whole.

Having Mickey around during this stage proved to be harrowing. We had both wanted to get me off heroin. But now that I was clean, this concern had morphed into constant, needy demands from him. As predicted, he wanted me to make a decision about our marriage and our life together. He had gone from bringing me into recovery to being the biggest threat to that recovery. I was in no shape to answer his endless questions about what would happen to us. I felt cornered, my back against the wall. I was drained. I didn't have the strength yet to fight him. Though somewhere within I was able to identify the emotion of anger. Mickey was nearly twenty years my senior, and yet here he was trying to get *me* to take care of *him*, to soothe *his* anxieties. It was so fucking typical, and so fucking inappropriate at a time like this.

As Mickey's demands grew, Clare and Andre intervened. They made it clear that I needed time to focus on my recovery without any interference. They were really quite firm with him about this, and I was so thankful to have them setting limits that I wasn't ready to set myself. It would be several years before I could successfully implement my own boundaries around Mickey. He wasn't pleased, of course, but he was forced to give me the space I desperately needed.

Andre had been right. My eyes were open. I was seeing a whole new world, and a whole new reality. Not all of it was pretty; in fact, most of it wasn't. And it was clear to me that by coming down to Ensenada to get clean, I had only just begun. Back home I had a big mess to clean up. I would have to deal with friends, habits, places I frequented; I would have to cut unhealthy ties (as I had done with Myka) and create new, healthy ones. I would have to deal with Mickey. But one thing was certain: I was on my way. I had taken the first and the hardest step.

When I had said yes to Mickey's request that I come to Ensenada, I had said "Yes!" to living. "Yes!" to changing my life. And I knew now that there wasn't anything I wouldn't do to stay on the path of recovery. You don't get many chances when you're a hard-core addict. You don't have many opportunities to find your way out. Heroin had brought me to my knees; Mickey had brought me to Mexico; Clare and Andre had brought me to this point of clarity. It was a powerful confluence of circumstances. It was a perfect storm in my life, a perfect storm that created an opening, a grace-filled clearing, for me to walk through. Once I was on the other side, there was no turning back. Although the task at hand—changing everything about my life—was daunting, I was determined.

Somehow Mickey and I managed to get through the last few days in Mexico without completely collapsing. He was hurt and scared. Now that I'd gone through the treatment, he was even more frightened than I was. He knew he had a lot to lose and that the likelihood of losing it had just increased. Between us there were many secrets and painful truths being revealed. But whatever the truth might do to Mickey, it was paving my way for a new life. As we left Ensenada for the long drive home, a new strength was rising up in me, giving me the courage and confidence to not only go home but to transform my life when I got there. I was readying myself for whatever might come.

And boy, oh, boy, was something coming.

EARLY SOBRIETY

A few months later, I was living in Beverly Hills, clean and sober. I had been on Tranxene to help with the detox and was finally feeling the kind of stability I had enjoyed at the farm. Outwardly my life still looked the same; I was living with Mickey again. But inwardly I felt that a shift was under way. Having found a chance at peace, I desperately wanted to maintain some sense of equilibrium in my day-to-day life.

I knew the odds. Living with Mickey had its risks. There was our medicine cabinet full of prescription drugs and there was the pressure of simply being in our incredibly volatile marriage that had me on edge. And that edge was a very slippery place for a newly sober individual. I was fighting to get my feet under me, create a routine, and interact with a newfound support system. Neither of us was ready for me to leave him behind. I didn't yet know that for me to continue my growth this was exactly what I would have to do. Nor did I know that my leaving him might actually benefit him as well.

In the meantime I waited and watched. Observing Mickey, I was beginning to realize that actions speak louder than words. He had decided to go to Paris and film the sequel to the famed 9½ Weeks with Angie Everhart. I was opposed to it. But again my opinion did not seem to matter. When asked if I would join him in Paris, I opted not to, knowing that if I made my life Mickey's life, I would end up in real trouble again. I'd seen how my drug use could escalate to the point that it threatened everything. I was taking my recovery seriously, and that meant not putting myself in a situation where I'd be likely to relapse.

Mickey seemed both relieved and furious. Relieved, in all likelihood that he would have the freedom to indulge himself in yet another sex-filled movie role without me watching over his shoulder, and furious probably because he was losing his control over me. I could see all this from the new perspective I had, and although I was not yet willing to leave him, the picture I was starting to see was far from pretty.

Just before Mickey left for Paris, I'd undergone a laminectomy for a back issue that had been bothering me for years. Unfortunately, post-surgery I began to experience severe pain in my foot. Night after night I would lie awake, a tickling sensation running down my leg and a maddening nerve pain thumping away. Because I was also on Naltrex-one, an opioid receptor blocker, pain meds were useless. Naltrexone kept me from getting high, but it also kept me from getting relief.

I don't even remember how she found me, but an angel walked into my life at that time, in the form of ex-model Rita Souki. Rita was a forty-year-old bombshell from New Jersey. She had modeled in the day with Janice Dickinson, Joan Severance, Kim Alexis, and Gia. Dark and gorgeous, with two beautiful kids, she was introduced to me at a dinner party for my old client Paul Guez of the Marciano Brothers and Guess Jeans. Rita and I had laughed loudly, gotten along easily, and exchanged numbers.

Mickey was gone for a few months, though he'd call incessantly, usually in the middle of the night California time. Despite my need to recuperate and find alternative and healthy options to manage my pain, he'd beg me to come visit him. Again, things were not going as well as planned on the set.

"Mickey, I can't. I need to heal," I would cry in the phone.

"You can't or you won't?" he would demand, angry that I wouldn't just get on a flight to take care of his needs.

"Sitting for ten hours would be the worst thing for my back, Mickey. I can't do it." And as I said those words, I heard his question again, and the answer came to me more clearly: "Actually, you're right, Mick. I *won't* do it, because it's not okay for me to do it." I was beginning to see his self-ishness and to really dislike who he was. What's more, I was beginning to see myself, too, and to recognize the need to make my own demands.

Then, for the first time ever, I hung up on him.

I was terrified yet exhilarated. I had power over myself, control over my life. I had a choice in what I did and how I lived. Imagine that. The phone rang again and again—until I finally unplugged it.

And this is when Rita appeared, dropping by for a welcome visit. Standing at the foot of the bed in which I lay recuperating, she put her hands on her hips and looked around our rental. "You've got to be kidding me. This is where you guys live?" she said. "This is your bedroom and that's Mickey's?" she asked, pointing down the hall, looking baffled.

"Yeah. What of it?" I asked, not understanding her point.

"You are how old? And you have separate bedrooms? Carré, you're young and beautiful. Don't you fucking dare give your life up to this shit!" she declared, her voice firm and yet matter-of-fact. "Get the fuck out of bed. You're coming with me." And with that, Rita was in my life. She was amazing, both empowered and empowering. She would save my ass in more ways than one.

We spent the next month hanging out at her house—by the pool, sunbathing, going to the gym, eating healthily. We had dinner with her husband and kids, making home-cooked meals and barbecuing. It seemed like forever since I'd had a girlfriend, an ally, a family. I wanted the life they had. It nourished me to the core.

I confided in Rita, sharing with her all that I couldn't share with anyone else. She, too, had sisters, had grown up witnessing abuse, and had her own secrets. She helped me see clearly where I was at and that the situation I was in with Mickey was neither normal nor healthy. She also encouraged me to get help and go to therapy.

I had a week before Mickey was due home. And I decided that a move was in store. Rita lived on San Vicente, so I had begun to know the beach area as well as Santa Monica. I wasn't ready to leave Mickey, but I was ready for a change. I wanted to get out of the neighborhood that we'd been living in for so long and settle in one that fed me, that supported the lifestyle I knew would help me remain healthy long-term. Beverly Hills had ghosts and shadows for me, whereas Santa Monica was untainted, fresh, and bright. I found a house on Ocean and Sixth, and when Mickey arrived back home, I announced that we were moving.

He was so stunned he couldn't argue. He sensed a profound shift in me, and in a way I know that it terrified him. I felt compassion toward that fear. Change is scary. The steps I was taking required a tremendous amount of courage on my part, but that courage was rooted in the realization that falling back and silencing myself ever again would only lead to my death. And I wasn't ready to die.

LEAVING MICKEY

The Santa Monica house was a charming two-story Craftsman with many rooms and hideaway spots. In all the time we were together, this was the first house I had chosen for us to live in, and it reflected my San Franciscan roots. The majority of my days were spent outdoors, running along the water's edge or working out at Gold's Gym in Venice. I could bicycle everywhere and loved the intimate sense of community the area provided.

Mickey, on the other hand, seemed unaffected by the new access to an outdoor lifestyle. He had a separate room on the main floor, with windows that he covered in tinfoil and an air conditioner that pumped freezing winds into his room. I would jokingly call it his igloo. I literally had to wear a coat whenever I went in to visit him.

I was thriving in this environment. And so were my beloved four-legged friends. Somehow, as depressing as Mickey's energy was, I was motivated to get up and out from the very first light of day. It wasn't unusual for us to pass each other at the front door; Mickey would be coming home from a night of raging, and I would be heading out for an invigorating morning jog. We were on two different planets, solitarily orbiting a shared sun.

My room was in the back of the house. French doors opened onto a small patio; there was a wonderful little loft above it with a second deck. Here I created my space, a small office and practice area. I could sit in silence and watch the sunset, hear the waves crashing on the shore. It was a slice of heaven. Finally.

It was clear that Mickey and I were growing apart and had become estranged in many ways. We hadn't had sex in over a year, which was fine by me. I was certain that he'd been sleeping around for some time and didn't trust that he was going to great lengths to protect himself or me from any type of STDs. I had grown tired of the fight. It was so much easier not to talk.

And so it was that one morning as we passed each other in our hallway, Mickey asked, "Aren't you going to say anything, Otis?"

"Like what, Mickey?" I looked him in the eye.

"Like, 'Where have you been?' Don't you wonder?" he asked me, trying to push my buttons.

"No. I don't. Not anymore, Mickey. I know where you've been." And as I said these words, I realized I couldn't continue to care in the ways I previously had. It was as if the spell was broken. The part of me that had been all-consumed, the part of me that was obsessed and addicted and hooked—it was liberated. I was free. Or well on the way to being free.

Mickey didn't like this. He tried to tighten his hold. I realized I was going to need support if I were ever to take the next steps in reclaiming my life. I needed to find a therapist, just as Rita had recommended; I needed to understand how and why I'd ended up where I was. And determine where I wanted to go next.

I found Dr. Nancy Sobel, and she soon became an integral part of my life and healing process. She gave me encouragement and steadfast support, and she invited deep reflection. She asked hefty questions that I didn't always know the answers to. She got me thinking.

Mickey was angry about this choice. He saw therapists—as well as friendships outside of those he had preapproved—as a threat. I was able to endure his constant verbal criticism of these people, although I was worried about the threats he made toward them. I was never too sure how far he would go with his violence.

I decided to hide my therapy sessions from him, willing to take the risk of being discovered. I knew that most likely Mickey was still having me followed and that the phones were probably tapped. I'd learned to navigate around these roadblocks. I had to continue to live my life and get the help and support I needed to stay sane and sober. My "normal" was unlike other people's. I'd learned to work with it.

One day, as I was sitting in Nancy's office, she said, "You know, Carré, you have really changed."

"How so?" I smiled, sensing that it was true and wanting to hear her thoughts.

"When you first came here, you were a shell of who you are now. Like a shadow. Now you embody yourself. I can be here with you. You are *present*." She smiled back.

"It must be scary to have to move between these worlds that you are in: to have to go home and not be this full and powerful." She looked at me with love and concern. I knew that she was holding a place for me to come into my full power. Somehow I knew that she could already see the woman I would become, even though I couldn't see it just yet.

I thought for a moment about what she was saying. The majority of my present life was spent living separately from my husband, even though we inhabited the same house. Now the hardest part of being with him was to lie and pretend that I wasn't growing. Why would I do that? Why would I need to? And why would I continue to make that choice? To be anywhere other than in my full glory. Why would I choose not to shine?

Nancy continued. "How would that look, Carré? A life without Mickey?" she asked.

The question made me nervous. My heart skipped a beat. My eyes misted. Free-associating, I began to speak.

"It would be scary. It would be unknown. I've been with him for so long. I would be scared for *him*. What if he wouldn't be okay? Who would take care of him? What if he took too many pills? What if he died? He doesn't really have anyone honest around him, anyone that gives a shit. . . ." My voice trailed off as I realized I was speaking only about Mickey and how it might be for *him* if I left. Talk about codependent! I was so conditioned to not think about myself. I laughed out loud.

"Okay. Let me try this again." I took a big breath and began. "It *would* be scary. It would be venturing into the *unknown*. It would be great. It would be freeing. It would be challenging. It would be my life. I wouldn't have to lie. I could really grow and become who I know I'm meant to be." The tears came again. There was some sense of grieving that was taking place. I was beginning to mourn the death of a relationship as well as the death of the unhealthy young girl who'd been ruling my life. "The problem is, I don't know how to get from here to there."

Nancy smiled and nodded. She understood. There was no pressure, just discussion.

"Would you like to talk about that? How to get from here to there?" she asked.

I thought for a moment, then looked up at her. "Yes," I said with absolute certainty. "Yes."

I knew that for me to leave, I would have to realistically address some of the concerns I had about Mickey's well-being. "Can you recommend a therapist for him? I don't know if he would ever go, but I would like to try to have a number for him to call," I said.

"Of course, Carré. That's a great idea. What else would it take for you to be able to leave?" I knew that this was one of her areas of expertise, dealing with domestic violence and finding safe houses for the women who were ready to leave their situations.

"I would want to take my dogs. I could never leave them behind. I would also need to . . . have a safe place where Mickey would not be able to find me." I was thinking it all through.

"Are you scared he might come after you?"

"Not so much that . . . It's just that I know how hard it is to be badgered by him. And that my chances of really leaving him, for good this time, will depend on my having a place he can't get to. Inside and out. Emotionally and physically." And it was true; I wasn't scared of him physically anymore, although several friends warned me that my mind-set was naïve. I was sounding to them like a textbook case of someone unwittingly falling into victim mode again.

I knew myself well enough to be honest about what it would take for my attempt to be successful. I had to cut him out entirely, extract myself from our very enmeshed lives. Down to our accountants and friends, he had infiltrated every aspect of my life. From past experience I knew that Mickey could get just about anybody to give him the information he wanted. He was an absolute master manipulator.

"What if I told you that I knew of a house that will be available in the next month? A perfect safe place with a backyard for your dogs, tucked into a quiet neighborhood in the Pacific Palisades?" Nancy asked, as if testing my sincerity.

Excitement sparked in me and I sat up eagerly, only to slouch back down with a sigh of doubt. "I'm scared," I said simply.

"I understand. I'm not going to lie and tell you it won't be scary. That is part of life and change. But I will tell you right now you can do this. And you are ready to do this."

I knew that it was true. I also knew that there had to be a method to the extraction process.

"Okay. Let me give it some thought. Let me see if I can convince Mickey to see a therapist. Let's go from there." With that, our session was over. I was out the door with a lot to consider.

Within a few days, I knew that I could and would do it. I knew that I was ready. So I began to organize the details that would enable me to leave. I got a new credit card with my own account that couldn't be traced. I made a reservation at a hotel under another name. I began to pack my belongings and then secretly took them from the house—a few boxes at a time—and put them into storage. I didn't have much. I didn't want to take anything that was Mickey's. I just wanted out.

Mickey agreed to go to therapy, and I set up an appointment for him to see an addiction specialist whom Nancy had recommended. My husband was at an all-time low, and the antidepressants and antianxiety meds he'd been on clearly weren't working. It was an enormous relief for me to know that at the very least he had someone to go to who was a professional and might really give him sound advice. I had tremendous compassion and concern, desperately wanting Mickey to have the opportunity to work on himself and his life. I wanted to see him happy. Even if from afar.

Within a week my clothing was moved out, and although Mickey didn't know it, my room lay empty. I organized a joint therapy session and, when asked, told him not to worry, that it was no big deal. Just a check-in on neutral ground.

It was on an afternoon in early March of 1997 that we met in the doctor's Beverly Hills office. Mickey and I came separately. When I arrived, he was already meeting with his therapist. Nancy was sitting in the waiting room. After a supportive hug, we entered.

Mickey stood up to greet me, then looked around. He hadn't known that Nancy would be there, and in a flash I could see his mind at work putting two and two together. He was panicked. He was nervous, and I was, too. I took a deep breath. My future lay before me. I was terrified.

"Thanks, everyone, for coming today," I said, attempting to open up the conversation. This was my call. I knew that it was up to me, and I had to take the lead. I swallowed hard, closed my eyes, and envisioned my life, my safety, and my love for Mickey as well as for myself.

"Mick. This is really hard." My lip trembled, and my palms were sweating. "Our life together, it's been full of so much. And so much hardship." I looked down at my shaking hands.

"What's up, Otis?" he asked. I knew he felt small. And I knew that his defense mechanisms would soon lead to his rage. I had to be ready for that, yet still be unwavering.

"I need to leave you, Mickey. I *am* leaving you, Mickey. That's what's up." I needed to summon all the strength I had to be able to look him in the eyes.

"No, Otis. No . . . What? What do you mean?" He was shocked. And began to breathe rapidly, the first signs of a panic attack coming on. Usually this was where I backed down. But instead I pushed onward.

"I'm sorry, Mick. I love you. But I cannot be with you. My things are already moved out. I'll be coming back in a few weeks for the dogs. I'm sorry." I started to weep. My heart was breaking, but I knew that there was no turning back. As painful as it was, I was ready.

"Wait, Otis. You can't do this. When did you move your things out?" Mickey began crying, too.

"That's the thing, Mickey—we're so far apart, you and I. My room has been empty for a week . . . and you never even noticed. That's where we're at. So far apart that you didn't even fucking notice your wife's belongings are gone! We haven't been together in a year! A whole fucking year. I'm twenty-seven years old! I'm your wife! We're married! And we don't even make love. . . ."

I was angry. I was hurt. I was crying, but I knew there was nothing more to talk about. It was over. I had mourned the loss of this relationship for the past few years. I could walk away.

I stood to leave. And Mickey did, too.

The doctor spoke. "Mickey, sit down. Let Carré go. And let's talk."

He had a wonderful and gentle manner. I knew that Mickey trusted him. And I knew that I could walk out the door and if there was any chance in hell Mickey might get on the right track, it was with this man in his life.

As I stepped past Mickey, he reached out and touched my arm. I looked at him, deep into his eyes, and lifted my arms to hug him. It was one of the most painful, honest, and relieving embraces we had ever shared. Our bodies shook with tears and with the pain we both held. My heart physically hurt.

"It's not that I don't love you, Mick. I will always love you. I'm doing this *because* I love you. And because I love myself." I pulled away and walked toward the door.

Stepping out into the sunlight on that busy street in Beverly Hills, I kept on walking. I didn't look back.

4

On My Own

Making Amends

There were many challenges in those first days, weeks, and months after I left Mickey. I was adjusting to a new way of being and to a new world, calibrating my life to my own rhythm—something I hadn't done since my teens. Moments of doubt passed like shadows. But I had a support system in place that was growing stronger every day. I was reassured repeatedly that "this, too, shall pass," and that I would gradually find firm ground. I was going back to the basics, learning to put one foot in front of the other, pushing myself forward one step at a time.

I'd been on several different medications to treat a multitude of symptoms. Most were antidepressants. And truthfully, for a time they saved me. They helped make me available for the psychological and spiritual work I needed to do. At this point that work consisted chiefly of attending therapy several days a week. Despite some setbacks, I was making headway.

My life was still full of secrets, but now the secrets were intended primarily to ensure my privacy and safety. I let no one else but my close inner circle know that I was staying at the Oceana Hotel in Santa

Monica during the first month after I'd left Mickey. Then, just as Nancy had promised, the quaint Palisades home became available to me, and I began the process of moving my belongings in. It had been a long time since I'd lived in a house that was truly and solely mine. And this was met with as much excitement as anxiety.

It took quite a while and quite a bit of work to get through a day without feeling as if doom would be walking through the front door any minute. With wonder I realized that I had a choice as to who could come into my home and who could not. I was finally allowed to tell people to leave if they were not welcome. I had endured nearly a decade of cohabiting with men, all sorts of men—the men who worked for Mickey, the men who did not, that damned omnipresent entourage. Away from all of them, it took me some time to accept and rejoice in my newfound freedom.

This new home was situated on a small cul-de-sac just off of Sunset in the heart of Pacific Palisades. It was smaller than any place I had lived in for years, and I welcomed the simplicity of it. Two tiny bedrooms, a bathroom in the middle, a charming living room, and a kitchen that led to a lush fenced-in garden with a deck and trellis. Once I had settled and carved out my space, I knew I was ready to go and retrieve my dogs. That had been one of the most painful aspects of leaving my Santa Monica home. I knew that Mickey would have someone take care of them, but the Chihuahuas were my one constant, and without them there was a void in my life.

I had a small convertible BMW and wasn't sure how I would manage to pick them all up and get them safely to my new place. A greater worry was getting them out from under Mickey's watch. I didn't want to run into him or have to confront him. So I waited until I knew he was away filming and drove several times around our old house to assess which assistant was on duty.

The door to the Ocean Avenue home was unlocked, and as I snuck in, my beloved herd greeted me. They were beside themselves, whining and shaking and wagging their tails. I gathered up the ones that were closest to me, trying to leave those pups I knew Mickey was closest to behind for him. Angel, Monkey, Romi, Esmeralda, and Raphael were led out to my car, and in an instant I was off, speeding home. Beau Jack, Choco, and Loki would stay. That much had already been decided.

And with the dogs, my home finally felt complete. I had victoriously reclaimed something that was mine. Bringing them to the Palisades was an enormous part of putting the puzzle back together. My dogs had taught me to love, and they had forced me to be responsible. They were the most consistent friends I had at that time.

I continued to work my ass off in therapy. There were moments of absolute loneliness, panic, and confusion. Finally I had the space and the strength to explore everything that had been suppressed. I grieved. I cried. And at times I even felt desperate. I experienced agoraphobia— for months, I was too frightened to get myself to the grocery store or to have any interaction with strangers. To overcome my fear, Nancy gave me simple assignments, such as going to the library to get a library card. The smallest tasks seemed monumental. Often I felt unable to follow through and get from Point A to Point B. I had to learn some basics, such as balancing a checkbook, something no one had ever taught me to do.

As I did this difficult work, I was transported back to the point at which I'd departed from myself, to that very moment in my childhood when I had first started running away. I finally spoke of the traumas I'd endured. The physical and verbal abuse I'd suffered for years. I was sick of the secrets, realizing that my silence had been killing me. As painful as it was, telling the truth was incredibly liberating.

But as I worked through all these things, the one issue that I wasn't yet addressing was my anorexia. It had become such a norm for me that I never for a moment thought that how I was eating—or rather how I was not eating—was problematic. As I would find out, recovery happens in stages. Even as I was doing important work, I wasn't ready to confront what would be my deepest and gravest problem. That would come later.

Not long after I'd moved the dogs into the Palisades house, I got a call from my sister.

"I'm getting married!" she screamed into the phone.

"Chrisse! Oh, my God! I'm so happy for you!" And I was. But I was also filled with dread. I knew she would want me at her wedding. And I hadn't been in communication with the rest of my family for some time. I was still having real issues being around groups of people. But I was determined to be the supportive sister Chrisse deserved. I had missed her and our connection. I wanted my family back, and as difficult as I knew it might be, I was going to show up and really be present.

Driving up toward Napa Valley, I was reminded of the magic of the California coastline. I was a California girl through and through. With the top down and Dave Matthews blaring on the stereo, a feeling of freedom had washed over me. It dawned on me that my whole life lay ahead of me. Why the hell wasn't I happy? Excited? Full of wonder and awe? Those were the qualities I wanted to have in my life. I, too, one day, wanted a happy and fulfilling relationship. Maybe I would be married again, to a wonderful man, in a real wedding? And I realized that it was possible. Anything was possible. I was on the right track.

My sister's wedding was held at a winery in the Napa Valley, a gorgeous setting against a warm June sky. Old friends and new were scattered across a vast lawn, as well as the family I hadn't seen in years. My father and mother had gotten divorced, and I could feel the tension between them. My brother, grandmother, and aunt were also there. Even though I felt like a stranger, I reminded myself of why I had come. It was part of the work of healing. And half of that work was just showing up.

The wedding itself was beautiful, a fairy-tale event. And as I hugged my sister in congratulations, she looked in my eyes and said, "Thank you. I've missed you so much." It was true for both of us. Sisters should never be separated in life. Chrisse and I needed to support each other. And I'm so glad to say our love and our relationship have only grown stronger from that day forward.

As the evening drew to a close, I headed to my car to leave. I heard my father calling out my name, hurrying after me. "Won't you stay, Carré?" he asked. It was the first time in so long that I had really looked at him, looked into his face. Dad was older, but still handsome and full of grace. I could only imagine how hard my marriage with Mickey must have hit him . . . and having to know of the very public abuses I endured. . . . I didn't know where to begin.

"No, Dad. I need to get going." I held back my tears. There was so much I wanted to tell him, but once again I didn't know where to begin. "I love you," I said quickly.

"Are you okay? I heard you left Mickey." He tried to sound brave. Tried to sound open. I knew he was concerned. And beneath that concern I could hear the lions roar in his tone.

"Yes, Dad. I've finally left him," I replied, looking beyond him at the rolling hills and setting sun.

He put an arm around me. "I love you, too," he said quietly. Then, even more softly, he whispered, "Call me if you get in a jam. I *am* here." And I knew he was. I knew our relationship was turning. He, too, was doing the work and showing up. He wanted to be a part of my life. I wanted that as well, trusting that slowly, very slowly, we could get there.

"Bye, Daddy," I said, kissing him on the cheek and sliding into my car. I waved farewell and sped off.

On a high from Chrisse's wedding, I was ready to confront issues and people I hadn't in years. Impulsively, I decided to call the farm and see if Nan and Ethan were there. I would have to drive back through Sebastopol, so why not stop in for a visit? I pulled out my cell phone and dialed a still-familiar number.

Nan picked up on the third ring. "Hello?"

"Nan, it's Carré!" I declared into the phone, expecting her to meet my excitement.

"Oh. Hi," she said flatly.

"Hi. How are you? How are the girls? Ethan?" I pressed on.

"Fine, Carré. Wow. I'm shocked. To hear from you, that is," she said.

"I know . . . gosh, it's been a while, hasn't it?" I said, trying to slough off the disappointment I felt by her lack of enthusiasm.

"Actually, it's been years, Carré." Her disappointment in me was palpable. I felt ashamed. How could I be so naïve? So self-absorbed to think that after all this time, after abandoning them for Mickey and Hollywood, she would be happy to hear from me?

"Yes. You're right. It has been years. I'm sorry. So very sorry, Nan. I've thought of you all so much. So much has happened." I tried to explain, to give her some reason where she might cut me some slack.

"I gather. I mean, we have heard and read about all that has happened. . . ." Nan's tone was still guarded.

"Hey, I'm just coming back from my sister's wedding. I'm practically just around the corner. Can I come by? Can we talk?" I pressed her. I wanted to see her. I wanted her to know how sorry I was and how much I respected her. She'd been like a mother to me, but it was true, in the years that had followed my time on the farm, in my true selfish style, I had scarcely looked back or checked in.

"That's probably not a good idea, Carré." Her words stung. I was speechless. I wasn't used to being rejected or denied so blatantly. "I mean, are you still with him? Have you left him? Do you know what trouble Mickey made for us? The whole farm was terrified. He threatened Ethan's life. We weren't even sure Ethan would be safe here. No, Carré. That's just not a good idea."

I could hear the fear in her voice. The closest that the farm had ever come to any kind of violence was from Mickey.

"Oh, God, Nan. I'm sorry I even called. I'm so sorry. Sorry for it all. I wish I could have done something. I wish I could do something now. . . . I love you." And with that, I hung up.

In a flash, fury surged. How could he? How could Mickey have made threats to Ethan? Ethan was a sweet and gentle man. What a pathetic piece of shit Mickey had been to do that, and to threaten the farm, too! I slammed my fist against the wheel. I knew I was partly to blame. The reality was that I had chosen Mickey and his violence over my loved ones' safety. That was the truth. In my naïveté and my need, in my want and in my grasping, I had made some terrible choices, choices that had caused great pain for others. The farm was a modern Eden, and Mickey was the snake in that garden. And if he was the snake, then I was the Eve who'd let him in. That realization was agonizing. It was time to begin to own up to what I had done and what I'd allowed to happen. It was time to be responsible

I drove straight back to L.A., pushing through the night, my tears whipped away by the warm summer wind. As painful as it was to face my own part in what had happened, I knew that it was time. Under the moon and the stars, I vowed to begin to do things differently. I vowed to consider not only my health and wellness but also the well-being of others and how my choices affected them.

Back in Los Angeles, I felt ready for a new round of life and a new round of responsibility. After the wedding and that painful conversation with Nan, I realized that in my process there would be a lot of time spent proving myself. My word had come to mean little to the people I cared most about. I was like the boy who cried wolf. It would take time, I thought—time for people to believe in me and time for me to believe in myself. That was okay. I was ready to put in that time.

SPORTS ILLUSTRATED AND THE HOLES IN MY HEART

I began to see that returning to work was another key part of the puzzle. I needed to confront all that I had left behind and reclaim my place as a professional woman. This time, though, I was determined to take a different initiative within the modeling industry. While I was older and wiser, I was still wounded in many ways. I knew that the wiser part would help me, but I wasn't so sure the older part of the equation would.

I had dedicated a year to getting my feet back on the ground, and in that time I had pursued little else. I felt completely out of the loop as to how to relaunch my career. I didn't want to go back to any of the agents I had history with; I knew I needed a fresh start, so I began asking around about who the players were and how they conducted their business. I was still legally married to Mickey, waiting for his signature on the divorce papers. I feared once more that he'd attempt to sabotage my efforts to work again. I knew it would take a strong individual to represent me with all the baggage I had. But I trusted that such an agent existed and that I would find him.

One name in particular kept coming up. He was a renowned "good guy," someone who stood out from all the usual suspects. Jeffrey Dash had been around for years and maintained an impeccable reputation as one of the few honest men in the industry. He piqued my interest. If I was going to get back in, I needed to do it on a whole new level.

I called to ask Jeffrey for a meeting, and in December 1997 I found myself sitting across from one of the first men I'd ever met who is exactly as he appears. No bullshit, no games, no promises. We candidly discussed the issues he saw as problematic in rebuilding my career—including, of course, the clear obstacles posed by my liaison with Mickey.

It was uncomfortable to hear my professional status summed up in this way, but it was a realistic assessment. If I wanted to get back in, I would need to deal with these details head-on. I needed a plan. And Jeffrey was a genius at building businesses. I could tell that he considered this a worthwhile project to take on—certainly it wasn't going to be a dull one.

Point-blank, I asked Jeffrey how he would feel if Mickey confronted him. This was usually the make-or-break question I asked of people getting involved in my new life. His answer would be important, because I knew that inevitably Mickey would step into the mix. I was still concerned about my not-quite-yet-ex-husband infiltrating my life and threatening the people surrounding and supporting me.

Much to my surprise, Jeffrey seemed less concerned about having to deal with Mickey than he was about getting me on top again. He looked me in the eye, and in a moment I knew I had met not only my new agent but a new friend. For many years there was no one who I could say truly had my back. From day one, Jeffrey Dash did.

As we suspected, every client had the same reaction during the first round of calls. They'd ask, "Is she still with Mickey?" As long as there was any thread of an association, the gig was off. No one wanted to work with me if they thought they might have to deal with that drama.

It was a frustrating period, during which it seemed impossible for me to separate from my past. While I wanted so desperately to be acknowledged for the woman I was without Mickey, I knew that this was part of the price I would have to pay to create my own identity and to earn back the trust and belief of others.

Patience is not one of my virtues, but thankfully it was Jeffrey's. He reminded me that everything takes time. And I was encouraged to sit back and have a little faith in him. "People will come around . . . you'll see."

Jeffrey had a system. And I had to learn to trust that system. Several rounds of calls were made, with time in between. New head shots would be sent out, and then after a wait he'd make more calls. I badgered Jeff incessantly. He would usually laugh and nod, acting as if he knew something I didn't. And he did. He knew I would work again. I, on the other hand, wasn't so convinced.

Slowly but surely, the calls came in, just as he'd said they would. Gradually, I began to work. Even the smallest job was a victory. The client feedback was favorable—I was consistent, professional, and easy to deal with. It was great to hear their compliments after all the effort I'd made to change things. I desperately wanted to prove myself in a way that had nothing to do with being the most beautiful. I had simply wanted to complete something, follow it through. I'd been on the run since I left home as a kid. I'd left school. Left the farm. Left business opportunities. Left my loved ones. It was part of my healing to be able to see something I'd started to completion. And to do so successfully.

I had just celebrated my thirtieth birthday when I got a call from Jeffrey with some good news. *Sports Illustrated* wanted to feature me in their Millennium Swimsuit Issue. We were both elated. It had been a steady climb to get back in the game, and the call from *SI* meant even more than that: We were back on top.

When I talked over the details on the phone with Jeffrey, he said, "Honey, just checking in, how is your weight? Where are we at?" Jeffrey was ever cautious and sensitive when it came to the subject of size, letting me know that no matter where I was, he would be right there by my side as agent and friend. By the time I'd begun to hit my late twenties, I found that my old methods of losing weight weren't working as well. It was getting more and more difficult to stay on the skinny side of life. And this warranted a realistic question a week before any shoot.

"It's okay," I replied nervously. The fact of the matter was, it was never where I thought it should be. Size, weight, and age were criteria that could either win or lose a job. Worries about my body had ruled my life for nearly two decades. The pressure was constant. And not being able to control even one aspect of my life was daunting. As I approached thirty, I saw hints that a change to my body was occurring. What was happening to me was normal, of course. Women's bodies change, inside and outside the modeling industry. And a body that has been in starvation mode for a decade will most likely shift into a holding pattern just to keep weight on. As far as the body is concerned, it's a matter of survival.

But what's normal for a model is different from what's normal for the rest of us. Normal is dictated by the industry's strict standards, and in my case by the additional concern that I could never be skinny enough to continue to work. The definition in my world has nothing to do with what actually happens to women's bodies in the real world. With the *Sports Illustrated* shoot approaching, my illness was about to peak, with life-threatening consequences.

I used the swimsuit issue as momentum to get into what I thought would be the best shape of my life. I felt I had more to prove than my fellow models hired for the job, because I had about ten years on most of them. I was also one of the few who was au naturel. I hadn't had my lips injected, I didn't have breast implants, and let's just say I had to work my ass off to keep my waistline. None of it was coming easily for me. Although I employed the advice of a trainer, the anorexic in me was convinced that for some reason he was lying. Lying about the number of calories I needed to eat in order to lose weight, lying about my body's needing rest for days. It was irrational, but I was in such a "go" mode that I was unable to see how my disease was in control, how *it* was running the show. Not me.

I was fearful of my food, convinced that I would gain weight overnight from eating even a modest meal. I was obsessed with counting calories and had insane rules for what I could and couldn't consume. I punished myself for losing control around food with laxatives; then, after purging myself, I would institute a whole new set of rules that were even stricter than the previous ones. Although I was working out at the same level as a top athlete, I limited my caloric intake, thinking that the combination of decreased calories and increased exercise would put me ahead of the game. Much to my dismay and frustration, my body began holding on for dear life to the few calories I had ingested, and instead of dropping weight I would retain or even gain weight.

Some of this was discussed in therapy, but the truth was that my eating disorder was my last little dirty secret. It had been with me the longest—before drugs and alcohol. It had been the first thing in my life that I had realized I could control. I wasn't about to let it go that easily. When I talked to Nancy, I kept the focus on my shoot. When she addressed some of my unhealthy habits, I would simply chalk them up to the requirements of my job. Not all a lie, but certainly not the entire truth.

After four months of intense training and dieting, I was ready for the *Sports Illustrated* photos to be taken. But I was also wiped out. I had begun to feel faint during the daytime. Nevertheless, I always pressed on. I didn't want anything to get in my way or slow me down. One morning at my gym, I stepped off the treadmill and in a flash felt the floor rushing toward me. The room went black.

"Carré!" I could hear my trainer, Mike, calling. He had a hand on my wrist and was checking my pulse. "Jesus, girl! Did you cool down?" he asked, nodding toward the machine.

"Yes, of course," I answered. I always tried to walk my heart rate down after a workout.

"Well, my dear . . . your heart is still racing. Let's just have you sit for a bit." In fact, my heart was pumping dangerously, at over two hundred beats per minute. Not the norm for a thirty-year-old supposedly in great shape. I didn't tell anyone else, but these episodes continued to happen with some frequency. I could usually feel when a blackout was coming and would try to get to the ground as quickly as possible to prevent falling. I'd lie to anyone who asked, insisting that I was just light-headed and needed some rest. I was concerned and did suspect that it had to do with my eating habits, but I wasn't willing to stop the momentum of my life right then to deal with it, so I chose to forge ahead and hope that it wouldn't get any worse. As far as I was concerned, it was still manageable.

The *Sports Illustrated* crew included my old friend, photographer Antoine Verglas. It was a great group of folks, and together we flew down to Puerto Vallarta, then made our way inland to an absolutely stunning resort. The backdrop was idyllic, with an enormous pool, waterfall, grassy knolls, and colorful cabanas. Hammocks swung in the gentle breeze, while an open restaurant complete with a bamboo bar stood as the hub of the resort. The rooms were more like suites, and there was a masseuse on duty to tend to anyone's needs. It was an atmosphere of style and decadence, exquisite cuisine included. We were waited on hand and foot, left to sun between shots or just float in the pool. While most of the girls opted to relax and take in the amenities, I continued my insane exercise regimen, thinking of it as more of a maintenance program. I ran in the midday heat under a blazing sun, did lunges across the grass and squats in the gym. I couldn't seem to stop myself; the fear of putting on even a single pound while on location had me running on empty.

During meals I would watch enviously as my young co-workers sipped margaritas and nibbled on chips. When I couldn't take it anymore, I would excuse myself from the table and from temptation. My illness was ruling my life.

CNN was filming behind the scenes to present a firsthand look at the creation of the Millennium Issue. They interviewed the models, too. And because I was one of the oldest models *SI* had used in its history, I became the poster girl for the thirty-something demographic. Outwardly I embraced the opportunity, but inwardly I was more and more uncomfortable with the constant comparisons to the younger models, as well as with the general fixation people had on age. I was thirty—so fucking what? *Why*, I wondered, *do we need to obsess about age in the ways that we do?* But clearly I had bought into it; I was uncomfortably aware that I was drawing near the expiration date I'd been hearing about since the day I arrived in the modeling world. Perhaps I was already there. Expired.

With the *Sports Illustrated* shoot completed, I flew back to Los Angeles and collapsed. I was beyond exhausted. It wasn't like me to have so little drive, even with a cold. But the energy reserves I'd once been able to draw from were all gone. Just as I was falling into a pit of despair, I received a welcome call from my brother, who was passing through town.

"Hey, Carré! It's your bro!" Jordan said cheerily.

"Hi!" I answered. It was so good to hear his voice.

"Can I crash with you for a couple of nights?" he asked. Of course. I was thrilled to have the company.

We hung out and watched movies that first evening. I tried to shake myself from my funk long enough to work out, but I was still too exhausted. Early the next morning, I tiptoed into the kitchen to make a cup of tea, but this time when I sensed I was about to black out, it felt very different. As I fell to the floor, I could hear a consistent and rhythmic banging sound. It was faint and in the background, but it was there. And as my confusion cleared just for a second, I realized it was my head banging on the floor. My body was flailing. I was having a seizure.

It was a miracle my brother was there. He immediately took me to the emergency room, where it occurred to me just how worried I was. The doctor in the ER put me through some tests, and I was referred to Dr. Anil Bhandari, a cardiac specialist at Good Samaritan Hospital.

After another battery of tests, Dr. Bhandari came into the room and asked if he could speak frankly with me.

"How is your diet, Ms. Otis?" he inquired.

I was stunned. "Well, it's fine, I guess. I mean, I am a model. I don't eat a lot. But I eat." I was trying to reassure him.

"What does that mean to you? Do you or don't you eat?" he asked me in a rather serious tone.

"Of course I eat," I said, laughing, trying to make light of the situation.

"Carré, I am asking you this because it appears you have three holes in your heart. I would like to try to understand why a woman at your young age would have them." He looked at me, and there was no smile in his eyes. This was serious. And all of a sudden, I was scared. My entire life flashed before me.

"Whoa . . . Can you fix them? Will I die? What can you do?" I sounded panicked. And I was.

"Take a deep breath. Yes, I will explain the procedure we can do. But let's go back to that last question about your diet."

He wasn't going to let me off the hook. I looked around the stark room, but there was no escape. There was nowhere left to go. I knew at that moment I needed to face that last dreaded little piece of me that I was still hiding, the one fragment of control I was still clinging to so desperately. I was as scared of the situation I was in now as I was of letting go and fessing up. The sad fact is, I was anorexic. And I had been for the majority of my life. After a long conversation and an honest intake of my history, I was admitted to Good Samaritan and underwent a noninvasive heart surgery. The three holes were ablated, and I was told to expect a full recovery.

Jeffrey was my chief confidant during that time. My family was still far away. It was the beginning of yet another layer of recovery. But this layer was different. I had managed to dig down deep enough to the place where the subtlest seeds of turmoil in my life had been planted long ago. I recognized a different kind of opportunity in arriving there. Everything in my life was about to change yet again.

PLUS-SIZE MODELING

I was on an emotional roller coaster during the weeks that followed my heart surgery. I had never felt so open, raw, or exposed. I reached out to friends and finally to family in an attempt to close the gap that I had created between the world and me. I could no longer compartmentalize my life into discrete boxes. I needed to have everything on the table, to open a dialogue about what it was I was going through. I began working with a new therapist, one who specialized in eating disorders, and I slogged my way through some painful truths. I needed to understand the origins of my illness—how, why, and when it had all started. The surgery drove home the obvious point that my eating disorder could cost me my life. I had no choice but to try to get to the root cause of its existence and to its solution.

At the "heart" of the matter lay a very fractured sense of self. The loss of connection I'd experienced with my mother and the absence of the feminine in my life at an important time had been the major impetus for my disease. I'd had no mentors, no warm hugs, no reassurances as my body changed. There were only unanswered questions, feelings that were forever suppressed, fears and concerns that were never voiced because there was no one emotionally there to receive them. I had never been taught that I could say no or have a say in anything. I felt that I didn't have any rights; my voice wasn't worth listening to.

As a result, my opinion of women was dismal from the start. I was repulsed by my own femaleness. I began to equate women with the meek and the weak. And from a very young age, I was not at all convinced that I had been born into the right body. I didn't want to be a woman. The vulnerability that lay there seemed unbearable. As puberty hit and my body began to change, a sense of absolute betrayal came over me. How could this happen? Breasts? Pubic hair? Hips? I was disgusted. And even further enraged that I had absolutely no control over any of it.

The open stares and furtive glances from older men taught me early in adolescence that a woman's body was not a safe place to live. That much was clear. It infuriated me. The repeated sexual and physical abuse I suffered from the men in my life was more proof that being a woman wasn't what I had signed up for.

I recalled the day I had run my hands over my rib cage, relieved that there were no breasts yet. I looked like a little boy. That lean, linear shape made me feel safe. As changes began to take place, I did everything in my power to maintain that flat chest, trying to keep myself looking like a boy for as long as I could. The only way of accomplishing this was through diet. And for years, even prior to modeling, voluntary and chosen starvation was something I endured almost every day. Not only did this work to keep me physically thin, but it provided me with a much-needed sense of control, too. Everything around me might have been out of my power, but I could at least manage what went into, or didn't go into, my mouth.

It wasn't until I met Nan and stayed with her on the farm that my beliefs about women and about my body were challenged. I had been impressed by the women I saw there. I'd even mimicked them to a certain extent, but I could never let myself go completely. Inevitably, I would scramble back to my haven of control, reining myself and my impulses back in. Though I had been drawn to these women, I hadn't been ready to soften as they had. I was not yet ready to embrace the beauty of the strength that lies within vulnerability.

I had never voiced these feelings before. And it was painful but relieving to finally be able to express my innermost secrets. I was sad that I felt disgusted with myself. Although it had been a long time since I'd felt disgusted by other women, I continued to disgust myself. I was mortified to go into a supermarket and get Tampax; it was humiliating to speak about my body. Anything that had to do with my being a woman seemed upside down and backward. It took a tremendous amount of courage to look into all of this, find my voice, purge myself of the loathing, and create a new and healthy inner dialogue.

As I worked endlessly in therapy, I also began to introduce something new to my system: calories. Per my doctor's orders as well as under the watchful eye of my therapist, I began to plan my meals. In those first weeks, I would sit down with my nutritious self-made meals and virtually fall to pieces. I was terrified, fearful that food would make me fat. The anxiety would swell and surge, usually resulting in a call to my doctors. It took a lot of coaxing for me to begin to eat three meals a day. At first I could handle only a few bites. As I moved through this period, I allowed myself the room to break down. I kept a journal, noting my emotional responses to learning to eat properly. I put nothing on my schedule other than the task of nourishing myself, and that looked different every day. I took long walks as opposed to hour-long runs through sand; I opted for a massage over time in the sauna. I was trying a kinder, gentler approach. It was around this time that a house came on the market in Malibu that was in my price range. I had been living for two years under the shelter of the Palisades home, and I was feeling ready to put down some roots of my own. Driving to Malibu one crisp fall day, I rounded the bend on the Pacific Coast Highway and smiled to see the view of Zuma Beach fan out below. "I could do this," I thought out loud. "I could live here." Within a month escrow had closed and I'd moved dogs, belongings, and myself to Broad Beach Road.

I continued my therapy sessions and worked on being present as I ate my meals. But a new challenge was soon in front of me. Part of the healing work resulted in a weight gain, a gain I'd never experienced before. And all the issues I'd once grappled with were now multiplied threefold. My body was in fact out of my control.

Because I'd been in starvation mode for so many years, my system could not trust that what I was putting into it wouldn't be taken away in a week's time. I had destroyed my metabolism. Only time and patience could repair it. In the face of the weight gain, I had to make a decision: Would I proceed with the protocol, trust my doctors and the fact that my body had the intelligence and wisdom to heal in ways I had yet to understand, or would I fall back on the same old patterns of control that would eventually kill me?

I was sick of the fight, so I surrendered to what was one of the most ironic and profound teachings in my life. My body did balloon. I gained close to thirty pounds. It challenged me in ways I had never been challenged before. But it was then that I had one of my most liberating revelations: I am *not* my body; I am so much more than my size.

I remember driving home from a therapy session and seeing a woman walking along the street where I lived. She stunned me. She awed me. She must have been my size at the time—a twelve, perhaps—and she moved with such sexiness and confidence. I wanted to stop her, ask her questions, and get to know her. Instead I held this image in my mind every time I had doubt and self-loathing. I recalled her boldness and pride. Beauty is not a size. Beauty is presence. Beauty is certainty. Beauty is the body.

I started to think about work. I felt this growing motivation to represent publicly all that I was going through. I knew that other models I'd worked with would rather be unemployed than work as a size twelve, but that route wasn't for me. I was finding my voice and purpose. Why should I have to hide myself away? Why would I be ashamed to come out as a larger-size woman? And with that, I decided to call Jeffrey.

"I want to work," I said boldly.

"Honey, you're still recovering," Jeffrey said quietly, not understanding exactly what I was saying.

I laughed. "No, Jeff, I'm not talking about losing weight to go back to work." I wasn't sure he would go for it, but I figured I would ask. If anyone was going to back me up in a controversial move, it would be Jeffrey.

"What are you talking about, Carré?"

"Well, what if . . . what if I started to work at the size I am now? What if I worked as a plus-size model?" I said excitedly. "I see the girls out there. There are a couple of magazines, and there's a ton of catalog work. Why not?"

My excitement was met with silence. I knew Jeffrey well enough to know that he was taking it in, ruminating over my idea. I pressed on.

"Jeff, I could make a difference. I can take a stance. Why should I stop working just because I'm bigger? First of all, I still need to work. Second of all . . . second of all, I have something to say. Something important." I waited.

"Actually, Carré, it's not a bad idea at all." He meant it.

And so we began to plan a course of action. I wanted to "come out" and do it with pride. There was no shame. I was ready to take on the role of a spokesperson for all the other women who had struggled as I had and whose bodies were not those of typical models. As I researched my role, I began to understand just how few women are anywhere near a size two.

And with a few calls, a lot of courage, and some great support, a new career began. One in which I was able to share everything I'd learned, to speak out loud and clear. This was one of the greatest lessons of all, and the irony of my situation never escaped me. It took my surrendering the control I'd clung to for so long and becoming what I'd feared most to actually find my voice and my purpose.

Discovering My Voice with Oprah

The funny thing about being a plus-size model, as I would soon discover, is that there is a certain emphasis on size in that world, too; if you fall below the minimum size expectation you could lose out on a job opportunity just as easily as you could if you exceeded the size expectation in my old modeling world. There was a time when I was in limbo between those two worlds. As my body finally adjusted to its new healthy regimen, I'd actually settled into a range between sizes eight and ten, depending upon the cut of the clothes and the designer. It was during that time that I received a call from Jeffrey saying that O magazine wanted to fly me to the Bahamas to shoot a summer story. I was eager to accept that particular job because I assumed I wasn't expected to show up rail thin. O magazine had an older demographic than most fashion magazines; I, just like everyone else in America, knew about Oprah Winfrey's very public battles with weight. She spoke out courageously about size acceptance as well as women's rights. A part of me felt flattered to be able to represent those values.

For the first time since my surgery, I was excited to get back on a plane. Harbour Island, Bahamas, awaited me.

I was met by the photographer's assistant at the small island airport and escorted to the quaint hotel that sat on the shore of a famous pink-sand beach. It was a treat to be there—in the balmy warmth, under the palm trees—and unlike on so many other shoots in my career, it was wonderful to be able to join the crew for a real meal. I retired early to get a good night's sleep, and when I awoke, I headed into hair and makeup to begin what I assumed would be a long day's work.

I endured the obligatory fitting to see what were the best looks for each location. It began to dawn on me as I shimmied in and out of outfits that the clothes were a bit on the tight side. Despite all the progress I'd made, I found myself struggling to manage the emotions that were welling up inside. The discomfort of being squeezed into a size six was both physical and psychological.

"Hmm." The stylist raised a brow as I sucked in my breath to zip up a pair of linen pants. "Things are not quite fitting as I hoped. Did you gain weight?" she asked in a tone that sounded to me as if she already knew the answer.

"I sent word along that I'm a size eight. These are all size sixes." I knew I was coming off as defensive, but Jeffrey and I were always careful to be truthful with clients about my size so that I could be comfortable and confident at all my shoots—especially during that transitional time. It was all I could do not to cry. I tried to hold steady and remember that this was all just part of the job.

"Well," she sniffed, "I think you're more of a ten or a twelve."

"Whatever the case, what I have on obviously doesn't fit. Shall we try to see what does, or should I just get on the next plane home?" My anger was rising. I was furious, after all the years and all the dues paid, to be in a fitting where I was treated like a newcomer or a twelve-year-old. I wasn't up for being belittled.

The stylist continued to huff and sigh her way through clothing options as outfit after outfit proved to be too snug. She was obviously upset, and I was, too—less because of the size than because of the way I was being treated. Finally we decided on several colorful bikinis, a wrap dress, and a few sarongs.

"If we have to, we'll just shoot close-ups," the stylist muttered under her breath, piling extra hats and oversize sunglasses into the bag.

Needless to say, by the time we started the shoot, I felt less than fabulous. The day went from bad to worse, and again my self-esteem was challenged. I knew I was recovering, but I still had my triggers. Being on a shoot and having it made evident that my size was unacceptable was definitely one of them.

"Carré, can you angle your hips to the side?" the photographer yelled to me over the waves crashing between us. I angled them and tried to deliver a natural smile. He scratched his head. "How about lifting the sarong just in front of your hips?" he tried again. And I did just that, angling and hiding myself as best I could. I wanted to cry. I wanted to throw the fucking sarong at him and walk away.

He lowered his camera and turned to the stylist, saying something I couldn't hear. I was done. I couldn't take any more.

Boldly, I walked over to him and simply said, "Hey, if this isn't working for you, let's call it a day. No one needs to be this uncomfortable." I looked him in the eye. I'd been doing this too long to pretend that everything was okay. "If you're not happy, just say it. Let's not go crazy trying to make it work if it's not gonna happen." I waited.

"No, no." He shook his head. "You're great, Carré. Let's just try something else. . . . Um . . . how about some head shots under the tree in the shade. Okay?" I wished he could just have left it alone. I wished I could walk away.

We worked for a while longer, and then as the sun began to set, much to my relief, we called it a day at last. I needed to get Jeffrey on the phone. I needed some support. As I walked back toward the hotel, I stopped in the lobby and ran into an old photographer friend of mine.

"Hi, Pamela!" I said, grabbing her by the shoulders and giving her a hug.

"Carré! Great to see you! What are you doing here?" She looked me over quickly.

"I'm working, Pam. And you?"

She laughed and shrugged her shoulders. "I'm working, too, but I just got a call from another client that the girl they hired is too fat. They wanted to see if I had an extra model to lend them." She looked around, and as I put two and two together, I casually asked her, "Who's the client?"

"O magazine. Why? Who are you working for?" she said, clearly not understanding.

I looked her in the eye. "O magazine."

We both stood there in silence, staring at one another. And in an instant she realized her mistake.

"Oh, God, Carré!" She quickly clamped a hand over her mouth. "I'm so sorry! What an ass!"

I shrugged and turned away. "Don't worry about it, Pamela. Good luck."

I was crushed, but also pissed off. First of all, I wasn't *fat*. Second of all, why couldn't they have come to me and said something instead of sneaking around and making it uncomfortable for everyone? I was sick of it. Sick of being put in this position. Back in my room, I packed my bag and cried. Really wept. I just couldn't keep it up anymore.

The job was over, and it was their choice if they wanted to re-shoot it all with a skinnier girl. I could no longer be what I wasn't. I was done.

Back in Malibu, Jeffrey called in to check on me. He had received a call from O informing him that they wouldn't be running the pictures. They said I looked too heavy.

"Are you fucking kidding me, Jeff? I mean, it's O magazine! As in Oprah Winfrey! I mean, who are her readers? Isn't it an older audience? It's still me! They know me and my story. If they had wanted a seventeen-year-old or someone a size two, why did they bring me out there in the first place?" I was furious.

"I know, Carré. It's ridiculous," Jeffrey responded. I knew he was as frustrated as I was.

"I'm going to write her a letter. I mean, I need to tell her that she hired someone who calls a size-eight woman fat. That's bullshit. And I'm sure that Oprah wouldn't stand for it if she knew. She's always been part of the solution, not part of the problem. How could this happen?" My anger was on the rise, but something interesting was happening simultaneously. I was exercising my voice. I had something to say about this. And I wasn't going to let it go. Whether the incident was occurring on the tail of my nearly two-decade-long career and I'd just had enough or whether it was the sheer fact that I was just seeing why I'd put myself through hell on a twenty-year diet, I was livid and super motivated to do something about it.

I followed through on what I'd said to Jeffrey. I wrote the letter to Oprah. And, in a way I had never done before in my entire life, I stood up and stood out. I told her what had happened and how I felt. I knew damn well I wasn't the only woman or the only model to have dealt with this kind of hostility and judgment. But I was going to use whatever influence I had to address the issue for us all. I was prepared for the photos not to run. The last I'd heard from our contact at O, everything had been reshot with another model. Truthfully, I didn't expect my letter to actually get to Oprah, nor did I expect to receive a response. But it was important for me to act, to take charge, to use my voice to be heard so as to help others.

Much to my surprise, a few weeks later the phone rang and the voice on the other end asked, "Is Carré Otis available?"

"Yes. Speaking," I said.

"I have Ms. Winfrey on the line for you. Hold one moment."

I gasped. I'd never imagined I would actually speak with her. I sat down, gathering my composure, recalling all the points in my letter that must have stood out.

"Carré." A booming voice sounded over the receiver. What a force; I felt it immediately.

"Yes. Hello, Oprah. Thanks for getting back to me. I assume you're calling regarding my letter."

"Well, I am. I wanted to clear up any confusion that you might have." She got right to the point. "You said in your letter that someone on my staff said you were too fat on the shoot for us to run the pictures. Who in fact said that, Carré?"

I tried to answer her questions just as directly. I told her that it was the stylist assigned to the shoot that day, and that the person who called to let us know that the photos would not be running had also implied that it was because I was too heavy. I took a breath and waited, then continued. I let her know that I found it hard to believe a woman with her history of battling weight would want only one body type in her magazine. That if anyone was willing to incorporate the shape of a real woman in a magazine surely it was her. Again, I waited and a silence hung heavy between us. I can only imagine that this news came as a big disappointment to her, too.

"I think there has been some miscommunication here, Carré," Oprah said.

"Really?" I asked. I was clearly just beginning to air my long-held frustrations with the industry because I then proceeded to tell her that I thought it was very unfortunate that within this industry, if you exceed a certain age and size, that is grounds for termination. To me that's discrimination. And of all the publications out there, I wished it hadn't been hers. I knew I was challenging her, but why not? This mattered.

There was a pause. "We will be running the pictures, Carré. And I do apologize for what happened. Obviously, I was unaware of what went on." Oprah was brisk but sincere. She wished me the best as she ended the conversation.

I was glad that O was going to run the pictures, but happier still to have the call from Oprah. The pictures were less important than being heard. What I felt best about was that Oprah had given me the opportunity to speak my piece. I'd found my voice and used it. Excitement percolated within me. From here on, I would be silent no more.

NEPAL

One summer afternoon in 2001, a small group of friends gathered at my home, and as we all laughed and joked, I overheard a tall blond woman say she was going on a trip to Nepal.

"Really?" I asked. "What will you be doing there?"

Nancy Rivard was an ex-model, six feet tall, and a genuine, kind-hearted soul. I was impressed with her and even more impressed as she told her story. She ran a foundation that focused on bringing toys and other aid to kids around the world. She had worked with and been inspired by the celebrated doctor and clown Patch Adams and called her organization the International Toy Bank.

I was struck by her work and drawn to the idea of traveling to Nepal. It was somewhere I had always dreamed of going. The Buddha himself had been born there, and I felt connected to Nepal in a deep, almost inexplicable way. Talking to Nancy, I realized how badly I wanted to go. I felt as if I *had* to go. And this seemed the perfect opportunity.

Nancy and I plotted our journey and decided to team up with Airline Ambassadors, which was headed by a former flight attendant who used her connections with the airlines to deliver much-needed medical supplies to remote areas across the globe. Airline Ambassadors has been around for thirty-five years and still does amazing work.

As I booked my tickets and packed my bags, I was beside myself with excitement. I had never traveled the world for myself. My trips had always been for jobs, and though I'd flown to some of the most amazing spots on the planet, rarely did I have the time to explore them beyond the airport and my hotel room. But now something in me was awakening to all that I might have missed. Surviving my heart surgery had opened me up to experiencing the world in ways I hadn't quite experienced it before. For the first time, I really understood my own mortality; for the first time, I had a deep sense of spiritual purpose. I sensed that my further survival depended on embracing that purpose. And I knew that making this trip to Nepal was part of doing just that.

After a layover at the airport hotel in Bangkok, I finally arrived in Kathmandu nearly two days after I'd departed LAX. Exhausted, I made my way through customs and out toward the smoggy and chaotic street to meet my driver. A young man wearing a bandanna waved a sign with my name on it, and as soon as I signaled that I was who he was looking for, he ran in my direction and grabbed my backpack.

"Otis, Otis, this way, Ms. . . . Please . . . to the car. My car. Come, come." He waved and smiled broadly. Happily, I followed along.

"The group waits, Ms. Otis. For you. At the hotel." The young man seemed unbearably excited, and in my daze I couldn't help but laugh. I could barely understand a word he said but realized it didn't matter at all. Like most Nepalese, he was unbelievably animated. That enthusiasm needed no translation.

We zigzagged through the crowded streets, rushing ahead, then braking sharply as our car approached cows and trucks that randomly stopped in the middle of the road. The flow of traffic made no sense. Most pedestrians wore masks to protect them from the intolerable pollution. But through the late-afternoon haze, something in the distance caught my eye. I strained to see beyond the buildings around me. I gasped. Dominating the skyline, an enormous dome rose up, and the fading light captured it in a fiery glow. I pointed and patted my driver's shoulder desperately. "What . . . what is that?" I cried.

"Ah!" He smiled. "Boudhanath stupa!" And there it was. I had heard of it, dreamed of it, and seen pictures of it. I had been taught the symbolism of stupas; From above they look like a mandala, or a diagram of the Buddhist cosmos. They represent the enlightened, awakened mind and the path to realization. Each stupa is a spiritual monument that contains at the very least holy relics; merely gazing at one is said to bring wakefulness.

And for some odd reason, I began to weep, overcome with emotion, relief, and a sense of security and ease. The sensation was similar to what I'd felt the first time I met my friend and teacher Tsultrim Allione. Everything was coming together and making sense. I was enveloped by the profound knowledge that I was exactly where I was supposed to be on my journey. I felt the certainty that had eluded me for so many years.

As we passed through the crazy streets of Kathmandu, I felt as if I knew what would be around each corner. It was all strangely familiar to me—the faces, the smells, the clothing and colors. I was remembering something but couldn't put my finger on it. It was like searching for that word that's resting right on the tip of your tongue. It's there, so close, just within reach. I looked around in awe.

"You must stop at the stupa," I begged my young driver, Raja. "I need to circumambulate it once!" He nodded in understanding. It is one of the great pilgrimage spots on this planet, with millions flocking to it every year from every faith and all walks of life. I, too, needed to express my gratitude.

Raja stopped just outside the enormous square that housed the sacred site. I slipped out of the car and into the flow of foot traffic around the stupa. Walking shoulder to shoulder with Tibetan refugees of every age, I felt as if I were being swept up into a current and pulled along by an immense collective energy. As I moved clockwise, my right hand reached out to turn the countless prayer wheels that were embedded in the walls. A murmured chant droned beautifully and ceaselessly, like the trickle of a stream bubbling away: *Om Mani Pedme Hung,* the six-syllable mantra of the bodhisattva of compassion.

Incense and the smell of butter lamps lit as offerings filled the air. In that last light of my first day in Kathmandu, I climbed up onto the great dome itself and sat, folding my legs under me, looking out at the ancient yet familiar city. The sounds, the songs, the language all coalesced, triggering again some faint memory within me. I was able to drop into *samadhi,* a quiet meditation holding me still, allowing me to open and dissolve.

I found Raja waiting in the car in the same spot where he had dropped me off. He nodded and smiled. "Good, Otis? Ms.? Good?" he inquired.

I grinned back. "Most excellent, Raja. Most excellent."

We laughed. There is an unspoken kinship with those on a spiritual path. In Nepal that path and that devotion are part of the fabric of everyday life. Whatever God you pray to, you're connected with all those who walk a true spiritual journey. For me it has always resulted in the feeling of having an extended family.

We made our way to the hotel in Thamel, a busy central section of the city. As I grabbed my backpack and slipped Raja a few American dollars, he smiled in thanks and ran toward the hotel doors to hold them open for me. I soon connected with my small group of dedicated travel companions, and that night they laid out the itinerary for the days to come.

Our plan was to stay in Kathmandu for a day, then catch a flight out to Lukla. We would go by foot through the region, stopping with our donated supplies at various drop-off points throughout the Himalayas. As far as we knew, there were only small stations that served as primary-care centers. There were rarely local doctors in these remote areas and few if any clean supplies. The majority of our donations were basics, but as statistics have shown, the basics in deprived regions can save many lives.

As we flew out of the polluted and busy capital and into the Himalayas, the change in scenery was marked. The vast expanses, sheer mountain drops, and wilderness of a kind I'd never seen before were awe-inspiring. Once we arrived in Lukla, I was able, despite my jet lag, to keep up with the group on the climb to Namche Bazaar. Namche is the main trading center in the Kumbhu region, sitting at an altitude of 11,286 feet. It is considered the gateway to the high Himalayas, and depending on the weather one can often glimpse Everest towering in the distance. We would be going higher still and would take a day in Namche Bazaar to acclimate to the altitude. Our final destination was going to be Tengboche Monastery. And as luck would have it, we were set to arrive there on the twenty-eighth of September. My thirty-third birthday.

It's not an exaggeration to say that every step of the way I felt blessed, joyous, eager, and alert. On one single-track trail that climbed alongside a throbbing river, I crossed one of the traditional hanging bridges and purposefully swayed side to side. The water raged in torrents beneath me, its roar deafening. Laughing, I looked up and to my amazement rested my eyes on the impressive Mount Everest through the parting clouds. It was breathtaking. I was reminded how tiny I was and how tiny my life was in comparison to the great expanse of nature surrounding me. There was a constant sense of surrender and peace as I walked along the craggy mountain trails. With each step I looked back at my life with a new perspective. It dawned on me how fixated we in the West are on ourselves. What was so important to me in the days before coming on this journey seemed so trivial now. As I began to laugh, Nancy gave me a gentle push from behind. "What, Carré?" she asked, laughing, too.

"Nothing. And everything." I smiled. "It's all perfect." I couldn't explain what was happening. I hadn't been this happy in years. And the joy was emerging in the simplest of situations. Imagine that.

As night began to fall, a chill swept through the air. A cold front was moving in, and in the Himalayas it happened fast. Although this was only the end of September, it was not unusual to experience some snowfall. Shivering, I pulled my hood up over my ears and zipped up tight. My body felt achy, and I was relieved to arrive at our stopping point. I could think of only one thing as I found an empty bed and un-rolled my sleeping bag. I needed to rest.

After just an hour of sleep, I woke with the dire need to get to a bath-room at once. I wasn't sure if I was going to throw up or crap myself, but I needed to move fast. Running down the hall, I threw myself into the bathroom and began vomiting violently. My body contracted in-voluntarily with each heave, and I could feel a fever beginning to rage. As disgusting as the bathroom was, I clung to the toilet bowl the entire night. I had never been so sick. I cried and trembled, and at one point I could hear some of my group gather around me, offering a wet rag, a sip of water. I just shook my head and purged. No one could help. Raja brought my sleeping bag to wrap around me. Sunrise found me asleep at last, curled up on the floor of the teahouse bathroom.

I was running an extremely high fever. The men carried me back to the room and placed me carefully into bed. I moaned out loud.

"You poor baby!" Nancy said, placing a smooth hand on my fore-head. I was grateful for all their help and concern. I felt like I was dying.

"We need to figure out what to do. The group needs to go on and stick with the schedule or we won't be able to drop off all our sup-plies. Carré, we can leave a Sherpa with you, and if you recover quickly enough, you can still try to meet us at Tengboche Monastery. Okay?" Mike was one of the leaders of the expedition and he was not only being practical, but he had everyone's best interests at heart. What he said was true: The group needed to go on ahead.

"Of course," I agreed, too sick to be sad that I might not be able to finish the mission.

"I'll stay with Carré," Nancy offered. It was an unbelievably gra-cious gesture, and I tried to convince her to go on, but she wouldn't hear of it. "Nope, we'll stick together. And maybe even catch up with them." She winked at me. Everyone blew kisses at me, not wanting to come too close, and I rolled over in my sleeping bag to get some more rest. I could only hope to wake up feeling better.

As I slept I dreamed of Tara, the female Buddha and Mother of Liberation. She appeared in her white form, luminous, floating above me. She whispered her mantra in my ear and offered me the branch of a tree. My body shook with delight, a warmth pouring over me, and when I awoke, I immediately thought of my first teacher, Lama Tsultrim. I also realized I felt better. By the next day, although I was still very weak, I felt well enough to walk, and with the Sherpa carrying my pack, I slowly made my way up the mountain trail.

We found a tiny horse that we rented for me to ride. I laughed, because my feet nearly touched the ground when I climbed onto his back. But the route we were on proved to be too treacherous for the animal, so I was soon left to rely on the strength of my own body. One foot in front of the other, I kept my head down and remained in a rather contemplative state. I held Tara and Lama Tsultrim in my mind's eye, calling on them for energy and strength. I allowed each step to be an offering. And when my suffering became great, I surrendered that burden so I could continue with this mission to help those less fortunate. Under the warm sun, I moved forward, gaining ground and speed as if some unseen force were carrying me along.

Since it was my birthday, my thoughts turned to my mother and father, and I was able to see a purity and goodness in them I hadn't acknowledged before. Compassion bubbled up, and in a moment I recognized that we are all products of our past—my parents, too. But how we proceed in our present and our future is our own choice. I was not a victim. I was not a slave. Only if I decided to be those things, would I be. I walked and cried, tears of forgiveness streaming out of me, mixing with the salty sweat on my cheeks. I was free. I was not my work. Not my parents. Not my past. I was I. A woman.

I realized how utterly self-obsessed I'd been and how, for the most part, the career I'd chosen—the career that had made me famous— condones, supports, and honors that self-obsession. I laughed and stumbled onward. I hadn't showered in a week. And I had never felt more beautiful and accomplished than I did in that moment. I wasn't tormented over what I was wearing as I climbed to the base camp of Everest. I wasn't concerned with what fit or what didn't. By offering myself, my services, and taking into account others' needs, I had shifted the focus. There were mothers along the way who couldn't feed their children. They didn't have the luxury of thinking about what to wear. They barely had clothes to keep them warm.

And just as the sun was setting and the moon was rising in the sky, just as the stars were being illuminated, I finally set foot on the rooftop of the world. The ancient walls of the monastery rose up, the wind whistled through the trees. . . . I had done it. It was a monumental feat for me. I had achieved what I set out to do—and I could rejoice and delight in those achievements. I was proud of my efforts and myself. As I made my way to my small group, I was greeted with applause and roars of excitement to have me with them.

Sitting under the impressive canopy of stars in that small mountaintop cabin at Tengboche, my companions presented me with a birthday cake. It was a small flat apple cake with a single candle. With enormous gratitude I closed my eyes, made a wish . . . and blew.

I had had it all—money, fame, privileges—but none of it had given me what I was looking for. I was ready for the next step in my journey. Ready to connect with my teachers again.

MONKS IN MALIBU

Winter seemed to have arrived early. It was October 2001, and I had just returned home from Asia. A torrential downpour left me in bumper-to-bumper traffic on the PCH, and I was daydreaming about my time in Nepal when I remembered I needed to pick something up from the health-food store I was just about to pass. I pulled over, stepped out, and attempted to run across the street. Big gusts of wind billowed up under my jacket as the rain fell in sheets all around me. I decided to duck into a doctors' office a few buildings from my destination.

"Wow!" I exclaimed to no one in particular as I shook the water off as best I could. I was chilled to the bone, and when I glanced out the window, I could see there was no letting up. The sky was black, and the traffic had intensified. I obviously had some time to kill.

"Hello. Can I help you?" A pleasant voice with a British accent asked from somewhere behind me. I laughed out loud—I thought I was alone in the waiting room. When I spun around to greet the person who was asking, I was surprised to see a table full of *mala*s and incense, much like the wares that were on display in Nepal.

"Hi. Actually, I just ducked in because of the rain and the traffic." I pointed to the highway.

"Yes. There must be an accident up ahead. It's been like this for a while." The woman couldn't have been much older than I was, and I found her quite beautiful. She had a shock of wavy red hair, a wonderful open smile that made her eyes twinkle. She actually looked like a model.

"You look really familiar to me," I said, realizing how silly that sounded. Usually people said that to me.

"I'm Rebecca. Rebecca Novick. My husband, Ronny, and I live up in Malibu." I looked down at the table where she was sitting, her black leather cowboy boots giving her an edge that went well with the accent. Just then two Tibetan Buddhist monks exited the office with a piece of paper and began to ask her some questions. They stopped, smiled at me, then continued to sort things out before wandering back behind closed doors.

"I'm sorry. You must be busy," I said, not wanting to get in her way.

"No, no. Not at all. I'm just helping this group of Tibetan monks who come from India every year to make money for their monastery. They travel all over the U.S. conducting Tibetan astrology readings as well as treating patients with traditional Tibetan medicine. What did you say your name was?" She smiled and extended her hand.

"Carré. Carré Otis," I said, returning the smile.

"Of course. I know you. Cool. And so interesting that you walked in when you did. The monks actually have an opening right now. Due to traffic, the next person on the list is a no-show. Interested?" she asked, nodding her head toward the door.

"Yes! Of course!" I cried. "What a funny day. I was wondering why I'd walked in here. Now I know."

She proceeded to lead me into one of the rooms, where a Tibetan *geshe* (a scholar with the equivalent of a doctoral degree in Buddhist scripture) sat. After we were introduced, I sat down across from him.

I smiled nervously. Again for some reason, I could feel my emotions rise to the surface. It seemed that whenever I was with Tibetans, I was alert to my deepest sentiments, even the most inchoate ones. The truth was that Nepal had been such an immense and impressive trip for me, I wasn't sure of where to go from there. I knew that I was on my path, but I was also feeling very isolated where I was living. I had big questions, the sort that were moving beyond the ones therapy could address. As I waited to hear what the doctor had to say, I knew that I was being guided. I just needed to sit back and relax.

The *geshe*'s translator stepped into the room, and I nodded quietly, not sure if I should do anything else. "Geshe-la is going to take your pulse, Carré. Can you give him both of your wrists?" He spoke kindly and quietly.

Without saying a word, I extended my arms. The warm hands of the *geshe* wrapped around each wrist, and I could tell as he stilled himself that he had found a pulse. He sat without stirring, his eyes focused on my chest, and as he did, something strange happened. For a moment I dissolved and felt as if I were in the *geshe*'s mind stream, or that he was in mine. There was no him, nor was there an I. I remained like that for some time in a profound sensation of nonduality.

The *geshe* cleared his throat. I blinked a few times as the room around me came back into focus. Behind him hung a beautiful *thangka* tapestry of the Medicine Buddha.

He spoke with the translator for a few minutes, then cleared his throat again. "Carré-la," the translator said, "Geshe says that your pulse is very weak. Have you had some heart problems?" I cocked my head to the side. Wow. *That was impressive,* I thought. And as I pondered his question, all of a sudden I didn't know how to answer. The *geshe* was speaking about more than just the body.

There was indeed an issue of the heart. My heart had been broken. My heart was filled with longing. The image of holes in my heart came thundering toward me. I was moved beyond words at the revelation. I understood that the *geshe* had seen all this when I'd allowed him into my mind. I had wanted to see this, and so the *geshe* had been able to as well.

"Geshe-la says he understands. You do not need to answer him. He has seen. Would you like help, Carré?"

I wiped my runny nose with the back of my sleeve and simply said, "Yes." I was overwhelmed with gratitude. My healing was continuing, and my path was perfectly unfolding. Had it not been for the rainstorm, I would not have been here.

"Geshe-la says to please take these pills. And he will see you again very soon." I was handed a box of Tibetan medicine, each pill an herbal formulation, individually and beautifully wrapped in silk and wound with a bright piece of string. I held them to my heart, and before leaving, I offered the *geshe* an envelope with offering money, and made three prostrations, as is the custom when you are in front of a teacher.

"Thank you, Geshe-la," I said as I backed out of the room. I didn't know when, but I knew that I would be seeing him again. As I turned around in the waiting room, I stood to face Rebecca. "Hi." She beamed at me. "That worked out well, didn't it?" she said.

I threw my arms around her, and she just laughed and hugged me back. "Thank you. Thank you. You have no idea. . . ." I sat to tell her a bit about myself. I'd had heart surgery, just come back from Nepal, and now lived alone in Malibu. I wasn't sure which way to go next. I recognize now, looking back, that I was in a spiritual crisis. My karma ripened at the perfect time to assist me along my path.

Just then Ronny, Rebecca's husband, walked in, shouting, "Bexie!" He grabbed her and smothered her with a bear hug. Ronny was over two hundred pounds, had gray hair that stood on end, a bad-ass goatee, and several silver hooped skull earrings. He was a delicious teddy bear of a guy, giving off the rare and genuine vibe of being super safe.

"Ronny, this is Carré. She lives in Malibu, too. She just saw Geshe-la." Ronny smiled and sat down, wiping the rain off his forehead.

"Geshe-la said he would see me soon. When are they back?" I asked.

"In a month or so. We're still booking their tour. We need to find them a place to stay in the meantime. Our house isn't big enough. . . ." Her voice trailed off. She was wrapping up and putting away the *malas* that were for sale. Their day was about done. It was almost five o'clock.

"Really? Well . . ." I looked outside at the rain, then at the box of medicine in my hand. I could see Geshe-la's smiling face saying he would see me again soon. "My house is big enough—I think. They could stay with me," I said, watching Rebecca's face closely. She smiled. Nodded. Looked at Ronny and winked.

"Wow, Carré. That is amazing. That would be incredible." And with that, I gave her my number. As I walked out into the dark evening, it didn't feel so dark anymore. My day had brightened.

In the weeks that passed, I thought often about the monks. Ronny, Rebecca, and I had gotten together to discuss the details of hosting them. I was getting to know this couple very well and liked the new world revealing itself to me. The monks were from Gaden Shartse Monastery, in India. They were, for the most part, Tibetan refugees, all skilled in the Tibetan arts as well as highly respected teachers, otherwise known as lamas or *geshe*. The Gaden Shartse monks were of the Gelugpa sect of Buddhism, the most recent of the four to be formed, focusing on a sequential path of practice as well as strict observance of ethics and discipline. Twelve of them would be coming to stay with me for a full week.

The rains continued to pour. The great eucalyptus trees behind my house bent in the winds. Malibu was howling. And I was readying the place for my new houseguests. On the day of their arrival, a huge pot of saffron rice had been cooked, tea and cookies were waiting. Rebecca, Ronny, and I sat in anticipation. At last we saw their van pull up, my gates open, and the maroon robes of the monks swirl about in the wind as they made their way to the front door. Rebecca opened it, smiling. *"Tashi delek!"* she said, greeting them in Tibetan.

Lobsang Wangchuk, the only Western monk in the group, smiled and graciously bowed down. "Ronny. Rebecca. And this must be Carré," he said, his sea-green eyes sparkling with a hint of mischief. "Geshe has mentioned you. Hello." He extended a hand, then waved an arm with a grand gesture to honor Geshe-la, who was just at that moment walking in.

"What can I do? What can I get you?" I asked Lobsang, thankful that someone out of the group spoke English. Just then my herd of four-legged friends ran in, barking and wagging their tails. Angel, Monkey, and Romi were my Chihuahuas, and Esmeralda and Raphael were my pugs. The monks looked terrified. Uh-oh. I hadn't thought about the dog factor. I laughed and reached down to pet my old friends. "They don't bite. Really!" I said, scratching Esmeralda behind her ears. I don't think the monks had ever seen such small, silly creatures living like humans in the comfort of a home before.

I showed Lobsang my house and the one private room where the *geshe* would stay with his attendant. Everyone else would stay on the living-room floor. As it turned out, the *geshe* remembered me quite well, and as I showed him the room, he grabbed my hand and pulled my head toward his in the traditional Tibetan greeting. Forehead to forehead we stood, the room hushed. I knew he was an old, old friend, and I was so glad he had come to stay.

The week was one of the funniest of my life, camped out with all those characters in my house. We talked, cooked, joked, and laughed. I had a sense that I'd known each of them before in a past life, and for us to all gather like this seemed completely normal. I drove them to their appointments to perform ritualistic house blessings and even took them to Cher's enormous mansion on the ocean's cliffs. It was wonderful, albeit a bit bizarre, for someone who'd done all the things I'd done in my life, including making a living as a model, to now be driving a dozen monks around Malibu blessing celebrity homes. But I didn't question for a minute my role in their lives and how natural it felt for me to serve them. I didn't second-guess a thing, and not once did I feel uncomfortable doing whatever it was they needed of me—cooking, cleaning, and making endless cups of tea. Even renting movies.

I took the ten of them (leaving Geshe-la and his attendant at the house) to Blockbuster one rainy night and walked through aisles and aisles of action movies.

"Lobsang, are you sure they want action? I mean, this is all really violent. Or really racy." I was concerned that it might negatively influence them. Lobsang just laughed.

"It's nothing they haven't seen, Carré! In the monastery that's all they watch! Steven Seagal's a big hit." I just laughed. Until Thinley pulled out and waved around the box for *Booty Call*.

"No way!" I grabbed it from his hand. "No way do you want to watch this!" Tears were streaming down my face I was laughing so hard. "Lobsang . . . please tell him!" I begged. And in Tibetan, Lobsang tried to explain what it was about, in a rather less-than-detailed way. We ended up leaving with *Die Hard*.

As the monks sat crowded on my living-room floor to watch the video, I went into the kitchen to count out my evening's regimen of medication: Paxil, Depakote, and trazodone. I'd been on my antidepressants for nearly a decade, rarely questioning the protocol my psychiatrists had recommended for me. Pills were a part of my life, and I assumed I needed them, just as I'd been told. Grabbing a cup of tea, I sat down in the background, the dim light illuminating my living-room table.

"What have you there, Carré-la?" Lobsang asked as he pulled up a chair and sat next to me.

"Oh, just my pills," I said nonchalantly.

"Why are you on pills?" he asked quietly, the look in his eyes capturing me by surprise.

"Oh, Lobsang, I've been on them for years. I used to suffer from depression." It came out matter-of-factly.

"And now? Do you? Still suffer?" he asked.

I thought for a moment, looking down at the small bowl I usually put my pills into before I took them. It was part of my ritual.

"That's a good question. I do. I mean, I still do suffer. It's not like it was, though. I don't want to die."

"Oh," he said simply. Geshe-la had come up behind him and in Tibetan asked a few questions. Lobsang looked at me, then at the bowl of pills. "Geshe is wondering if you still think you need them," he translated.

"I'm not sure. What happens if I go off of them and . . . ?" I didn't finish the sentence. I hadn't really contemplated that before.

"Geshe-la says he can't see why you take them. Suffering is part of the human condition. Sadness is part of being alive. As is joy. Do you feel joy?" he asked.

"I hadn't for some time. Now, with you all here, I suppose I have." I laughed. It was true. I'd been feeling immeasurable joy throughout their visit.

"So why not see what it is like without them, Carré? Geshe would like to give you a meditation practice that can help you stabilize your mind."

I wasn't at all convinced I could stop taking my meds cold like that. But I was open, and I sat gratefully as Geshe walked me through a basic meditation practice.

"We will help you, Carré. You just need to reach out to us."

The very next day, I called my doctor and spoke with him about it.

"I've been on this stuff forever. It's not like I don't still feel sad sometimes, but it's not like there's one pill that is a cure either," I pointed out to him.

He didn't agree. "Carré, statistics say that within a month you are very likely to end up in the hospital with depression. This is serious business. You will also have to contend with withdrawal. You need to be monitored. I realize you've made headway, but I cannot ignore medical statistics." It was obvious he didn't like my decision. But something in me rose up in response to his words.

"All due respect, but I'm not a statistic. I don't want to be on this stuff anymore. I'm going to get off." And with that, it was decided. I began my withdrawal.

It had been more than a decade since I'd felt such intense emotion—the good, the bad, and the terrifying. The numbness that had once helped me move past my fears was replaced by a sharp and almost painful awareness. I felt like I was on LSD. Colors became vivid, smells almost overwhelming, and feelings stronger than they'd ever been. I wasn't sure I could manage them without the constant hands-on support of my newfound friends.

Lobsang reassured me daily, and before leaving, Geshe-la handed me a box of what he called Precious Pills—a unique blend of healing minerals. "Geshe says you will be fine. You can do this. Don't forget to practice. This intensity will pass." I wept as I said good-bye to them and watched, holding my beloved Chihuahua Angel as they drove away early one morning.

When I stepped back into my home, the silence was deafening. How the hell was I going to do this? But day after day I remembered what I'd been told. I was to practice, breathe, and call my support system, including Ronny and Rebecca. I knew that my pills were only a step away; I knew that I could always return to them if I needed them. They wouldn't disappear. But what I wanted more than anything right now was to be in touch with the complete me, and that was going to take courage and perseverance. That me was outside the box of my old thinking and outside the box that my therapist could support. I was on my own to make the transition, and I was determined to do it successfully.

When the waves of emotions washed over me, I'd make my way to the safe island of my meditation cushion. My pups would gather around in concern, and we would wait there together until the fear passed, like clouds in the sky. I began to understand that all does eventually pass; each and every moment is fleeting and impermanent. Just as I couldn't hold on to my moments of happiness and joy, the moments of my fear and sadness wouldn't stay in my life forever either. In this way I came to understand and trust myself. I sat in the meditation posture that I had been taught, counting my breaths, watching my emotions come and go. And in a month's time, the intensity of it all had subsided and the ups and downs became manageable.

As the New Year approached, I gathered all my pill bottles that were collecting dust and piled them up in front of my shrine. I was ready to throw them out. I knew that I would not need them again. Saying good-bye to my medication was like saying good-bye to the last remnants of the Carré who was dependent upon outside forces to make her well.

I knew I could reach out and get support. I also knew that I could turn inward to find the stillness and safety that hadn't been cultivated enough in me before. After having left my childhood home at such a young age, I'd spent so many years seeking home in other people and places. But I realized at this moment that wherever I was, I was home. I had finally created that safe harbor where I could exist peacefully. The indestructible one that exists within. There would be no more searching for it, as it would be with me all the time.

GESHE GYELTSEN AND THE VOW OF CELIBACY

As I did more and more work as a plus-size model and gathered strength from the painful but transformational *O* magazine experience, I began to speak publicly about eating disorders. I was eager to converse with the women whose paths I crossed about the subject of body image and the pressures our culture puts on young people. I began to hold a regular circle at the Monte Nido Eating Disorder Treatment Center, which wasn't far from my home. Carolyn Costin, an extraordinary author and therapist, founded Monte Nido. I met Carolyn in a yoga class, and we easily hit it off, often having to take our conversation outside in our excitement. One of the many things that struck me about Carolyn was that she was the first professional I'd met who would say, point-blank, that "you can *recover* from eating disorders." I was so grateful to hear that.

I had also been traveling with Ronny and Rebecca every week to Thubten Dhargye Ling, a Buddhist temple and study center in Long Beach. The Venerable Geshe Gyeltsen was teaching the Stages of the Path to Enlightenment (also known as the *lamrim*), and as we sat before him listening intently, I couldn't help but wonder if he was *my* teacher. Of course I'd had instruction by several wonderful teachers so far, but when a student finds that one with whom he or she is more profoundly connected than all others, that is said to be this person's "heart teacher." I was intrigued by this notion and was always on the lookout for that rare occurrence. This took nothing away from the love and respect I had for Geshe-la. He was incredible—sweet, funny, and skillful. And the discipline of the Gelugpa school was helping me immensely. For the first time since grade school, I was formally studying, reading texts and learning an incredible amount about the basics of Buddhism. The foundation I was building was priceless. I was grateful for it all, but a small part of me was curious about the pull I was feeling toward this teacher who now had my rapt attention.

One afternoon I had a private meeting with Geshe Gyeltsen, and it went in a direction I never expected. Geshe offered me tea and motioned for me to sit down on the floor before him.

I blurted out a question, my own words taking me by surprise. "Geshe, do you think I should become a nun?"

A part of me was very serious, not knowing how else I could offer myself fully to the path. I felt I had already seen so many things in the world and now was ready to root myself in just one thing, Buddhism.

But the part of me that was an extremist was searching for the next bold direction to catapult myself into. And, thankfully, Gyeltsen was able to see all this.

His eyes twinkled, and he threw his head back in laughter. Then, rubbing his chin, he nodded and said, "This is so wonderful, Carré. For you to have such deep devotion. But let me ask you this—for this is where most Westerners have trouble. . . ."

I nodded and waited.

"Have you ever been celibate?" he asked, looking me right in the eye. I choked on my tea. "Um. No. Never." I thought for a moment. I didn't have to think too far back into my past to recall my last sexual encounter. It had been another one-night stand. And then before that it had been with a female friend, leaving our friendship in ruins.

I must have made a sad and confused face, because Geshe laughed again. "Yes. This is a problem. It is very hard for people in the West to separate from their sexual 'identity.' And this really must be explored before one takes robes."

I knew he was speaking from firsthand experience. Geshe was one of the few Gelugpa monks who had taken robes, then given them back to pursue a relationship (through which he'd had a son), then later returned to monastic vows.

I had actually not given much thought to the dalliances I'd had. In my head it was just what people did: Have sex. Have affairs. It certainly was what I'd done for a long time. But what had eluded me was that none of these affairs—including my marriage—had been successful. I certainly hadn't reached a point where a sexual union with another human being was a mutually aware or liberating experience. Quite the contrary, it almost always felt more obligatory than exalting.

"My suggestion to you, Carré, is that you take a vow of celibacy," Gyeltsen said.

"Really?" The prospect excited me. I liked vows. I looked at them as challenges. "How long, Geshe?" I asked naïvely. I had no idea what I was in for.

"Start with a year," he replied, and with that, he smiled and then abruptly dismissed me.

Our conversation was over. And out I walked with a new mission. Little did I know just how hard it would be. Nor did I remotely comprehend that the greatest challenges would come in areas that were not at all obvious.

Sex for me wasn't about pleasure, it was about power. Or what I thought was power. I equated sex with approval. And someone's wanting me physically meant that I had the upper hand in the situation. Since I was young, it had been something that had given me an in. It was how I got some level of the love and attention I craved.

Sex was at the heart of the modeling industry. "Sex sells," I was told over and over again. How many times had I heard a photographer say, "Look at the camera like you're making love to it; look like you want me to fuck you." This unending, vulgar dialogue was part of my everyday professional life, and I'd had to endure it, whether I liked it or not. I couldn't show disgust or discomfort; I'd learned to hide my intense dislike of the sexualized discourse of the industry.

I knew how to appear sexy. The kind of sexy that comes at the expense of real feelings—fears, wants, desires, likes, and dislikes. I'd learned what to do on the job and figured out the rest on my own. I recognized from the start that there was power in sex. There was power in giving a great blow job. But what kind of power was it? How long did it last? And what was the cost?

Sex had never been about intimacy for me. Walking out of Geshe's office, I realized I had no concept of what intimacy really was. My whole life's work was wound up in my being a sexual entity. But it was a game. Even with my friends, it was a game. I'd lost plenty of friendships in just this way. My approach to life for years had been all about seduction—I would seduce everyone: you, your brother, or your mother. I didn't know any other way to relate to people or get the attention I so sorely needed.

Sex wasn't about an orgasm. It was about faking an orgasm. And the only orgasms that I'd ever had were by my own hand. How could I ever surrender enough to another person to actually let go and come? That was incomprehensible to me. It hadn't bothered me, because I never gave it any thought. Being sexy and being good in bed was part of my persona; it was just what I did. It was always about obligation, never about connection or my own pleasure. I set out to make every man I was with feel like a superhero, but little did he know that for me it was always an act.

And so I embarked on one of the most intense and revealing journeys of my life to date. I shed every vestige of my sexual self. Rather than feeling clothed, I felt naked, exposed for the world to see in all my discomfort. I had no idea who I was without the power of sex, without the tool of seduction. I had no idea how to relate, even to my friends. I realized early on in my celibacy how much I had played the role of sexpot throughout my life. Without that mask, social interaction was excruciating—I had no idea who I was.

Living a celibate life taught me many invaluable lessons. It freed me to discover that real intimacy could be had with friends. By sexualizing everything, I'd created veils of illusion that had separated me from other people. Celibacy allowed those illusions to slip away. I could be close without being sexual; I could show up for other people and let go of my self-centered need for validation. It was an ongoing revelation. Geshe Gyeltsen had known exactly what I needed.

Through this process I was getting ready for something more. I wasn't sure what that was, exactly, but I knew that all this was integral to living out the rest of my life in an honest, authentic, radically healthy way.

RECONNECTING WITH TSULTRIM

In February 2001, just after I'd gotten back from the O magazine shoot in the Bahamas, I had a dream. In it I could see my friend and teacher Tsultrim Allione clear as day. I was watching her being driven in a car around winding roads high up in some mountain range. The sky was the brightest blue, and the air around me was crisp. In an instant the car was gone. I ran to the edge of a sheer cliff only to see it tumbling over and over to the ground below. I was consumed with grief. But out of the grief sprang a well of love and devotion. The scenery changed suddenly, and I was walking toward a cabin high on a mountaintop, tall pines rustling in a steady wind. "Tsultrim!" I called out. And then she appeared, one finger to her lips to quiet me, the other beckoning me to come sit by her, a cushion already waiting.

I awoke with a desperate feeling that I had to speak with Tsultrim immediately. I felt rather wild and out of control. Why had I waited so long to reconnect with her? Why had I not thought to call her sooner? Our bond had always been so strong, but as I had traveled through my life, carried by one current or another, the shame I felt for having gone against her advice, for having left the Ojai retreat to meet Mickey and Zalman all those years ago, remained. That decision had cost me so much. The remorse I subconsciously felt had kept me from her for so long.

Turning on my bedside light, I checked the time. It was 4:00 A.M. I picked up the phone and dialed information. Where had Tsultrim said she was going when I spoke with her last? Where did she live? I was stuck for a moment, knowing she'd left upstate New York years earlier, but to where? And then, as the sleep receded further, I remembered the name of a place I'd seen in one of the occasional newsletters I still received. It was clear as a bell.

"City and state," a voice asked over the phone.

"Pagosa Springs, Colorado," I said, smiling to myself.

And I found her. Just like that. I waited a few hours to place the call and was surprised to get an answering machine with a pleasant woman's voice welcoming me to Tara Mandala Retreat Center. Clearly, a lot had happened since last we spoke. I waited for a beep, and as I left my message, a flood of tears sprang forth.

"This is a message for Tsultrim. . . . It's her old friend and student

Carré Otis. I really need to speak with her. It's really important." Choking on emotion, I hung up. It felt as if my very life depended on talking with her once more. I was worried. The dream had made me feel as if I would never see her again. I was terrified that might be the case.

Several hours later I tried the number again. Finally someone answered.

"Tara Mandala."

"Hi! I am so sorry to bother you. . . . I left a message earlier. . . ."

"It's Carré?" the woman asked, cutting me off, not unkindly.

"Yes," I said, relieved.

"Hi. I have given Tsultrim your number. She will be calling you. But she is getting ready to go into long retreat, so things are quite busy here." I was dumbstruck. I was desperate.

"I have to see her. I have to talk with her!" I cried.

And the woman on the other end reassured me that I would be able to speak with her very soon.

So I sat and waited. And paced. Finally the phone rang. I knew it was her before I even picked it up.

"Tsultrim," I whispered into the phone.

"Beauuuty," she purred, affectionately calling me what she always had. We were both silent for a moment, as if our breaths were matched and our minds were merging. I felt as if she were holding my entire being in the warmest embrace.

I told her what I was doing, where I was living, and that I was practicing again. Somehow I could tell she knew that this time was different from all the other times I'd called her. Things had really changed for me. I also learned that she had moved and was living near the retreat center she'd founded, in southwest Colorado.

"I had a dream, Tsultrim," I said, giving her the details.

"Carré, I was in an accident. I was in Bhutan, and my car rolled off a cliff. It's a miracle I'm alive."

I let out a long exhale. "I need to see you. That was the other part of my dream. That I was in retreat with you."

"Well, this is true, too. I'm going into retreat March ninth for a year," she replied.

"No!" I wailed. So close yet so far away! I felt I'd missed the boat! How could I wait to see her for that long? "What should I do?" I cried. "I mean, where do I go from here?"

Tsultrim laughed. I was ready for instructions. I was ready to commit.

"There will be a very special teacher coming from Tibet when I return from my retreat next year. But all our students will have had to do some preliminary practices in order to meet him and attend his teachings. Actually, most of the schools of Tibetan Buddhism require a practitioner to do at least one full cycle of these practices before proceeding along the path. This is called *Ngöndro*, or the Preliminary Practices; if you would like, I can give you these over the phone and you can work on them throughout the year."

I was overjoyed. I felt as if I were receiving the greatest gift, a flawless jewel. And indeed I was. With paper and pen ready, I took down notes on the basics of *Ngöndro* and vowed that I would come to be with Tsultrim in a year.

Hanging up the phone, I shed tears of relief, of sorrow, of longing, and of joy. And every day I practiced. With the start of each Ngöndro session, I focused on four thoughts: the preciousness of life, the certainty of death, the flawed impermanence of this world, and the basic principle of cause and effect. I came to see how wrapped up I'd been in the minute and immediate details of my life and how I had missed so much of what really mattered. These practices became my lifeline.

FINDING MY HEART TEACHER

The year Tsultrim was in retreat had a profound effect on me. Ironically, I felt that I had finally been thrown a lifeline, but the person who'd thrown it to me could not be reached. It motivated me. It inspired me. And it made me desperate to somehow stay on course.

I took the instructions that Tsultrim had given me over the phone and began, day by day, to create the time and space to "sit." I was finding a rhythm. Through practicing what she had given me, I realized I was showing my appreciation as well as my devotion. Many Buddhist teachers speak of how precious the teachings of the Buddha are and that to be given a jewel and not do anything with it is a true pity.

I took my practice on the road, and no matter where I traveled for a job, I awoke early enough to fit it into my day. I made sure that it was a priority. The value of stabilizing one's mind is terribly underrated. I wouldn't be where I am today without having taken that discipline seriously.

Just as Tsultrim promised, in a year's time I received a call. She was back. I could go and see her.

"Why not come for the Dzogchen retreat we're having? You can stay up at our house," Tsultrim offered. I was beside myself with excitement and booked my tickets to Durango, Colorado.

The tiny puddle jumper landed in the heart of the Rockies, and as I stepped out onto the tarmac, the single runway seemed dwarfed by the impressive mountains that circled it. It felt more like the Himalayas than the Rockies. I was impressed.

The drive to Tara Mandala was stunning. The colors along the way seemed exceptionally vivid. I felt alert and awake and happy to be evidencing my change to people I respected and cared about so deeply. It had taken me decades to pay my dues and return to this place of spiritual family.

I reached the small town of Pagosa Springs as the sun was beginning to set. I was careful to follow the directions very closely. This was the wilderness in all its raw glory.

There were no road signs to guide me, just a red barn at the gate where I was supposed to enter. As I began to panic a bit in the shadows of dusk, I reminded myself of my unyielding connection with Tsultrim. I had come this far. There was no way I wouldn't get to her, even in the darkness of the nighttime Rockies. Just then, down the road, I saw a twinkle of lights. And farther beyond, a row of enormous prayer flags, the kind you only see in Bhutan or Tibet. I had arrived.

I parked the car and turned off the engine. Silence. Then, rising above it, the drone of Tibetan chants. I followed the sounds to a large earth-colored stupa, and there, under a brilliant moon, sat Tsultrim. Her son Costanzo, whom I hadn't seen since he was seven, was there as well, an empty place next to him. Cos smiled at me, reached out, and gave me a hug. "Welcome home, sister." He winked. Gratefully, I snuggled in next to him, sitting happily on the earthen floor, sharing a prayer book so I could join everyone. I had come in at the conclusion of Tara Mandala's regular feast offering. I waited quietly as everyone wrapped up, knowing that Tsultrim hadn't seen me yet.

And then our eyes met. Everything seemed to grow quiet. I knew she could see through it all. She could see me.

"Carré!" She grinned. And we held each other tight, then rested our foreheads together in silence.

I traveled many times to Tara Mandala in the years to come. Practicing, taking teachings, following Tsultrim's advice and instructions. Then one afternoon in the fall of 2003, she called.

"You must come. An amazing teacher is visiting from Tibet, and I just feel you will have a strong connection with him." I took her advice to heart and made a plan to go. The retreat would actually end on Christmas Day, and I couldn't think of anything better to do than be with my dharma family. I wasn't yet as fully reconnected with my own biological one. We had made inroads in our relationship, but were nowhere near spending holidays together.

"Bring warm clothes, Carré. The teachings will most likely be held in a tent outside. There is already snow on the ground, so it will be cold."

I had no idea what I was in for. No idea, really, about this person I was about to meet. At that point I had met a great many teachers who had brought elements of profound illumination into my life, but I wasn't certain if one actually needed to or could ever find a heart teacher. I knew that many students never found one. At this point I was just grateful that I'd been able to receive teachings from so many inspiring masters.

I had arrived in Pagosa yet again, this time staying at the small Spa Hotel. I would be driving out to Tara Mandala every day for the retreat. That first morning I was shocked to see the thermostat in my rental car read just nine degrees. I had never been in nine-degree weather. That was cold.

I carefully drove along the icy road out to the center and made my way to the tent that had been erected for this particular retreat. Outside, there was a large fire. Juniper was being burned to dispel spiritual obstacles. There were approximately forty students all lined up, waiting for this teacher to arrive. They were waving white *khatas* (offering scarves) in the air and singing the guru's mantra. I found my place with the others and waited. The air was bitter cold, and I tried to move closer to the fire. Just then the smoke seemed to part and an unusually tall lama began walking toward us. He had dark hair, glasses, large feet, and long earlobes. I was immediately drawn to him. And I, like many others present, was moved to cry. He walked slowly, taking big, careful steps, holding one hand to his brow, nodding and smiling, giving his blessings as he made his way past our line and into the tent. (Because he still lives in Chinese-occupied Tibet, I'm choosing not to reveal his real name for his protection.)

In an instant I was certain, sure as day, that I had just met my heart teacher. The tears I shed were those of absolute gratitude. My karma had ripened, enabling us to come together once again in this life. Every cell of my being knew this. I felt utterly devoted.

The week was magical and full of learning. I was formally given my preliminary practice instructions and vowed to finish these; all one hundred thousand of three different accumulations plus one million recitations of another. (This is what it sounds like, and more. It can take years to complete. It was well beyond what Tsultrim had given me when we first reconnected.) I was excited to have a concise practice, one where I had a specific goal. A new world opened for me. And I took it very seriously.

Leaving Tara Mandala after that visit was harder than ever before. I knew I wouldn't see this formidable teacher again for a full year, and my heart broke as I watched him leave. But I realized the profundity of working with someone long-distance. To maintain the connection, faith must be present. I knew that no matter what, my heart teacher was only as far from me as my mind projected. In reality we were inseparable. And so in this way I practiced, seeing my lama in my heart center. Wherever I was and whatever I did, my lama remained with me.

My celibacy took on a new meaning and a new purpose as I saw how rich my life had become. I was learning how to really take care of myself and eradicate the fantasy that always and so conveniently suggested that someone or something else could do it better. I was building a foundation, one that in this life I had not been taught or encouraged to do.

I was beginning to feel like a nun, although I hadn't taken my robes. Never before in my life had I been so devoted and disciplined. I had found a groove that went with me wherever I went. I awoke at 4:00 A.M. and had my first practice session; then I'd do my Ashtanga Mysore yoga, break for a snack and tea, and resume my sitting practice. My days were spent like this for quite some time, and although it was a grind, it helped me to focus and get through those last years of living in Los Angeles. I came to realize that for the most part it is only ourselves as individuals who can get us to practice and get us *through* practice, too. We can have friends and partners and business associates, but in the end we're in charge of creating the lives we want to live. I was living that out.

The following year my heart teacher returned to the United States. I was just about halfway through my *Ngöndro* accumulations and eager to report this to him. I was also eager to speak with him about my ongoing desire to take my robes as a nun. I was feeling more and more at ease with and empowered by my life as a celibate. I was on a path that fulfilled me.

The fact that I loved celibacy didn't shield me from the incessant questioning and the frank bewilderment of family and friends.

"What? Are you nuts?"

"Why would you do that? You're in your prime!"

"What a waste. You're such a beautiful woman."

Kimora Lee Simmons famously said to me, "What's *up,* girl? You got cobwebs in your coochie or *what?*" That was only slightly less classy than the typical remark.

The bottom line was, most folks just couldn't fathom why I might make a choice like that. Our culture has rigid criteria for women and their bodies. By being celibate I was making it clear that I wasn't abiding by those criteria. I wasn't worried about having a baby, wasn't worried about having a lover, and didn't feel obligated to give my body to anyone. Just my being open about celibacy pushed people's buttons. I'd begun to realize why monks were meant to live in the monasteries. There was not much support for that life in our modern world.

Sitting quietly with my heart teacher and a translator, I fidgeted around the subject until I finally had the courage to ask.

"Rinpoche, I have a question."

He nodded, a warm smile pulling his round cheeks upward. "Yes, Carré."

"I wanted to know what you would think of me taking my robes? I have been celibate for three years now. This is not a problem for me. I feel very drawn to becoming a nun." I waited.

He looked at me hard, his gaze penetrating. What if he were to say yes? Was I really ready? But then he smiled. He lifted a finger and shook it at me, his head following the movement as his grin grew wider. It was clear he did not approve of the notion.

"Why?" I asked, laughing with him. The second time! Turned down! What did he know that I didn't? Obviously, everything under the sun.

"Finish your *Ngöndro.* That is all I will say. Now it's not the time. Finish your *Ngöndro.*"

I didn't argue. Part of me was relieved.

I had another question for him. I told him I thought it was time for me to leave L.A. "I'm thinking of returning home to Marin," I said. "I want to reconnect with my family." I knew that this was a change I needed. I also knew I needed his blessing.

My teacher looked at me and through me, his eyes far away. The room seemed more illuminated as we sat quietly, waiting, while he found the answer. He came back, his eyes focusing and his head nodding emphatically.

"Yes. This is very good. This will complete a karmic cycle for you. It is time to return home." He nodded and smiled and then, with a wave of his graceful hand, dismissed me. It was like that every time. Loving, spacious, open, then matter-of-factly dismissed. I appreciated that. His clarity and practicality affected me and quieted my drama every time we met.

I thanked him and slipped back out of the room, pausing in the dark hallway to take a breath and steady myself. Okay, finish my *Ngöndro*. That much was clear.

And in my spare time look for a new place to live in Northern California, pack up my house, and move. I wasn't so sure it was going to be that easy.

LAST MEETING WITH MICKEY

Leaving Los Angeles was more complicated than I thought it would be. Returning from that winter retreat at the end of 2004 with my heart teacher's blessing, I was eager to move back to the Bay Area. I had never felt L.A. to be my home, being the Northern California girl that I am. For many years I'd missed the rain, the weather, the leaves that turn brilliant colors in the fall. I'd missed the fog and the hikes through redwood forests. I'd missed the cliffs and the crashing waves. The Bay Area represented my roots, and I was now ready to return and reclaim them.

But with each step I took toward extricating myself, it seemed as if Los Angeles were wrapping its tentacles around me all the tighter. I was beginning to see some of the wonderful things I'd created in my time there. I had found a sweet routine within a yoga community and had doubts that I would ever be able to find another community like it elsewhere. I had made my professional home in L.A. as well, and it gave me a comfortable lifestyle. Could that still work after a move? Fortunately, my agent reassured me that I needed to be happy first and foremost. Jeffrey said that when clients wanted to book me, they would simply have to bring me in from San Francisco.

"Honey, you have to be happy. This is your life. Live wherever you feel supports that!" And I knew that Jeffrey was right. It was the truth. But somehow I was also looking for reasons not to go. I knew that I needed to move, but I also knew that the road might be rocky. I was going home to make amends with my family; we had visited and corresponded in the years since my sister's wedding, but I was ready to have them more fully in my life again. And I knew that before that could happen, there might be some painful truths to revisit.

I remember one of my teachers once giving me the advice to "act as if" when I wanted to manifest something. So I acted as if I were going to be moving soon. I packed all the things I needed and sold those that I didn't need. I was determined to fit my entire life and belongings into one U-Haul that I could drive myself. I also called my family to tell them my news. I was coming back home.

My mother wanted to help. In fact, everyone in my family wanted to. So I agreed to have my mother take a look at some rentals for me. My father was simple and sweet.

"Carré, just tell me what you need."

I laughed. It was amazing to finally be in ongoing communication with them all. "Actually, Dad, there is one thing. When I find the place I'll move to, could you fly down to L.A. and help me drive the U-Haul back?" I honestly couldn't think of a better way to make the move. It seemed fitting. And I really did need the help.

My father agreed, and while I continued my house hunt, I kept "acting as if." When I got closer to leaving, my certainty seemed to be repeatedly tested. It was as if the universe knew that something big was about to happen and threw some mighty obstacles my way to be sure I was ready for it.

I had just gotten home from my yoga class one afternoon when my cell phone rang.

"Hello?" I answered.

"Um, hi," said the male voice. I didn't recognize it.

"Hi?" I said back. And then it dawned on me. It was Mickey.

"Wow. Hey, Mick. How are you?" I asked. I was startled but not surprised.

"Hey! Otis. Carré. It's great to hear your voice. I . . . I was thinking about you," Mickey said.

"And you called." I wasn't too sure how I felt yet.

"Yeah. I wanted to see if you wanted to get a cup of coffee? We could hang out. See a movie." It was both great and terribly confusing to hear him. I had always hoped we might find a way to be friends. Mickey had been such a big part of my life and my growing up. In ways both good and bad, my time with him had shaped me irrevocably.

I didn't answer immediately. I was feeling it out, checking in with myself to see if the call felt right. It did.

"Actually, Mickey, it would be great, really great, to see you." I was hesitant, but also hopeful. I didn't want him back as a husband or a lover. But perhaps we could be friends, or at least friendly. I owed it to both of us to be open to the possibility. We met at the Promenade in Santa Monica, the bustle of kids and tourists around us.

He smiled sheepishly when he saw me, and I reached out to give him a bear hug. He mussed up my hair affectionately, then grabbed me again.

"Damn, it's good to see you, Otis!" And it was for me as well. He was still my old friend, even though it didn't look like him anymore. I couldn't help but notice all the work he'd had done on his face. Of course I'd seen pictures of him in magazines, but I wasn't prepared for how different he looked up close. I felt sad for him. And still loved him the way one loves a brother. As I looked at the face I'd once known so well, I realized that the surgeries represented his pain and his constant attempt to mask what it was he was feeling. I had compassion. It made me wonder how well Mickcy was really doing.

"Let's sit and have some tea," I said and walked with him, arm in arm, over to one of the quieter cafés.

We found a seat in a corner. I couldn't help but notice that Mickey was looking at me longingly. I was uncomfortable. He placed a hand over mine, and I studied his fingers as I once had, his long nails arching over the nail bed. His hands were still strong. I pulled mine away and cleared my voice, looking him in the eye.

"Okay. I just want to clear the air about something. I'm not sure if you know, but I'm celibate. I've been celibate for years. So with your call, I was hoping you just wanted to reconnect—as friends."

I waited. I had found my voice and didn't want it to leave me now. I had the power to make myself heard, and that would keep me safe. But it was fascinating to feel my own angst well up as I sat there in front of him. I'd spent years working on myself, working to be able to handle this very moment. Yet still some faint triggers of fear and doubt crept over me.

Mickey laughed, grinning broadly. "So you're telling me you haven't been with anyone for years?" I was surprised that out of everything I'd just said, this was what he was focused on. "That's great news. I wouldn't want to hear you'd been with anyone."

And in a flash my instincts were confirmed. He was still holding out for me. No doubt he thought it was good news that I was celibate, because perhaps that meant *I* was holding out for *him*.

"Wait, Mickey, I just want to be clear with you. I'm here as a friend. . . . I mean, I would love it if we could be friends." I took a deep breath, closed my eyes, and opened them again. "I'm not interested in you as anything else. And if you can understand that, then I'm happy to continue this conversation."

I knew I was challenging him. But the fact of the matter was, I wasn't at all interested in playing games. Boundaries were clear to me now; I had worked my ass off to be able to create and honor them. After all the work I'd done, I wasn't willing to be around anyone who couldn't be in alignment with that.

But Mickey placed his hand back on mine. He stroked it fondly, testing my words. Again I pulled away. "Mickey . . ." I said in a stern tone. This was going nowhere fast. And just like so many time before, I saw the telltale signs that he was ready to blow. His eye began twitching. He tapped his nose a few times. He didn't like to be reprimanded. Or rejected. He couldn't handle the fact that I had changed while he had not. He could no longer control me, and he was pissed off.

Mickey suddenly snapped. He slammed his fist down on the table and looked at me. "You know, Carré, you are a fucking piece of work." His hostility was escalating fast. "You are a fucking bitch. A real bitch."

I stood carefully and started to back away. I didn't have to sit there and listen to that anymore. I could just walk away.

"No, actually, you are a cunt. A fucking cunt."

I didn't even blink. Step by step I backed out toward the door. Customers were starting to move out of Mickey's way, as he looked like a bull ready to charge. Then he stood up and flipped the table onto its side, sending our glasses crashing to the floor, where they shattered into a million pieces. I thought, *That's us, our relationship. It's done. Shattered. You just showed your true colors, Mick. Good-bye.*

"C-U-N-T! Fucking cunt!" he bellowed, raging on to no one in particular. And in a flash I turned and ran through the doors, out onto the Promenade, disappearing as fast as I possibly could into the sea of people.

I was out of breath. I was stunned. I felt shell-shocked and blindsided. I raced around a corner and stopped, grabbing the side of a building to steady myself. And I began to sob. I wasn't crying from disappointment or shock. I was crying from pride. I was so proud of myself to have walked away. It was over at last. Whatever final little test I needed to pass, I had. I wept because I knew in every fiber of my being that I never needed to go there again. Not in any relationship, not with anyone.

I reached into my purse for my ringing cell phone and saw it was Mickey calling. I hit "ignore" and instead dialed Jeffrey's number. I wailed into the phone, trying to tell him what had happened.

"Can I do anything? Are you okay?" he asked quietly.

"I'm scared, Jeff," I sniffled. "Not of Mickey. But of moving on. Of moving away. I'm scared right now. I think that's why I agreed to meet with him. I was hoping that somehow something about seeing him would make me less scared." I knew that Jeffrey understood. He knew my fallbacks. He knew what I'd been through. He had actually been with me almost every step of the way.

Jeffrey told me that he didn't know anyone stronger than me. He told me what I needed to hear and what was true. That I'd worked incredibly hard, that I'd made bigger changes than anyone he'd ever seen. And he told me that I was ready and able to make this move. He added one more thing.

"Don't take his calls, Carré. Be done with that. You don't need to learn that one again."

After I hung up with Jeffrey, I checked my messages. There were several from Mickey. My ex-husband was frantic, and the sequence of messages he left progressed predictably, from abjectly apologetic to furiously threatening as he realized I was not going to take his calls.

Walking back toward my car, I laughed out loud. I felt exhausted yet victorious. I knew I had just passed a very serious test, one that would allow me to leave Los Angeles at last. And I was reminded of the old saying that a leopard cannot change its spots. I'd changed mine. But Mickey hadn't changed his, and at last our story together was finally, completely, and utterly over.

5

A New Beginning

COMING HOME, MEETING MATTHEW

Just two weeks after my last meeting with Mickey, in January 2005, I found a place in Northern California. "Acting as if" had worked. It was a rental in a small but lovely Victorian, set in the hills of Sausalito, overlooking the bay and a harbor full of sailboats. It was so picturesque that it was ideal, as were the owners. For the year I lived there, I would fondly call them my fairy godparents. They had appeared at a time when I'd needed an easy and wondrous transitional space, and that's exactly what they offered me. From the moment I walked into their San Carlos Avenue house, there was a sense of comfort. It was within walking distance of the little town and some great restaurants. The area felt like a small village compared to the vastness of Los Angeles. It also had a perfect room for practice. As I was unpacking, I created my shrine with the knowledge that this was where I would finish my *Ngöndro*.

As he had promised, my father flew to Los Angeles early one February morning and made the journey home with me. The preciousness of that did not escape me. Ten years earlier I could never have imagined

a day when my father would caravan with me back to the Bay Area.
It was quite the testament to all the work we'd each done on ourselves
during the many years we were out of touch. We had each wrestled
with our demons and were making incredible strides in our sobriety.
Forgiveness was sweet indeed.

I drove my black Jaguar filled to the brim with two Chihuahuas
and one pug. My father followed close behind in the U-Haul into
which I had fit everything I was willing to take home with me. The
weeks before I left had been a free-for-all, as friends and neighbors
came by to score the loot I was giving away in an attempt to lighten my
load. I didn't need much at all. I wanted very purposefully to let go of
my possessions. I wanted a fresh start in every sense of the word. I had
learned to live happily on the basics, even though my basics were still
so much more than what my spiritual teachers needed.

After a few weeks of solitude had passed, I began to wonder what
the hell I was doing. I didn't have my busy Los Angeles routine. Being
in Sausalito reminded me of the first few days of a retreat; it took some
time to unwind, to let go and quiet down. I hadn't anticipated how
intense and emotional it would be, returning to the place where I'd
grown up and to be in such close proximity to my family. It was what
I wanted and where I knew I needed to be, but at times it was also excruciating. So many memories resurfaced.

Slowly I began to piece together a routine, including practice sessions, walks through the hills with my dogs, and short but fulfilling
visits with my family. I was becoming a part of the fabric of their lives
again and they a part of mine. And just as Jeffrey had promised, clients
didn't blink an eye when they were told they had to fly me in from San
Francisco.

Some days when the fog rolled in, I would watch as the dewdrops
gathered on the spiderweb outside my window, and I'd listen as the
foghorns I remembered from childhood bellowed outside on the bay. It
was a magical time, filled with discipline, courage, and isolation.

Just before the full moon came in May, I realized I might finish my preliminary practices on Saga Dawa itself: the day Buddha had been born, had reached enlightenment, and had also passed from this world. For some reason the coming culmination of my many years of practice sent me into an odd panic. What would I do then? I had been so singularly focused on this one task of finishing my Ngöndro, and I was now beginning to wonder what it all meant. I knew that my doubt was just another obstacle presenting itself, my ego's way of trying to sabotage the feelings of accomplishment and joy.

The evening before Saga Dawa, I finished my practice and calculated that the next morning's session would indeed bring me to the one-hundred-thousand mark of accumulations. Standing up to stretch, I saw the clouds gathering, a menacing dark sky on the move, and a single bolt of lightning illuminating the hills across the bay. I remembered the story of the night before the Buddha had attained enlightenment. The *maras* (Buddhist demons) had thrown everything they could at him to attempt to distract him from his dedicated focus. A chill ran over me, and I knew I had to try to get in touch with my teacher and ask him to please pray for me, to be thinking of me. I knew that it was a long shot, but I ran to my computer and e-mailed my friend Lisa, who was his attendant in Tibet at the time.

"*I am just about to finish my* Ngöndro, *and I feel all of these obstacles coming up. I am scared.*" I pressed send, and, astonishingly, there was a two-word response in my in-box less than five minutes later: "*Call NOW.*"

I picked up my phone and dialed Tibet; Lisa answered seconds later.

"*Tashi delek!*" she shouted at me in Tibetan.

"Hi!" I screamed. I began to cry from gratitude and apprehension. I knew that I just needed to hear my lama's voice, or at least have him know how I was feeling. But a part of me also knew that was ridiculous. He already did.

"Wait just a moment, Carré," Lisa said. "He's here. He wants to talk to you." And in a flash I could feel him, his presence, and his blessings. A moment later I heard his precious voice.

"Carré-la! Osel Wangmo!" He sang my Tibetan name to me, and in an instant I was reminded of all that I was, my true Buddha nature. Just hearing the name he'd given me was inspiring and reassuring. "I love you! I love you! I love you!" He laughed as he said this, full of joy, full of knowing, full of prayer. He couldn't speak English, nor could I speak Tibetan, but those were three words he knew. Tears streamed down my face. I was so grateful. And I knew that in the morning indeed I would, without any further obstacles, finish my *Ngöndro*.

"I love you, too! Thank you!" I wept.

"*Tashi delek,*" and he hung up. I sat for a moment, watching as the clouds parted and the last rays of sunlight touched my face. "Thank you," I whispered.

By seven the next morning, I had completed my first *Ngöndro*. It was a mighty accomplishment and had carried me through several years of my life. The changes that took place on every level of my being during that time were remarkable. I'd learned to steady my mind, find the courage to face my memories, see what was in the deepest crevices of my heart, touch all that was there, and then let it all go. Slowly and painstakingly, I had liberated myself, taken responsibility for my life, cleared out the blockages. It was the most extraordinary thing I'd ever done.

I decided to celebrate that monumental day by taking myself on a hike, one that I'd been going on since I was a child. I headed out to Tennessee Valley Road, first deciding to stop at the Whole Foods Market in Mill Valley to get some water and a tea. The day was already warm, and I had on a pair of orange shorts, a white tank top, and sneakers. I skipped happily into Whole Foods and placed my order for a yerba maté latte. I waited at the coffee bar, watching the traffic coming in and out of the store. It was a Saturday, and people were moving slowly and going sleepy-eyed through the motions of their morning routines. I, however, had been up since before sunrise and felt unbelievably energetic.

Out of the corner of my eye, I noticed a tall man with dark hair scanning the shelves, a confused expression on his face. I watched him for a moment as he fumbled about. He seemed uncertain about what he was looking for. There was something familiar about him. It was uncanny. Had I met him before? Did I know him? But it wasn't that. It was something much subtler. As he turned down the aisle toward me, I turned away. I wasn't yet ready to engage with the opposite sex. I wasn't yet ready to end my celibacy. Though saying hello to a man wouldn't necessarily mean the end of my sexual hibernation, I reminded myself of my boundaries. I knew how powerful energy could be. I also didn't want anyone to mistake my friendliness for sexual receptiveness. I was aware, from experience, just how often that happens.

But when I turned back around to grab my tea, there he was, right next to me, watching. He scratched his head and flashed a wonderful, open smile.

"Hi," he offered.

I looked away, then back at him. "Hi," I replied, my voice strangely tight.

"Do I know you?" he asked innocently. It was a line I'd heard so many times before from men who I knew perfectly well recognized me. But I sensed at once that there was something different about this guy. He hadn't a clue as to who Carré Otis was.

"Nope," I said with a laugh, turning to walk away.

"Wait!" he tried again. "Wait a minute. Is it too early to ask for your number?"

I looked back. He was really adorable, undeniably handsome. I looked into his big eyes and saw something striking: One eye was black and the other a stunningly bright blue. It reminded me of David Bowie. But this man was better-looking.

I couldn't help but play with him a bit. He was too fascinating not to. "Do you mean too early in the day or too early in our 'relationship' to ask for my number?" I shot back at him, my grin letting him know I was teasing.

I could tell by the way he was looking at me that he wasn't going to let up. I knew that we were both powerfully attracted. And I also knew I wasn't at all ready for it.

Before he could answer, I spoke again. "I don't give out my number."
And before I could think through what I was doing, I followed that
with "But I'll take yours."

I was blown away by what had come out of my mouth. For so long
I'd been on my guard with men. I hadn't been cold or rude, but I knew
how to keep my distance. And at that coffee bar on the morning I finished my *Ngöndro,* something was happening that I didn't entirely
understand.

He happily handed me his business card, holding it for a pause
while I held the other corner, capturing me in his gaze. And then he
let go.

"Thanks. Have a great day." And with a quick wave, I walked out
of the store as nonchalantly as I possibly could. Oddly enough, there in
the parking lot, before I even reached my car, I had a hand in my purse
searching for my phone. And as I climbed behind the wheel, I was dial-
ing his number. It was totally unlike me, but something was driving me
to connect with this person. I needed to know him.

Every bone in my body already knew I wouldn't let him go.

Sexual Healing

Mysteriously, since the first days of my celibacy, my menstrual cycle
had ceased. It baffled the doctors I went to see. And it puzzled me, too.
I was no longer unhealthily thin; this wasn't the amenorrhea that often
accompanies anorexia. Yet there was something perfect in this as well,
something I recognized. A doctor of Chinese medicine I consulted had
a theory that due to my gunshot wound and the excessive blood loss
suffered, losing more blood on a monthly basis was not high on my
body's agenda. Of course, that shooting had happened years before
I chose the celibate path. Whatever the reason, I felt a sense of divine
peace about it; I trusted that my body knew exactly what it needed. I
intuitively knew that the absence of this cycle was linked to my sexual

healing. After several consultations with different practitioners of both Eastern and Western medicine, I decided to stop trying to fix what clearly was not broken.

During my celibacy I'd learned to quiet my need for validation; I'd unlearned all my old unhealthy behaviors. So when I met Matthew, I saw it as an opportunity to deal with my sexuality differently than I ever had before. With Matthew, I challenged myself to have a healthy, spiritual, truly intimate sexual relationship.

We courted for months, talking easily on hikes up Mount Tam, walking along the ocean's edge, watching the wind rustle the trees and the sun set from his home in Mill Valley. We listened to each other's stories with rapt attention over wonderful dinners and bottles of red wine. As I got to know this unique and gentle man, I allowed him to get to know me as well. Not the me that existed at any time prior, but the woman who stood before him then. I didn't hide my past, as it was no longer who I was. My career neither impressed nor intimidated Matthew, and we rarely even spoke of it. Sometimes he asked me, teasingly, "What was it that you used to do?" I would just laugh and shrug. From my new vantage point, my past and my career seemed irrelevant. I loved that I could be the amazing and strong woman I'd worked so hard to be in recent years. And that's exactly who he saw.

Throughout the summer we met almost every day. A feeling of never wanting to be separated from him washed over me. I knew I was falling in love, but a part of me was still unsure that I was ready for that step. I wasn't certain anymore what "love" meant. I had redefined most of my old ideas about love and intimacy, and I had actually become quite comfortable with platonic relationships. What I hadn't been able to see up until that moment was that I was now on the opposite end of the spectrum from where I'd once been, and I was finding it difficult to move back to a healthy and happy medium. Whereas earlier in my life I had known no boundaries sexually—my behavior had been wildly inappropriate—and whereas more recently I had focused on nothing but boundaries, living a completely celibate life, I was now left wondering how I could still feel safe and experience intimacy at the same time. Achieving that balance was an essential part of my growth. I knew if I could find that place, I would reemerge into a sexual being who could love another as I loved myself, with consciousness, integrity, and radical honesty. It was such a terrifying but necessary leap to take.

While I sought the path to that balance, I kept Matthew at arm's length for months. We would regularly have early dinners at great restaurants, and after a wonderful time together I would ask to be dropped off outside my front door by 7:00 P.M. To me this seemed a normal request. I'd neglected my boundaries so much in the past that I was now overcompensating with strict rules that I knew would keep me safe. To his everlasting credit, Matthew didn't press me. I'm not sure he even realized that his growing fondness for me was actually reciprocated, because of how coolly I felt compelled to play everything.

I wanted to share my life with him. I felt an indescribable urge to love him and let him in. But as much as I felt those things, other frightening feelings arose. I wasn't sure I *could* be with him. I was no longer sure of how to physically love someone. The thought was agonizing, evoking memories of abuses I'd suffered. Sex in the past was always equated with either violence or a disconnectedness; neither was a place to which I ever wanted to return. I'd always been a performer in bed, acutely conscious of what I was supposed to do and how my body looked and felt to my partner. I had no idea what real lovemaking was like; I'd never done it. I was afraid that if I were sexual with Matthew, I would slip back into old patterns of disassociation. "Checking out" was how I'd endured the acts that I mistook for intimacy. And even after all my years of spiritual work, I had only reframed the concept of intimacy to the point of realizing that it wasn't something you "endure." I hadn't defined it beyond that yet.

One evening Matthew and I lay clothed on his bed. I was staring up at the ceiling, thinking of what to do. I wanted him. I couldn't be with him. I wished he would kiss me. I was terrified he might. I was such a nervous wreck, filled with contradictory wants and fears, that I burst into tears. I was completely blindsided by the emotions that were welling up in me, horrified to be so unable to control myself next to this man with whom I was so clearly falling in love.

"Talk to me," he gently suggested as I lay there racked by my sobs.

"I . . . I can't. I mean . . ." I couldn't figure out how to say what it was I wanted. I wasn't even sure. Matthew knew how much he was up against. But by now we both knew that we loved each other. He was ready to work.

"Let me ask you this: Would you be willing to see my therapist with me?"

I sighed. It sounded like a good idea. This trying to figure things out on my own wasn't working out so well. And we both wanted so badly for it to work.

"Yes." I nodded, burying my face in his chest and crying all the more.

Matthew held me like that for hours and then kissed me and nodded toward the door. "I know you need to go, Carré. It's okay." He was tremendously sensitive. He knew that pushing or pressuring me would only backfire. He genuinely cared. And through those months the trust that was built by his loving patience became the solid foundation for our relationship.

We met at his therapist's office in Greenbrae. I got there first and sat in the waiting room. Matthew arrived a moment later, straight from work and still dressed in a suit and tie. As he walked in, I was reminded of how much I loved everything about him, the suits included. He was such a lovely, handsome, striking man. We sat silently until a door opened and a gray-haired and bespectacled man emerged, a smile on his face and one hand outstretched in a warm introduction.

"Hi. You must be Carré. I'm Michael. Please, come in and make yourself comfortable," he said, and stepped aside to let us into his office. An amazing view of the sparkling bay lay before me. I found a single chair and sat back, taking a deep breath to calm my nerves. What if Matthew had brought me here because he wanted to break up with me? But were we even officially dating? A million thoughts went through my mind, and I placed a hand over my mouth as I tried to clear my throat. I needed to get something out.

"Okay. Can I just jump in and tell you about myself? Where I'm at?" I looked Michael in the eye and then over to Matthew. Both nodded in agreement, and Matthew smiled encouragingly at me. I took a deep breath and said a prayer for the clarity to be able to articulate my wants and fears.

"So, to be clear, I *want* this relationship. I want love. Matthew, I want to be with you. I'm also scared. I'm not sure anymore, after such a long time of being on my own, just how to do that. Not because of you, but because of my past and all the pain. When you and I move toward intimacy, I become overwhelmed with fear. It stirs in me like an aversion. I can't imagine having sex again. It's as if, to be that vulnerable, I have to be with all that has happened. . . . I have to let go. And that has never been a safe thing for me to do before."

I began to cry. But there was relief in my tears. Relief to be letting out what I'd been keeping inside. I gathered myself and pressed on.

"I want to be *free*. Free of the fear. I want to be free sexually. Free to explore, to be passionate, to have an orgasm. I want that with you, Matthew. I honestly just don't know how to get from here, where I am, to where I want to be. And I don't want my fear to be what fucks this up."

I looked at Matthew and the therapist, my eyes pleading for a solution. I couldn't even begin to express my gratitude that Matthew was willing to go through this with me. They looked back at me with kind and inviting eyes. I took a deep breath and continued.

"I realize that by most standards we should be having sex. I just don't want the typical things that make a relationship 'right' and 'okay' to be what dictates how or when we're intimate. I know, Matthew, that for you as a man there must be certain things that happen that either confirm or deny our love. But for me, I need to redefine that as well. I want there to be room on a day-to-day basis for me to either want or not want to be close, and I want that to be all right. I've never had the room in a relationship to even get in touch with that. . . . I've never been able to be the one to initiate or deny sex. I've just always done what's expected of me," I continued. I was hoping I was making sense. And finally I admitted my whole truth: "I've never had an orgasm with a man. And I don't want to feel that I need to fake it ever again. So I guess I'm asking that if—I mean, *when* we do make love, that if that doesn't happen, I just don't want you to be angry or have you get your ego wrapped up in it. I mean, I've never just made love without feeling as if I have to perform. I don't even know what that's like. I want to linger and feel, without agenda or expectation. Is that even possible?"

I was crying even harder as I finished. Part of me felt like a silly kid instead of a woman of thirty-six years; another part of me was ecstatic. I was revealing myself, and although it was uncomfortable, it was tremendously liberating.

When I looked at Matthew again, he had tears in his eyes. He was enormously relieved as well to at last be able to better understand me. He had needed to hear that it wasn't about him.

Before we left our session, Michael gave us what he called homework. We were to schedule our homework and time it. It was basic and simple.

"Twenty minutes," Michael said. "Lie down together for twenty minutes and just hold each other. Nothing more. But you must be together for the entire twenty minutes, and whatever comes up is okay. Talk about it. Let it be. Don't make love yet. Just hold each other." Matthew and I both started laughing nervously. It sounded ridiculous, but it also sounded doable. "Do you think you can do that, Carré?"

"Yes. Oh, yes."

And with that, Matthew and I left, headed to his house on the hill, agreeing that our first homework session would start right away.

I have to admit I felt like a twelve-year-old. But the beauty in it all was that I was able to go to someplace so pure and simple and sweet, someplace I'd never had the chance to experience. We visited Michael for several more sessions, and each time he added to our assignment so that soon we were lying naked with each other for twenty minutes at a time. And so it progressed. Each time we would begin like shy kids, and each time progress was made. We were again and again able to return to the structured shelter of a set task that was pushing us in the direction we both so wanted. What we desired was to be together, free of our pasts, free from expectation and society's labels of what it was we were supposed to do as a man and a woman in a sexual relationship.

The time and care we put into building mutual trust and friendship fueled the passion we felt for each other. And at last we made love. For the first time in my life, I was fully present with a partner. I was able to let go of an agenda, let go of the need to perform, let go of the idea that there was anything to achieve. I was rewarded with an earth-shattering orgasm, the first I'd ever had in the presence of another human being. As that thunder rolled through me, I felt that everything that had ever happened, everything that had wounded, wronged, and harmed me, was healed. In the profound silence that followed, I finally understood what true sexual healing meant. No woman can have an orgasm without being able to let go. And no woman can let go unless she knows she is safe. Safety cannot be found through "trying" or "doing." It is found, or rather it is built, through trust, through the willingness to be present in the stillness.

Most of us are so busy trying to "get" somewhere to "get off." That's true of many aspects of our lives, especially in the bedroom. And the wonderful truth that I finally found was that if we can just slow it down, slow it *all* down, the bliss is right there for the taking.

Matthew proposed to me in October of that same year on the island of Maui. Two months later, on December 17, 2005, we were married in a wonderfully intimate ceremony at my father's house in Mill Valley. My closest friends and entire family were present, able to witness and rejoice in my life's coming perfectly full circle.

SURGERY, PREGNANCY, JADE

During the months we courted, Matthew and I had discussed having children, so once we were married, we decided to see a fertility specialist to better understand how my still-absent menstrual cycle might factor into our plans. The consensus of the specialist and his colleagues was that I would be unable to conceive without artificial means. The doctors walked us through various procedures and options, none of which came with a guarantee that I would conceive. And although a part of my heart felt heavy and let down, I truly felt that if Matthew and I wanted to have a child, we could just as easily adopt. Matthew's warm hand on mine was reassuring, reminding me that we were doing this together, no matter what. We both felt that although we were older than typical first-time parents, we were not in a rush. We both had absolute faith in the perfect unfolding of a divine plan.

In that last week of December 2005, we got word that my teacher would be able to get out of Tibet and lead a retreat in Texas starting January 1. This was another auspicious sign and an amazing blessing. Matthew and I agreed that we would rather be in Houston with our lama than honeymooning in a typical fashion. Due to the political situation in Tibet, we never really knew for certain if or when our teacher would be able to get out, so we jumped at the chance to spend the first weeks of the New Year in his presence. Our time in Houston was wonderful; Matthew and I were able to sit and practice together, solidifying our vows, as well as receive a formal blessing from our teacher.

Back in Marin, winter had set in, and with it one of the biggest storms of the year. The winds howled, shaking our house on the hill, trees came down around us, and much of Mill Valley lost electricity. Matthew and I would sit by our fire, cozied up, reading or practicing. At that time I had a dedicated home yoga practice, and Matthew would watch in awe as I would drop into backbends or stand on my head for long spells. But there was a problem that just didn't seem to quit: I'd been afflicted with back issues for years, and no matter what I did—Pilates, massage, yoga, acupuncture—I was in pain.

I refused to take medication and for the most part had simply resigned myself to the fact that I would be someone who simply had to tolerate a certain amount of pain in my life. But the truth of the matter was, it was agonizing. The pain extended to my right hip and leg. Sometimes it was so bad that my toes would curl involuntarily and my foot would turn ice cold, as though the blood or energy just didn't flow through that channel anymore. Muscles on my right side had begun to visibly waste away.

I had been diagnosed almost a decade before with foraminal stenosis and had been told I would eventually need surgery. But what the doctors had shown me at the time had dissuaded me. I did not like the idea of having hardware in my body. I was a yogini. Metal rods didn't belong in me.

But that week, as Matthew and I were housebound, we discussed the matter at some length. It was clear that at least for the time being we were not going to focus on starting a family. I was young and healthy enough to recover from a surgery. We both agreed that I ought to get it over with, as my quality of life really depended on it.

By the end of January, I'd met with one of the Bay Area's best orthopedic surgeons, Dr. Robert Byers. After an initial consultation, Dr. Byers scheduled me for a spinal fusion on March 6.

Oddly enough, on February 1, 2006, shortly following that first meeting with the orthopedist, and after nearly seven years of having no menstrual cycle, I got my period. I looked at it as proof of the blessings and healings that were occurring in my life and body. I had rediscovered a liberating, sensual life. I had married an incredible man. I had just seen my lama. The timing of it all was perfect.

But the operation was far more intense than I could ever have imagined. I spent eight hours under anesthesia and emerged with four four-inch titanium rods in my lower back. I was wheeled into a post-op room where my beloved husband anxiously awaited me. I was scared.

While I was under, I felt certain I had died. I could feel myself hovering near my body, watching the doctors and nurses work on me. What's more, I felt as if I wasn't alone. I sensed that someone else was watching with me.

As I came crashing back into my body and into some semblance of awareness, I knew that a great deal of trauma had occurred. I understood the physical part but wasn't prepared for the psychic impact of such major surgery. It was terrifying.

"Carré, how does your leg feel? Can you wiggle your toes for me?" Dr. Byers asked.

I looked down at my pale feet and did just that, wiggled my toes, and noticed that the nagging pain was definitely not there.

"I hurt everywhere else but my toes!" I cried, still under heavy pain medication.

"That's what I want to hear. That's great." He smiled at me encouragingly. Then added to Matthew, "Oh, by the way, I was really glad I got you on the phone. Can't believe we almost missed that." He patted Matt's back and exited the room.

"What?" I asked sleepily.

"Oh, Dr. Byers called me while you were under. They weren't sure if you had decided to have your bone grafted or if you wanted to use some synthetic material that hasn't been proven safe in pregnancy," Matthew replied.

"What did you tell him?" I asked.

"To use your own bone." And that was all I heard before falling back into a deep slumber.

I stayed in the hospital for several days, each day meeting the unbelievably painful challenges my physical therapist pushed me to get through. My first steps were shaky. As I learned to walk again, I felt as if my body was made of lead. But I progressed slowly and in time was able to return home with a walking cane and a back brace.

As Matthew continued his schedule of getting up early to beat the traffic as he commuted to his office in the East Bay, I would bundle up in warm layers and a raincoat and walk along the small dirt path on the crest of the mountain, looking out at the gray skies and the ocean below. Winter lingered, the rains hadn't ceased, the wind was still howling, but nothing could deter me from fully recovering. Although my life felt as if it had been put on hold, an old motto came in handy: "When in doubt, wait it out." I didn't press to go back to work. I knew that a time would come when I would either decide to return to modeling or move into some other as-yet-unknown new career. I just let myself be, wandering the mountain and regaining my strength.

One late morning as I was heading out on my hike, I felt an intense burning sensation in my nipples. I'd never experienced anything like it before. It was so painful that it brought me to tears. I cupped my hands under my shirt, trying to soothe myself. It didn't seem to help. It made no sense, and so I chalked it up to a possible side effect of my medication. I decided that when I returned from my walk, I would switch to Tylenol. Anything was better than burning nipples.

But the next day and the next, the same pain returned, and finally, on the third day, I broke off the hike to go home and call my doctor.

"I can't imagine that having anything to do with either the medication or your surgery, Carré," Dr. Byers said. "Call your OB. That sounds more hormonal." And so I did. As I explained my symptoms over the phone, I could practically hear my obstetrician scratching his head.

"Well, that does sound hormonal. I'll tell you what. Why don't you come down to the lab and we'll run a full-panel pregnancy test," he said.

"A what?" I asked, baffled. "You told me I couldn't get pregnant," I reminded him in shock.

"It's a long shot, but it might tell us what's going on."

I called Matthew on my way down, and he laughed off the notion. It seemed preposterous.

I went into the lab, came home, and waited for the call. My symptoms remained, painful and debilitating. I was incredibly irritated that something like searing breast pain could halt my efforts at rehab and hiking. I just wanted someone to tell me how to get rid of it. The next evening, with Matthew home from work, I stood half naked in the kitchen while my husband sponge-bathed my back and re-dressed my incision.

Just as he was finishing, the phone rang.

"I got it," I said, leaning over and answering. "Hello?"

It was my OB in San Francisco. "Carré. Hi."

"Hi?" I replied, waiting. There was a long pause.

"I have . . . some big news," he said. I looked at Matthew. Matthew looked at me. He mouthed, *What?* while I just waited, silently.

"I'm calling to tell you that you're pregnant." My heart jumped. I was stunned. And then elated. And then terrified.

"What?" I asked again excitedly. It couldn't be. Matthew's eyes locked on mine, and in an instant I knew he knew. His eyes welled with tears. I didn't know what to say.

"Now, let's not get too excited. Let's get you in tomorrow for an ultrasound and see what we have. Don't get me wrong—this is an ab-solute miracle, and I'm thrilled for you. . . ." The doctor's voice trailed off. And I jumped in.

"What does this mean? Is it okay? I mean, I've been in surgery, under anesthesia, radiation, for hours. I'm recovering from a fusion." As the words came out, my heart sank. I was naturally concerned. A miracle, yes, but one that arrived under what seemed the worst possible circumstances. The doctor assured me we'd talk in the morning, and I hung up the phone and dove into Matthew's arms. He held me as I sobbed and worried and also laughed with joy. We were both beside ourselves with a strange mix of elation and fear. The uncertainties spread out before us like the big blue sea.

The days that followed were harrowing. It was true, I was preg-nant and had been about six weeks along at the time of my surgery. According to the experts, this timing corresponded with some critical fetal developments that could have been adversely affected by all that I underwent during the operation. But there was no certainty. Matthew and I sat with a genetic specialist who crunched some numbers to determine the radiation to which my baby had likely been exposed. Her prognosis was neither good nor clear. The bottom line was, the doctors and specialists could only give me their medical opinions, opinions based on statistics and their professional expertise. In the end I'd have to make the final decision based on my beliefs, my faith, and what was in my heart.

After several weeks of tests and consultations, I realized I had to pull away from all the medical input. No one could look into a crystal ball and tell me what the outcome of carrying my baby to term might be. There was no way of knowing how my newly fused spine would handle a pregnancy or labor. Somewhere within myself I had to find the answer and the conviction it would take for me to go against all the medical advice I'd been receiving and bring my child into this world. And that's exactly what I did. I understood without a doubt that my pregnancy was part of a spiritual agreement. I had karma with this being, and I had no right to step in to alter what had taken place. That this child had stuck with me through the invasion of a major surgery and was still holding steady was miraculous. I recalled the sense I'd had during surgery that I was not alone. It was my baby who was with me then, and I knew it. I looked back over the events that had taken place in the six months since Matthew and I had gotten engaged. Everything, it seemed, had been leading up to this very moment. This was part of an abundant blessing. And no doctor could tell me otherwise.

And so I made a pact with my baby. I did it out loud as the rain pounded on the roof of our home. I placed my hands over my belly as I spoke. This child had chosen me, and I had chosen this situation. We had karma together, and no matter what that meant, what that looked like, or how it panned out, I promised that I was going to show up and be the best vessel, protector, and mother that I could be. I recalled how when I'd seen my heart teacher in January in Houston and introduced him to Matthew, he had nodded and laughed. "I told you. Finish your

Ngöndro!" he'd said with a wink. He had known all along that my path was not as a nun but as a mother and wife.

In the months that followed, I continued to walk the mountain. The spring came and went, the long hot summer witnessed my body swell to a great round shape, and on November 11, 2006, my daughter Jade Yeshe Sutton was born into this world.

ENDURING COLIC

Although I'd always had a vision that I would be birthing my babies at home, we'd decided that, given my recent back surgery, the safest place to deliver was in the hospital. It turned out to be the right decision, too. By the last week of my pregnancy, I could no longer walk without a cane; the pressure of my baby on my pelvic floor and spine was more than I could bear. The doctors wanted to induce. I worried that might very well result in a C-section.

On the eve before my due date, I lit a candle and spoke with my baby. I told her that it would take the two of us together to get through what lay ahead, and I needed her help. I was ready, I told her, but she was going to have to initiate her entrance into the world. Each day that went by, it was becoming harder and harder for me to function.

One November evening Matthew came home from work and took me to dinner at a wonderful restaurant in downtown Mill Valley. I sat across from him, keenly aware that we were sharing the last moments together of being a two-person family. As I lifted a forkful of food to my mouth, I felt a gush of liquid splash forth between my legs, and my eyes widened in surprise.

"What, Carré?" Matthew asked, knowing that something had happened. We'd been reading what seemed like a million birthing books, and as I felt my water break, one of the funniest terms—one that had never failed to send us into fits of hilarity—came to mind.

"It's a sock soaker!" I burst out laughing. "My water just broke!"

He stared at me, wild-eyed. "What do I do?" I asked, standing up and looking down at the drenched and stained leather chair I'd been sitting in.

"Just throw your napkin over it!" he said, and I did exactly that. Matthew paid the check, grabbed my arm, and as I clutched my cane, he helped me to the car.

After sixteen hours of labor and an epidural, Jade was born. She was literally the first baby I'd ever held. The mothering instinct kicked in, but with it came a certain degree of doubt. I really didn't know what I was doing. As much as I wanted to leave the hospital and begin privately enjoying the magic of nesting together, I was scared. And when we returned home, things became even more challenging.

Jade had colic. I had read all the baby books and felt I could handle anything but that. "Please, please, Buddhas! Just not a baby with colic!" I had heard the horror stories.

Like clockwork from 2:00 till 8:00 P.M. each day, Jade would scream. She would cry, moving into fits that were terrifying because there was no fixing it. I brought her to our pediatrician, and as Lindy held her, swaddled her, shushed her, and rocked her, she just nodded sympathetically to me over the ear-piercing shrieks. "Sorry, hon. It's your classic case of colic." I was devastated.

I tried every remedy under the sun: homeopathics, tinctures, swaddling, better burping techniques. I would hold her in the bathroom with the shower and sink running. I tried a white-noise machine. But finally I had to surrender to the fact that there was nothing I could do except wait it out.

One evening Matthew and I stood shoulder to shoulder in the laundry room, our dinners on the dryer, each of us with a glass of wine in hand. Jade was swaddled, strapped in her car seat, both washer and dryer going for sound effect. Matthew was as frustrated as I was and possibly as frustrated as Jade! On and on our daughter wailed.

My nerves were frayed. I was sleep-deprived, still figuring out how to nurse and how to burp. My body was a blob. I was beside myself. And then I heard Matthew say:

"I'm not sure I'm cut out for this."

I looked at him, bewildered. Bad fucking timing, buddy! I could feel some crazy primal rage bubbling to the surface, and in a flash it unleashed itself.

"Don't you even fucking tell me this *NOW*! Too late, Matthew—think again. Not an option. *Make* yourself cut out for this, because there is no other option!" I was furious, but I also totally knew how he felt. He spoke the words we'd both been thinking for weeks. It's just that some things, even between a husband and wife, are better left unsaid.

It is clear to me that a marriage or a partnership that can survive a child with colic can survive anything.

And we did. Like clockwork, just as our pediatrician predicted, the colic disappeared when Jade turned three months old, What didn't divide us made us stronger. We had passed the first of many tests.

Round Two: Body Image and Weight Gain

I had always been certain that if I were ever to be pregnant, I would enjoy it thoroughly, embracing all the wonders that came with it. Knowing a number of powerful midwives throughout my life had made an impression on me, and I was inspired by the form of every pregnant woman I came across. Marveling at the great protruding bellies of pregnant friends or strangers on the street, I saw nothing but beauty and the evidence of miracles.

But when it came my time to be the pregnant lady, the all-giving mother goddess, I had definite challenges accepting what was happening to me. Though I was in awe of my changes, proud first of my little baby bump and then the enormous swell it grew into, there were some tough feelings I had to reckon with and talk myself through.

As a woman who had recovered from an eating disorder, I knew that I wasn't entirely free from old habits. I could feel the need to scrutinize and monitor each of my changes as my body grew. I used the tools I'd been taught, making sure that at every step I processed my feelings with my support system. There was a lot of dialogue regarding the rapid and drastic transformations my body was undergoing, changes beyond any I'd ever dealt with before. The changes were gorgeous, but they were also outrageous and shocking. That's the bottom line: What happens to a pregnant woman's body is absolutely wild.

Fortunately, by the time I conceived, I had done so much work on myself that I was well trained to observe and appreciate these changes. Every day I would stand before the mirror in wonder. My breasts were massive, my hips were slightly padded, and my ass was bigger than it had ever been. And of course my belly was like an enormous mountain, proudly protruding from it all. I knew and trusted that my body was doing everything it needed to in order to prepare itself to birth a child. Body wisdom is mighty and impressive. But each day I had to consciously let go a little bit more. It was about softening. And even for women, softening is not what our culture wants us to do. We are taught to muscle through, dominate, and remain in control. We are taught to be hard. Yet to birth a baby out of your vagina and into this world absolutely requires softening and letting go. Trying to dominate and power your way through the process is impossible.

When I visited my ob-gyn's office early in my pregnancy, it was the first time in what seemed like forever that I'd been on a scale. I had thrown mine away long ago as part of my healing. When the nurse slid the weight bars forward, I experienced all-too-familiar dread: What would I weigh? Would it be too much? Too little? It took me several visits to the doctor to find the voice to say that I didn't want to be weighed unless absolutely necessary. And even then I turned my face away when I was on the scale. I did *not* want to know the number.

Most of the pregnant women I knew seemed thrilled. There was so very little conversation about the more frightening aspects of watching one's body change that I felt as if I should be beaming, too. And even though I did feel terrific as I entered my second trimester, I still had a lot to contend with and surrender to. It took a conscious effort on my part not to completely freak out. I was blown away—and I was blowing *up*, too.

Some women don't gain weight. Some do. Some women lose it right away. I happened to gain fifty pounds with both my daughters, and it took at least a year to get it off. The many tabloids that so rudely harassed new Hollywood mamas, reporting on the race to lose the baby weight, incensed me.

Like so many women, I was disgusted and horrified to find my body become a subject of discussion and unwarranted comments from complete strangers. As a culture we are fascinated with pregnant women; think of the entitlement that leads many people to freely put their hands on a woman's expectant belly. People also feel it's their place to criticize or offer suggestions about diet, as if the health of the unborn child requires their unwanted and unbidden intervention. As a model who was still regularly recognized and remembered from my thinner days, I heard quite a lot of discussion about my weight gain.

Going to my local Whole Foods became a nightmare. I actually started driving to one farther away in San Rafael so that I didn't have to engage with anyone or endure unwelcome intrusions.

"You look like you're going to explode!"

"Wow, I gained weight just like you. My thighs and ass got huge!"

"Oh, you'll drop the weight, don't worry."

"When are you going to pop that thing out?"

The remarks came from both men and women. I began to wonder if the miracle and the reality of the pregnant form was just too much for people to handle. Does it expose us to the unknown? Does it push our limits of how we believe the world to be? Does it test what it is we can and want to see? Whatever it is, I'm convinced that there's only one thing that you should ever say to a pregnant woman: "You look great." Other than that, keep the comments to yourself.

As I moved through my pregnancy, I realized I was again being given the opportunity to assert healthy boundaries around my body. In my last trimester, before people could open their mouths with those unsolicited comments, I would hold up a hand and simply say, "My body is off-limits for discussion or review." I wouldn't wait for a response. I knew that I needed to protect myself and was finding my footing as to how to do so.

No one had discussed how I would feel or look after I'd given birth, and this came as a surprise. I just assumed that postpartum I would somehow shed my belly, rolls, and love handles. But this wasn't the case at all. For at least four months after Jade was born, I still looked pregnant, and I just had to accept that the mirror was not a place I needed to linger. Many women and doctors today tout breast-feeding as a way to take off the baby weight. A slew of promises are made, and the experience of many women bears this out. But it didn't work that way for me. The fact is that breast-feeding is a great idea, period. Hoping for quicker weight loss shouldn't be the reason to do it.

It helped to have tools in place to deal with the angst that arose around my less-than-perfect body. I sought advice and received great comfort from those mothers who I knew would be honest about their struggles to accept their changed bodies. And I was also given realistic encouragement. I was told that it took nine months to put the weight on and that I should expect for it to take at least that long for it to come off. I was also assured that in time everything on my body would go back "more or less" to the way it had been. That was helpful to hear.

I worked hard to enjoy both of my pregnancies and not let my previous body issues rule that time. I do feel that there's so much about the process of pregnancy that we need to do a better job of honoring. Women's bodies are not public property, even when they have other growing bodies inside them. Despite living in a supposedly open era, we need to have much more discussion about body image and pregnancy.

BIRTHING KAYA

That first year of my life as a new mother went by in a flash. The days were long, but the year was short. Just before Jade turned one, I realized I was pregnant again. My previous state of infertility had clearly passed! But I was as worried as I was thrilled. How the hell was I going to manage with two kids? I was just learning the ropes and finding my rhythm with one! I wasn't sure at all that our house could hold our quickly expanding family. This time I was showing within the first two months, so I couldn't keep the secret. But, fortunately, everything seemed easier that second time around. The worries of the unknown didn't haunt me; I knew that my back could hold up. I trusted that my body would know what to do in labor. My old desire to have a home birth seemed more and more like a possibility, and after I'd sat down and talked about it with Matthew, he agreed to meet with some midwives.

We interviewed several and felt most connected to a woman named Nancy. She'd been practicing for over a decade and felt confident that I was a good candidate for a home birth based on my labor with Jade. I began the wonderful and intimate process of building a relationship with her so that we might move in synchronicity on the day my second child was due.

Being pregnant with such a young child at home left little time for rest or naps. I did my best to find the magic in it all and would continue my walks up and down the mountain, often with Jade on my back. I carried her until it was impossible, and then we continued by way of a stroller. I hiked like this up to the last days of my pregnancy, using the time as a moving meditation. With each step I envisioned my baby dropping lower and lower into my pelvis and imagined my labor filled with ease and grace.

For Christmas 2007, Matthew, Jade, and I traveled to Colorado to visit Lama Tsultrim and meet our teacher, who had come from Tibet for our annual winter retreat. We stayed at a small condo in town so that we could have room to cook for Jade and we'd be able to maintain her napping schedule. Winter was heavier than usual that year. The snowfall was incessant, and the roads seemed always to be covered with thick ice. We had come knowing that there was a chance Matthew would have to fly back to the Bay Area on a moment's notice. He was in negotiations to sell his company, affording our family a great opportunity for change. Indeed, the Mill Valley house would be too small for the four of us, so as we considered upgrading, the discussion about where it might be best to raise our girls began.

The day after we arrived in Pagosa Springs, Matthew received the call. The meeting needed to take place the next day. He would have to return to California and leave me in snow-laden Colorado with Jade and our new baby growing steadily inside me. Come hell or high water, I was set on attending the retreat, desperate to see my beloved heart teacher after my crazy year and before I was about to enter another.

I hugged Matthew tightly as soft flakes fell in the dark of the morning. It was a bold move on my part to stay. "I love you," I whispered. "Be careful and come back quickly!" I watched, fighting back my tears, as he drove off slowly through the winter storm.

When the sun rose, I packed Jade up in her new snowsuit and set off down the snow-covered dirt road to Tara Mandala. How I made it through that retreat is beyond me; it seems now a distant wonderful memory. That I made it through was a testament to my practice and connection with my teacher. I managed to juggle Jade's needs with my own, nursing her when she was hungry, pulling out my endless bag of tricks and snacks to engage and occupy her when she became fidgety so that I could practice as much as possible.

Matthew returned just as the retreat was wrapping up, and although I had missed his presence and help, we were thrilled that the company was going to be sold. It meant we could plan our next move. But before leaving Colorado, Matthew and I decided to stop and see a house that had just come on the market. We hadn't seriously talked about Colorado as a destination—that was a dream well in the future—but we decided to see the place anyway.

The home was impressive, bigger than what we had expected and unique in that it was crafted and designed unlike anything else we'd seen in our house hunting. There was nothing that needed to be done to it. It was perfect.

In the months that followed, Matthew and I made the big decision to move. We realized that we didn't want to raise our family in California. We loved the idea of having access to a Buddhist community and the chance to be in such close proximity to our teachers. Matthew and I were both outdoor enthusiasts, loved adventure, and knew that the Rockies would provide all that and more. Thankfully, we saw eye to eye on the environment in which we wanted to raise our children. California had grown crowded, and even the small town of Mill Valley was becoming too busy a location. We made an offer on our dream home in Colorado in March and closed within a few weeks. The process of putting our Mill Valley house on the market wasn't easy for the already busy six-months-pregnant mother of a toddler. But somehow I knew that everything would fall into place. I trusted that it was time to leave California. I trusted that our house would sell. With this in mind, I packed up the majority of our Mill Valley home and made arrangements to move three months after our second child was born. We already knew we were having a girl; we had named her Kaya. As I set up the nest in preparation for a home birth, Matthew looked at me in both wonder and concern. "Are you sure you'll be ready to move when the baby is just three months old?" He asked this more than once.

"Absolutely," I would respond, unwavering in my resolve.

"What if our house doesn't sell?" he would ask.

"Not an option. It will. Just wait and see." And just like that, it did, right before the market crashed. It was unbelievable how things all came together for us; the move was simply meant to be.

When June came around, I felt enormous. Of course—I was. But I was also ready, physically and psychologically. I had continued my hikes up the mountain and felt stronger than ever. The only thing that could get in the way of my having a baby naturally at home would be my mind. And that's something I knew I could work with.

On the morning of June 7, 2008, Jade had woken me up early. The sun was just peeking out, the late-spring heat already on the rise.

"Mama, come read me a book!" she said, pulling me from my bed and Matthew's slumbering body.

I sat up and smiled. "Okay. What do you want to read?" I asked, padding softly into her room behind her.

"*Frosty the Snowman*," she said, pushing the book at me. We lay down on her bed, snuggled up together nice and tight. She had wrapped her body around my humongous belly, as she loved to do.

I began to sing the words to the song by the same name, as out of season as it might have been. Just then I was stopped by a strong cramp. "Ohh. That was strange. I need to go to the bathroom, Jade," I said. But before I could get up from the bed, another "cramp" tore through me and a wave of nausea rose up. Whoa.

In a flash I knew that I was in labor. And something about this was different from before.

"Matthew," I called out as I began to breathe heavily. "Matthew!" I screamed as he came running in, wiping sleep from his eyes.

"The baby's coming," I said quickly.

Jade started jumping up and down. "Baby's coming! Baby's coming!" she squealed in delight.

"Call Nancy. Call Catherine." Catherine was the doula whom we'd known since Jade's birth, an amazing woman who'd been a great nurturing support to us all in the previous months. I had wanted her to be at our home birth to do whatever was needed to keep Jade comfortable. We had agreed that if Jade wanted to be by my side, she could, or if she wanted to go to the park instead, that would be fine, too. It was up to Catherine to help either way.

As Matthew got busy making calls and filling the birthing tub in our living room, my labor quickened. I could barely speak, and within twenty minutes my contractions were coming on the heels of one another. I made my way to our bedroom, where I proceeded to rock back and forth on all fours on the bed, roaring loudly, trying to work with my baby, who seemed to be fast approaching. I had never, ever felt anything like it. With Jade I'd had an epidural. I was unprepared for the wild intensity I was feeling at this moment.

"Forget the fucking birthing tub, Matthew!" I shrieked. "I *need you!*" He had up until that moment been in the other room readying things. I somehow knew I wouldn't make it there. Matthew came rushing in. He looked confused and concerned. I moaned loudly and was relieved to hear Catherine's songbirdlike voice in the background.

"Help me!" I screamed. "I don't think I can do this!" I was in terror. I really didn't think I could go through with it. Another contraction rolled through me, and my body arched involuntarily as I roared again. I was being transformed into a primal birthing animal. I had no control.

Catherine climbed onto the bed beside my naked body and soothed me. "But you *are* doing it, my dear. You are," she said.

I was finally able to catch a breath. As I looked wildly into her eyes for some clarity, she held me in her gaze and in her certainty. By the time the next contraction came, I was able to breathe a bit more calmly through it.

"I have to pee," I wailed. "No, I have to poop!" I screamed. "I don't know what I have to do! Help me to the bathroom," I begged. The last bits of my desire for dignity were gripping me; I didn't want to crap on the bed! Matthew and Catherine brought me into the bathroom, and I sat on the toilet, wrestling and writhing in the unknown sensations, not at all sure what it was that would relieve me, praying that something would. I started to groan again. Involuntarily, my body was pushing and heaving.

Catherine called from just outside the bathroom door. "Are you pushing?" she asked.

"I don't know!" I growled. I hadn't felt the sensation of pushing with Jade. I didn't know what it was.

"You need to stop, Carré. Slow down," she said in as collected and firm a tone as possible.

"I can't!" I sputtered. And I couldn't. Just then I felt a burst and a gush. My water broke. It was such a relief that before I realized what I was doing, I had flushed the toilet.

"No, Carré!" Catherine screamed, rushing in. She needed to look for signs of meconium to be sure that there was no chance that the baby had inhaled any. On the toilet lid, she found a small splash of a greenish black substance. I panicked and dropped to all fours.

"Are we okay? Is the baby okay?" I cried. I could hear Catherine instructing Matthew urgently as she knelt down behind me to get a better look. Just then it felt as if my hips had popped and as if Kaya had dropped down an inch.

"Oh, my. Matthew . . . the baby is coming now! Call Nancy!" Catherine was as calm as could be, but I knew we needed help. It was all happening too fast.

On the bathroom floor, my body began to pulse uncontrollably. I was moving like a wave with each contraction. I was vaguely aware that Nancy had finally arrived and that she had slipped into the bathroom and dropped to her knees as well.

"You're doing great, Carré," she whispered. "Let's try to take a couple of long, slow breaths. Your baby is crowning."

I could feel my world splitting open. My life, my heart, my body.

"She's coming out my asshole!" I screamed. I was certain she was.

"I promise you, she will take a sharp turn. Just bear with me. Give me a few breaths here." And in my silence I tried to pause, to rest in the moment of splitting wide open. It was a hell of a place to hang out.

And right there, with me wedged in the doorjamb between my bathroom and bedroom, right there on all fours, in one last contraction Kaya Elizabeth emerged into the world. I reached down between my legs and caught her, that slippery body and crazy shock of jet-black hair. My labor had been an hour from start to finish.

I rested in one of the sweetest victories a woman can know: I had endured a natural labor, and I'd had my baby at home. And almost as important, I'd found the real power and grace that rested in my body.

COLORADO BOUND

On September 15, 2008, when Kaya was just three months old, we made our move. It took courage to pack up my entire family, including two children under three years of age, and drive across California, the deserts of Arizona and New Mexico, and into our new life in Colorado. But I've learned that with every step in life there are gambles and sacrifices, risks and rewards. We will never know what's on the other side unless we take that leap of faith. My years of dedicated spiritual practice and hard work on myself had given me the ability to trust my judgment and my instincts. And it was now clear to me where it was we were supposed to be. Not just me, but the entire entity my family had become. The entire unified, functioning energy that we are collectively. I was becoming accustomed to thinking of myself no longer in the singular but in the plural. It was no longer "I" but "we." This move we made together has proven best for all of us.

As much as California was and will always be my home, I realized that it was time to move beyond what was convenient for me. I knew in my heart that our daughters deserved what all children do: their childhood. It was my job and Matthew's to provide them with that and protect them from growing up saturated with the messages and expectations of urban and suburban American culture. I had been a child who was in a rush to grow up. And I did grow up prematurely, forced as much, if not more, by circumstance as by choice. I knew that my childhood was not something I could get back. I could heal and forgive, but reclaiming those formative years was impossible. I accepted that for myself, but I wanted—we wanted—to make a different choice for our daughters. I understood the sacrifices that we were making as parents to move to such a remote place, yet I felt absolutely certain that these were the right sacrifices. We have been rewarded abundantly.

I was thirty-nine years old. I had come further than I'd thought I could. I'd had a lifetime of challenges and adventure, and as we drove away from the setting western sun, I realized how utterly grateful I was. I was ready to give up all else for the happiness of my family and the simplicity of a small-town existence. I was relieved that my life was no longer just about me.

Two weeks after we left California, and under a big southwestern sky in our new Colorado home, I turned forty. My friends and family were with me to celebrate. My teachers close by, my children playing in the field of wildflowers that make up our backyard. They do not yet know my story, my daughters, but as time unfolds, they will. They have a chance at knowing *me* now. The simple me. The recovered me. The extraordinary me who worked intensely for years to be able to stand exactly where I do today, with no regrets, no shame, and with absolute forgiveness. To say I had a hand in it all is true. To know I made choices along the way, and to own them, sets me free from being the victim I once thought I was.

I am at peace, too, with my ex-husband. We haven't spoken since the day he threw that fit in a Santa Monica restaurant, but from afar I have rejoiced in the resurrection of his career. I'm pleased to see Mickey working again as an actor. Matthew and I sat and watched *The Wrestler* together. Everyone has said that Mickey put so much of himself into that part, and I think that's true. I laughed in surprise to see so many traces of his real self come out in the film. At the end of the movie, I was filled with compassion for this man whom I had once genuinely loved. Mickey was and is a remarkable talent, and I hope that he continues to be well and continues to enjoy success.

My happiness at his comeback turned to anger, however, when Mickey repeatedly brought up my name during interviews to promote the film. He discussed aspects of my history without care to accuracy, the life I have since built, or the public forums in which he was sharing those details. I was furious. I was even tempted to speak out then. But I chose instead to wait, and to put my energy toward writing this book. Many parents can choose to hide their pasts from their kids. I can't. My daughters deserve to know the truth about my life, and when they are old enough, they deserve to find out that truth from me, in context, and not from the Internet or from stories told by my first husband.

Today I have a healthy relationship with all the members of my family. I've worked hard, and so have they. After all I've been through, I'm not a child anymore. I'm a powerful adult woman with excellent boundaries, boundaries I've worked very hard to create and maintain. And this work has afforded me a chance to give Jade and Kaya wonderful relationships with my parents and with their Aunt Chrisse and Uncle Jordan. Since becoming a mom myself, I've gained enormous insight into my parents, and I have a great deal of compassion for them. They parented without the tools that I am blessed to have today.

I take responsibility for my life and my choices now. What wisdom I do have was hard-earned. Earning it cost me and many who loved me years of pain. It nearly cost me my life. If there's one thing I believe, it's that while suffering is indeed part of life, the kind of suffering I endured to get where I am is not something I want any other young woman to go through. The path to wisdom and joy doesn't require degradation, despair, and misery. That's a message I'm ready to share.

As the great Mahatma Gandhi once said, "Be the change you wish to see in the world."

Anything is possible.

Acknowledgments

When I first began writing this book, the collective events of my life were almost too big to get my arms around, so I tackled the task story by story. I knew that one day I would somehow piece all the elements together to represent the whole, but I was never quite sure how. My sincerest appreciation goes to Hugo Schwyzer, for meeting my intense pace and passion in the writing of this book and for providing some much-needed balance and insight.

Thank you to HarperCollins for seeing the value of my story and standing behind me so I could tell it the way I wanted to tell it. And to Frank Weimann, my literary agent, for your support and for pairing me with my publisher.

I would also like to acknowledge my dearest friends, who have encouraged me along my path, assuring me that a time would come when I would be ready to tell my story. Without their steadfast support, I might not have recognized the opportunity when it presented itself. Carolyn Cavallero; Nan Koehler; Lama Tsultrim Allione; Anne Klein; my mother, Carol Otis; Clare Waismann; Dr. Nancy Sobel; Dawn Agnew; Catherine Stone; my dearest sister, Chrisse Otis Sahadi; Karen Young; Liza Boles; Michelle Peck; Jody Kemmerer; and Marie

Christine Kollock. Without all your love, support, and belief in me, I'm not sure if this book would have come to fruition.

Thank you to Ellen Serrano, with whom I shared the first edits— she encouragingly held my hand and caught my tears as I adjusted to my story being "out."

And to my dearest teacher, whose name is in my heart even if for the sake of his safety it cannot appear on these pages, I thank you for guiding me flawlessly along the path and pointing out the most precious teachings one can have revealed to her.

Thank you, David Petite, for the profound lesson your life and death has brought to my life over the past summer.

To my father, Morrow Otis, who is one of the most courageous men I've known: Thank you for your love and support as well as for your heartfelt efforts to walk such a clean and honest path, one day at a time. Many thanks also to my brother, Jordan. And to Jeffrey Dash, for being one of the first safe, honest men I met on my journey. My trust was renewed in the male gender as our friendship and work partnership grew.

Warmest thanks, of course, to my beloved husband, soul mate, and consort, Matthew Charles Sutton. You have rocked my world and provided inspiration, safety, love, trust, nurturing, and many laughs along the way. Truly, if it were not for your profound place by my side, the better half of this book would not have come to be.

Finally, to my daughters, Jade Yeshe and Kaya Elizabeth Drolma: Carrying and birthing you both into this world has completed my cycle of healing and brought me onto the path of profound compassion and radical truth. Your presence has blessed me with the opportunity of looking deep into myself and having the courage to make changes where otherwise I might not have. You both have graced my life in innumerable ways and no doubt will continue to do so.

Photograph Credits

All photographs courtesy of Carré Otis, except for:
Insert page 10, top, photograph by Ron Galella, Ltd., courtesy of WireImage.

Insert page 10, bottom, photograph by John Roca/New York Daily News Archive, courtesy of Getty Images.